MODEL **ANSWERS**

A Thematic Approach

Acknowledgements

I would like to thank some of the many people who have made this book possible, particularly Vera Kerrisk for her invaluable comments and advice, and Peter Malone, who coordinated the publication.

I would also like to thank my colleagues at Hewitt College, Cork, especially Principal Patricia McGrath, Vice Principal Aidan Cleary, Aoife O'Driscoll and John O'Brien.

I'd like to thank all my past and present students, who were unwittingly a key part of this project, and Dr Barry Brunt in UCC, who had a very positive influence on my own interaction with geography.

Finally, I would like to thank my publishers, Educate.ie, for the great commitment they have shown this book.

Eleanor Solon

LEAVING CERTIFICATE

Geography

MODEL **ANSWERS** – *A Thematic Approach*

ELEANOR **SOLON** MA PhD

educate.ie

PUBLISHED BY:
Educate.ie
Walsh Educational Books Ltd
Castleisland, Co. Kerry, Ireland
www.educate.ie

EDITOR:
Jane Rogers

PRODUCTION EDITOR:
Kieran O'Donoghue

DESIGN:
The Design Gang, Tralee

PRINTED AND BOUND BY:
Walsh Colour Print, Castleisland

Map of Carrick-on-Suir reproduced by kind permission of Ordnance Survey Ireland © Ordnance Survey Ireland and Government of Ireland, Permit No. 8733.

Aerial photographs reproduced by kind permission of Peter Barrow, Inniscarra Dam by permission of John Herriot, weather maps and satellite image © by permission of Met Éireann. Other photos: Stockbyte/Getty, Bigstock Photos, L. Wedekind/IAEA, E.R. Schiffahrt/Nordcapital.

The author and publisher have made every effort to trace all copyright holders, but if some have been inadvertently overlooked we would be happy to make the necessary arrangements at the first opportunity.

ISBN: 978-1-907772-55-9

CONTENTS

INTRODUCTION

THIS BOOK PROVIDES MODEL ANSWERS TO ALL ESSENTIAL QUESTIONS asked in the Higher Level Leaving Certificate geography examination since the present syllabus was introduced in 2006. It covers Physical, Regional, Economic and Human geography, as well as two options – Global Interdependence and Geoecology. It aims to give students a structured framework for answering examination questions and encourages them to develop their own answers based on their studies at home and in the classroom.

Leaving Certificate Geography: Model Answers is designed to help students and teachers really get involved with their geography course. This syllabus is wide ranging and demanding, and requires students to:

- gather
- understand
- analyse
- examine
- and explain key geographic themes and concepts.

In order to help them do so, the book adopts a thematic approach to topics in geography. This allows students to focus on the key concepts and encourages them to develop an organised approach to learning and revision. Students are asked to recognise the interrelationship which exists between core, elective and option units, and for that reason this book emphasises the need to engage with the entire syllabus. Students' attention is also drawn to the importance of being familiar with the official marking schemes, which are provided here alongside each question.

A variety of answers are given here to individual questions, and a large number of regional settings are utilised throughout the book. Detailed essays are provided for Higher Level candidates for the two most popular options, namely Global Interdependence and Geoecology.

The text also illustrates clearly the key skills required of Leaving Certificate geography students, including map reading and interpretation, aerial photograph reading and interpretation, graph design and interpretation, regional sketching, and physical illustrations.

Attention is of course drawn to the importance of using past examination papers in order to prepare properly for the real exam.

In designing the present geography syllabus, great emphasis was placed on broadening the knowledge base of Leaving Certificate students and increasing

the links between the Junior Certificate and Leaving Certificate syllabuses. In addition, there was, and continues to be, a very strong commitment to the belief that the Leaving Certificate course should be syllabus-driven rather than examination-driven. Therefore, it is critically important that students and teachers are very familiar with the syllabus content and learning outcomes of all sections of the course.

The syllabus contains:

- compulsory sections including Physical, Regional and Skills
- geographical investigation
- electives
- options.

EXAMINATION STRUCTURE (HIGHER LEVEL)

The fieldwork investigation is externally assessed and accounts for 100 marks, or 20 per cent of the total marks for the exam.

The written examination in June accounts for 400 marks (80 per cent of the total). Total time allowed is two hours and 50 minutes. The paper is divided into distinct sections. Students must make sure they are familiar with:

- layout of the paper
- time allowed
- question structure
- mark allocation
- marking schemes.

THE WRITTEN PAPER

PART ONE: SHORT-ANSWER QUESTIONS 80 MARKS

- 12 short questions, of which you must do ten. (You can attempt all 12 questions, but you will be marked on your best ten answers.) The questions are based on Unit 1 (Physical), Unit 2 (Regional) and Unit 3 (Skills).
- Marks: eight marks for each question, so the total for Part One is 80 marks (20 per cent of the total marks for the paper).
- Recommended time: 30 minutes.

PART TWO

Section 1 – Core (Questions 1 to 6)

You **must** attempt **two** questions: one from *Patterns and Processes in the Physical Environment* and one from *Regional Geography*.

Patterns and Processes in the Physical Environment (Questions 1 to 3)

- Three multi-part questions, of which you must do one.
- Marks: 80 marks (20 per cent of total marks for the paper).
- Part A of each question is generally worth 20 marks; parts B and C are worth 30 marks each.
- Recommended time: 30 minutes, plus five minutes to read the questions.

Regional Geography (Questions 4 to 6)

- Three multi-part questions, of which you must do one.

- Marks: 80 marks (20 per cent of total marks for the paper).
- Part A of each question is generally worth 20 marks; parts B and C are worth 30 marks each.
- Recommended time: 30 minutes, plus five minutes to read the questions.

Section 2 – Electives (Questions 7 to 12)

You **must** attempt **one** question from **either** Patterns and Processes in Economic Activities or Patterns and Processes in the Human Environment.

Economic (Questions 7, 8 and 9) and **Human** (Questions 10, 11 and 12)

- Three multi-part questions, of which you must do one, from chosen elective.
- Marks: 80 marks (20 per cent of total marks for the paper).
- Part A is generally worth 20 marks; parts B and C are worth 30 marks each.
- Recommended time: 30 minutes, plus five minutes to read the questions.

Section 3 – Options (Questions 13 to 24, Higher Level only)

- Three essay-type questions on each optional unit.
- You must answer one question from one option.
- Marks: 80 marks (20 per cent of total marks for the paper).
- Recommended time: 30 minutes, plus five minutes to read the questions.

The options are:

- Global Interdependence: Questions 13, 14 and 15
- Geoecology: Questions 16, 17 and 18
- Culture and Identity: Questions 19, 20 and 21
- The Atmosphere–Ocean Environment: Questions 22, 23 and 24.

MARKING SCHEME

The allocation of marks in the Physical, Regional and elective section of the paper is currently based on Specific Relevant Points (SRPs). In the Higher Level paper an SRP is worth two marks, so for a 30-mark answer the examiners will be looking for 15 SRPs in order to award maximum marks.

An SRP is deemed to be a combination of

- a factual piece of information
- a statistical fact
- a geographical definition

➜

- a clear and concise explanation of a relevant process
- a relevant example.

Note: SRP marks have been utilised since the introduction of the present syllabus in 2006. At that stage, examiners also had to allocate Overall Cohesion marks (OC). These were based on the logic, presentation and structure of answers. In 2006, OC marks accounted for six marks in a 30-mark question. In 2007, the use of OC marks was withdrawn from all sections of the paper with the exception of the field investigation and essays. It is possible that OC marks may be reintroduced into marking schemes, so students should avoid writing too many answers in bullet points, which can lack cohesion and structure.

ESSAYS

The marking of essays is based on the number of aspects (paragraphs). Students are given the following instruction in the examination paper: 'It is better to discuss three or four aspects of the theme in some detail, rather than to give a superficial treatment of a large number of points.'

The marking scheme is worked out according to the number of aspects examined in the essay.

	THREE ASPECTS	FOUR ASPECTS
Total marks for each aspect	27 + 27 + 26	20 marks each
Identifying the aspect	4 marks	4 marks
Examination of the aspect	8 SRPs at 2 marks each: total 16	6 SRPs at 2 marks each: total 12
Overall coherence	7/6 marks graded	4 marks graded

STUDY TIPS

- Make sure you know the requirements of the syllabus.
- Be very familiar with past examination questions.
- Break topics into key components: Where? Why? Consequences.
- Prepare a study plan with clear, concise learning objectives.
- Plan to spend no longer than 40 minutes revision time on any one topic.
- As you read, write down key points and short notes.
- Use memory maps or spider diagrams to organise information or to test recall ability.

- Practise exam questions within the time allowed.
- Vary the topics you study: do not always start at your favourite section.

EXAMINATION DAY

- Focus on the positives – what you know rather than what you don't.
- If you want to check over notes, use pre-prepared revision notes, e.g. memory maps.
- Make sure that you have everything you need for the exam: pens, pencils, ruler, etc.
- Make sure you know your seat allocation in the examination centre.
- Get to the examination centre at least ten minutes before the exam.
- When you receive the paper, read all the questions carefully.
- Choose the questions you want to answer, and proceed according to a prearranged plan (e.g. start with the options and finish with the short questions, or start with your best section in order to gain confidence).
- It is critically important that you clearly address the questions asked – 'A' students are generally the students who are able to display the key skills of analysis, relevance and time management.
- Watch your timing throughout the exam. If you are exceeding the time allowed for a particular section, leave space in your answer book and move to the next question.
- Do not leave the examination centre early. If you finish before the allocated time, re-read and re-check your answers.
- When the exam is over, it's over. You can't change anything you have written, so don't waste time on post mortems – move on and focus on your next exam.
- Remember: the key to success in exams is preparation, preparation and more preparation. The only place success comes before work is in the dictionary!

FURTHER MATERIAL ONLINE

Questions and model answers to the 2011 examination paper are identified in these pages by an icon *(see opposite)* and can be downloaded at http://www.educate.ie/downloads.php

rotation

abrasion happens as rocks
are scraped along base

1

PHYSICAL GEOGRAPHY

PLATE TECTONICS 2007 QUESTION 1 PART B

'Plate boundaries are zones where crust is both created and destroyed.'
Examine the above statement, with reference to examples you have
studied. (30 marks)

MARKING SCHEME ✓

Name one example of each boundary: **2 marks + 2 marks**
Discussion recreation/destruction: **7 (6) SRPs or 6 (7) SRPs**

HOW CRUST
IS CREATED

Crust is created at divergent plate boundaries. One example is the diverging plate boundary where the Eurasian plate and the North American plate diverge as a result of convection currents. These convection currents originate in the mantle, where there are high temperatures. The liquefied rock rises towards the earth's crust, cools, slips sideways, becomes denser and slowly sinks back into the very hot mantle. The movement of these currents causes the over-riding crustal plates to move: this process is known as slab pull. As the crust is pulled apart, it is stretched and weakened and eventually breaks. This allows liquid molten material (magma) from the mantle to upwell and break through the crust. The magma, which is now known as lava, cools and solidifies to create new rocks. If this occurs underneath the sea, mid-ocean ridges such as the Mid-Atlantic ridge or East Pacific rise are created. The rock at the point of

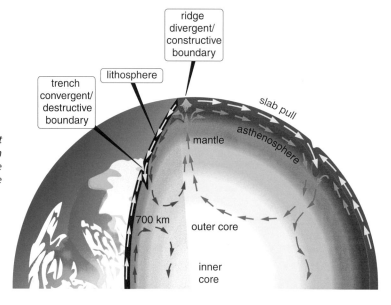

Plate movement
due to convection
currents in the
mantle

divergence is young, and it gets older with distance from divergence.

HOW CRUST IS DESTROYED

Crust is destroyed at a number of converging plate boundaries, including ocean-to-ocean, ocean-to-continent and continent-to-continent. As two plates collide, the heavier ocean plate subducts under the lighter plate (e.g. the Pacific plate subducts under the Eurasian plate). The edge of the subducting plate descends into the hot mantle, where it experiences intense heat and pressure. This causes the edge of the plate to melt, resulting in the destruction of the crust. A deep trench marks the point of subduction. Parallel to the point of subduction, liquid molten material may rise up under the lighter plate to create volcanic landforms. The collision of an ocean and continental plate results in subduction and destruction of the edge of the heavier plate and the creation of fold mountains and volcanoes parallel to the point of subduction on the lighter continental crust (for example the Nazca and South American plates).

Destruction of the crust also occurs as two continental plates collide (for example the Indo-Australian and the Eurasian). Limited subduction occurs because the plates are of equal weight and thickness. As the two plates collide, sedimentary rock on the ancient ocean floor is compressed and folded to create fold mountains.

PLATE TECTONICS 2009 QUESTION 1 PART B

Explain, with reference to examples you have studied, how plate tectonics helps us understand the forces at work along crustal plate boundaries. (30 marks)

MARKING SCHEME ✔

Name two forces: **2 marks + 2 marks**
Name examples of different boundaries: **2 marks + 2 marks**
Discussion: **11 SRPs**
– *Credit one named example from SRPs*
– *Give credit to relevant diagrams for a max of 1 SRP and credit extra annotated information on diagrams*

The theory of plate tectonics proves that the lithosphere is composed of 16 (seven major) floating plates, which are moved by convection currents originating within the mantle. These plates can: move apart, diverging; collide, converging; and move parallel to one another.

PLATE TECTONICS

The movements of these plates have huge implications for the earth's crust, as it can be either created or destroyed: the boundaries of these plates can be destructive or constructive. In some cases, the crust is neither created nor destroyed, and these locations are known as neutral plate boundaries. An example is the North American and Pacific plate at the San Andreas faultline.

CONVECTION CURRENTS

The movement of the earth's plates is made possible by convection currents, which originate in the mantle. There are high temperatures in the mantle, which result in the creation of liquid molten material. As the liquefied rock rises towards the earth's crust, it cools and slips sideways, becomes denser, and gradually sinks back into the very hot mantle, and the cycle continues. This cycle of convection causes the overriding lithospheric plates to move through a process known as slab pull.

The movement of plates allows us to identify a number of plate boundaries.

CONSTRUCTIVE/ DIVERGENT PLATE BOUNDARIES

Constructive (or divergent) plate boundaries result in the creation of new rocks as the plates move away from one another. As this occurs the crust is stretched, it becomes thinner and weakens and eventually breaks. This allows liquid molten material to upwell and break through the crust, and it now becomes known as lava. This molten material cools and solidifies to create new rocks, and mid-oceanic ridges are created. At the point of divergence, the rock is young, and with distance from divergence the rock increases in age.

MID-OCEAN RIDGES

Mid-ocean ridges are formed by rising molten material or plumes, which cool and solidify on the earth's crust, and the process of divergence is known as rifting. These landforms are volcanic in nature and are composed of basalt. As the continents move apart, the edges sink, creating shallow continental

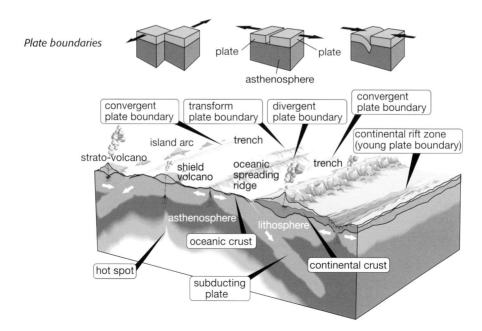

Plate boundaries

shelves. Examples of divergent plate boundaries include the North American and Eurasian, resulting in the creation of the Mid-Atlantic ridge; and the Pacific and the Nazca, resulting in the creation of the East Pacific rise.

DESTRUCTIVE/ CONVERGENT PLATE BOUNDARIES

These result in the destruction of rocks or a change in their composition. There are a number of destructive/convergent plate boundaries, including: ocean-to-ocean (e.g. Pacific and Philippine); ocean-to-continent (e.g. Nazca and South American); continent-to-continent (e.g. Indo-Australian and Eurasian).

SUBDUCTION

As destructive plates collide, the heavier plate sinks under the lighter through a process known as subduction. The point of subduction is marked by the presence of a deep oceanic trench. The edge of the descending plate melts due to heat. Magma rises parallel to the point of collision under the lighter plate and volcanoes are formed. Over time, due to the accumulation of material, these may eventually result in the creation of volcanic islands or island arcs (e.g. Saipan Island) or volcanic mountain chains, for example the Andes.

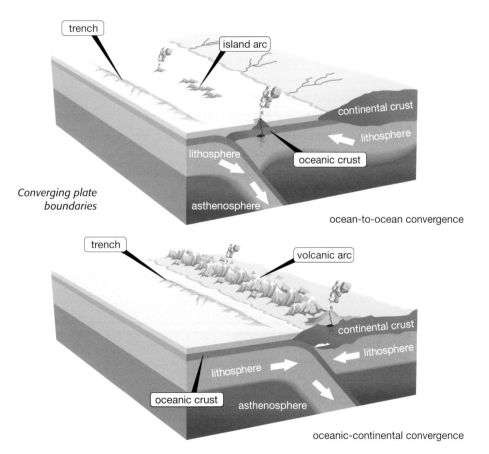

Converging plate boundaries

ocean-to-ocean convergence

oceanic-continental convergence

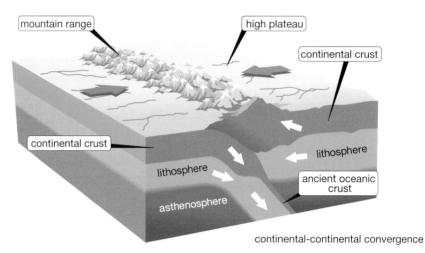

Converging plate boundaries

mountain range

high plateau

continental crust

continental crust

lithosphere

lithosphere

ancient oceanic crust

asthenosphere

continental-continental convergence

CONTINENT-TO-CONTINENT PLATE BOUNDARIES Both plates are of equal thickness and weight, so limited subduction occurs. At the point of collision, sedimentary rock material is forced upwards. This results in the creation of fold mountains. One example is the fold mountain range in the north-west of Ireland, which dates from the Caledonian folding period that occurred when the American and Eurasian plates converged 400 million years ago. A more recent example is the Himalayan mountains, which were formed by the convergence of the Indo-Australian and Eurasian plates. These plates started to collide 50–70 million years ago and folding continues today. The presence of marine fossils on the top of these mountains shows that these plates were once separated by an ancient sea.

The movement of tectonic plates causes volcanoes, folding, faulting and earthquakes.

VOLCANOES 2006 QUESTION 3 PART C

Examine the processes that have led to the formation of any ***two*** *volcanic landforms.* (30 marks)

MARKING SCHEME ✓

For each of two landforms:
Naming landform: **2 marks each**
Processes discussed: **5 SRPs**
Overall coherence (over both landforms): **6 marks graded**
Unless there is reasonable difference in processes, reduce the overall coherence accordingly

OR (where processes are dealt with as a unit)
Volcanic landforms or examples identified: **2 marks each**
Processes discussed: **10 SRPs**
Overall coherence: **6 marks graded**

Landform A: Mid-Atlantic Ridge

The Mid-Atlantic ridge is an example of a mid-oceanic ridge created by volcanic activity. Mid-oceanic ridges are created as a result of the separation of plates on the sea floor. The Mid-Atlantic ridge was created due to the divergence of the North American and Eurasian plates. This occurs due to a process known as slab pull, which is caused by convection currents in the mantle. The force of this movement, or thermal convection, causes the plates to move apart, resulting in a stretching of the earth's crust. Cracks or fissures appear and liquid molten material upwells and cools, resulting in the creation of mid-oceanic ridges associated with diverging plate boundaries under the sea. Rocks at the point of divergence are young, and with distance from divergence the rocks increase in age. The Mid-Atlantic ridge is composed of igneous extrusive volcanic material, and the main rock is basalt.

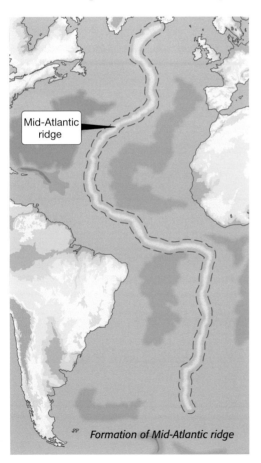

Formation of Mid-Atlantic ridge

Landform B: The Giant's Causeway

The Giant's Causeway in Co. Antrim is a highly distinctive volcanic landform. Sixty-five million years ago a fissure eruption occurred, which caused liquid molten material to break through the earth's crust. The earth's crust had been weakened and stretched by plate movement caused by convection currents. The two plates which diverged were the North American and Eurasian plates, and this divergence took place due to slab pull associated with the movement of convection currents in the mantle. The liquid molten material which upwelled had a low silica content and therefore low viscosity, which caused it to flow over a large area. As the lava came into contact with the sea, it began to cool rapidly. This caused the minerals in the lava to contract around regularly spaced centres, and it cooled to form hexagonal columns of basalt. Basalt is a volcanic, igneous extrusive rock, which is very hard, smooth and contains very small crystals – resulting from rapid cooling. Today the Giant's Causeway is a major tourist attraction due to its unique volcanic landforms.

Basalt columns in the Giant's Causeway, Co. Antrim

VOLCANOES **2008 QUESTION 2 PART B**

Explain how the study of plate tectonics has helped us to understand the global distribution of volcanoes. (30 marks)

 MARKING SCHEME ✓

Global examples: **2 marks + 2 marks**
Plate tectonics examined: **6 SRPs**
- *Examination all on plate tectonics: maximum of 6 SRPs*
- *Give credit to relevant diagrams for a maximum of 2 SRPs and credit extra annotated information on diagrams*
- *No credit for the effects of volcanoes*

The study of plate tectonics is important in understanding the global distribution of volcanoes. It helps us understand how volcanoes form and thus where they are most likely to be present. The three most likely places for volcanoes to occur are at divergent plate boundaries, convergent plate boundaries and hot spots.

CONVERGENT PLATE BOUNDARIES

Of these three locations, volcanoes are most prevalent at convergent plate boundaries. One example is the convergence of the oceanic Pacific plate and continental Eurasian plate where the islands of Japan and the Japanese trench were formed.

SLAB PULL

Convection currents originating deep within the mantle cause the plates to move in a process known as slab pull. When an oceanic plate meets a continental plate, the heavier oceanic plate is forced down, and it sinks into and is destroyed in the mantle in a process known as subduction. Liquid molten material rises parallel to the point of subduction underneath the lighter plate and can result in the formation of a volcanic island arc. These volcanoes form as pressure builds below the continental crust due to the increased volume of magma when the descending oceanic plate is melted. Magma upwells and eventually breaks the surface as lava, forming a volcano. Volcanoes can be identified all around the perimeters of the Pacific plate as it converges with the North American, Eurasian and Indo-Australian plates. This area is known as the Pacific Ring of Fire.

Plate boundaries and volcanic hot spots

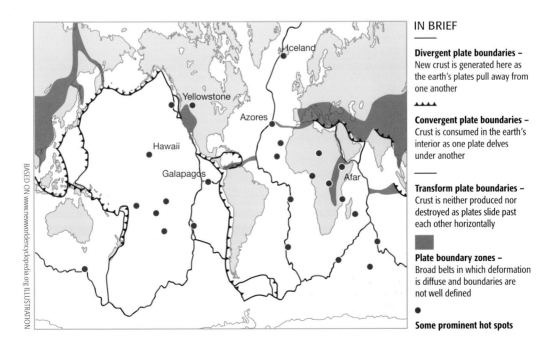

BASED ON www.newworldencyclopedia.org ILLUSTRATION

IN BRIEF

Divergent plate boundaries – New crust is generated here as the earth's plates pull away from one another

▲▲▲▲

Convergent plate boundaries – Crust is consumed in the earth's interior as one plate delves under another

Transform plate boundaries – Crust is neither produced nor destroyed as plates slide past each other horizontally

Plate boundary zones – Broad belts in which deformation is diffuse and boundaries are not well defined

● **Some prominent hot spots**

CONSTRUCTIVE PLATE BOUNDARIES

Volcanoes also occur at constructive or divergent plate boundaries. One example is the Mid-Atlantic ridge and, more specifically, Iceland. In general, eruptions at these points are less violent, normally occurring as lava flows or fissure eruptions. This is due to the lower viscosity of the lava, a fact related to its low silica content. In Iceland, the North American plate and Eurasian plate diverge, and lava upwells, forming new land (e.g. the island of Surtsey in 1963).

HOT SPOTS

Although most volcanoes are found at plate boundaries, a number do occur away from the extremities of plates. These are caused by the presence of hot spots within the mantle. Hot spots are areas of extremely high temperatures originating deep within the mantle. Due to the process of slab pull, volcanic islands are formed over these hot spots as magma upwells and eventually breaks through the crust. The Hawaiian island ridge is a result of the slow-moving Pacific plate moving over a fixed hot spot.

EARTHQUAKES 2006 QUESTION 3 PART B

Explain how a study of plate tectonics helps us to understand the occurrence of earthquakes. (30 marks)

MARKING SCHEME ✓

Plate tectonics examined: **12 SRPs**
Overall coherence: **6 marks graded**
– *Credit relevant labelled diagrams as new information (do not double-mark information)*
– *Do not give credit for the effects of earthquakes*
– *If all plate tectonics but no earthquakes (or vice versa), overall coherence: 0 marks*
– *Give credit for a maximum of two examples from the SRPs*

Plate tectonics is the study of the movement of the plates that make up the earth's crust. Earthquakes take place as a direct result of tectonic activity. Due to convection currents in the mantle, plates move, and they can collide, separate or move past one another. However, these movements do not occur smoothly: the plate margins can jam or stick, and this causes a huge build-up of pressure. This pressure is released with a sudden earth movement (earthquake), which causes a series of vibrations on the earth's surface (surface waves) and below the earth's crust (body waves). Ninety-nine per cent of all earthquakes come about at plate boundaries due to plate movement.

SAN ANDREAS FAULT

One area where earthquakes occur frequently is the San Andreas fault in California in the USA. This faultline is on a passive plate boundary where the Pacific and North American plates slide past one another. Sometimes the plate

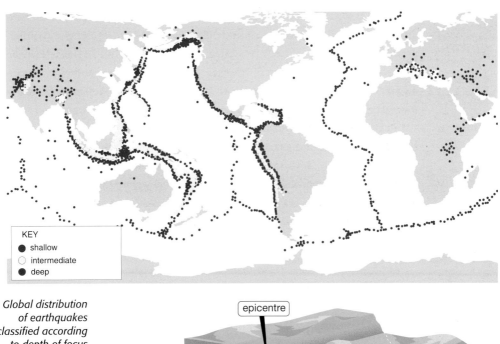

Global distribution of earthquakes classified according to depth of focus

KEY
● shallow
○ intermediate
● deep

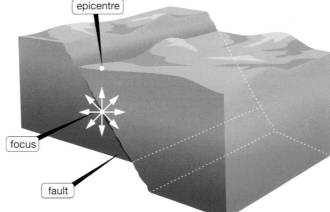

Epicentre and focus of an earthquake

margins jam together, and this leads to a significant build-up of pressure, which is released through a sudden earth movement, resulting in an earthquake (e.g. in 1906).

JAPAN   Japan also experiences many earthquakes. Close to Kobe, the denser oceanic Philippine plate is being subducted beneath the lighter continental Eurasian plate at a rate of about ten centimetres per year. Earthquakes are very common here due to friction as the two plates converge along this destructive margin.

Earthquakes are also associated with plate boundaries of separation (for example Eurasian and North American). As these plates diverge, the earth's crust is stretched and will eventually crack, and this movement can result in shallow earthquakes.

EARTHQUAKE PREDICTION AND PLATE MOVEMENT   Following significant research into the causes of earthquakes, scientists are able to predict areas most at risk, and planners are able to implement building regulations, including the use of reinforced concrete and tilt angles which can reduce damage to buildings and lessen the loss of life. Evacuation plans can also be developed for areas most at risk. Seismologists monitor plate movement using tilt meters, lasers and other scientific equipment.

Yet not all areas at risk have the economic resources to take precautions, and regions in Asia and India which are on plate boundaries are poorly equipped to deal with the devastating effects earthquakes leave in their wake. Earthquakes can be classified according to depth of focus, which is the underground point of origin. Shallow, intermediate and deep are associated with subduction zones, while diverging and passive zones are associated with shallow quakes.

EARTHQUAKES 2008 QUESTION 3 PART C

Examine, with reference to actual examples, the measurement and effects of earthquakes. (30 marks)

MARKING SCHEME

Measurement identified: **2 marks**
Effects identified: **2 marks + 2 marks**
Named examples: **2 marks + 2 marks**
Discussion: **10 SRPs (5 SRPs per aspect)**

The earthquakes I have studied are the Japan earthquake of magnitude 8.9 on the Richter scale that struck on 11 March 2011, and the earthquake in Christchurch, New Zealand, on 22 February 2011. This measured 6.3 on the Richter scale and occurred close to the passive plate boundary of the Pacific and Australasian plates which are responsible for the major Alpine fault line.

Measurement

Earthquakes are measured using two types of scale.

RICHTER SCALE   The Richter scale measures the magnitude of earthquakes. A scale of 1.0 to 10.0 is used, and with each increasing number the magnitude is multiplied by ten. Two is considered to be a mild tremor, while 7.0 represents a major earthquake. This is the scale most commonly used by seismologists.

THE MERCALLI SCALE   The Mercalli scale is used after the size and location of an earthquake has been identified. It reflects people's perceptions of the degree of damage, so it is not considered to be scientific. It is based on a 12-point scale: one represents no damage; 12 represents complete devastation.

Effects

JAPAN EARTHQUAKE Japan is located on the Pacific Ring of Fire, which is one of the most active tectonic zones in the world. At this location the Pacific and Philippine plates are subducted beneath the lighter continental North American and Eurasian plates. The epicentre of the earthquake occurred west of the Japan Trench, 125km off the eastern coastline of Japan, at a depth of 10km. The quake was the fifth largest ever recorded and resulted in a ten metre high tsunami which devastated the Japanese coastline, causing huge structural damage to boats, houses, transport infrastructure and telecommunications. Four of the six reactors in the Fukushima nuclear power plant experienced meltdown. An estimated 11,500 people were killed and 16,500 are still missing.

CHRISTCHURCH EARTHQUAKE The Christchurch earthquake struck at lunchtime on 22 February 2011. The epicentre was only 4.8km from the city and the focus was shallow at a depth of 4km. Six months earlier, the city experienced an earthquake of magnitude 7.1, which resulted in some structural damage but no casualties. The second quake in February 2011 resulted in 131 deaths when many of the weakened buildings collapsed as a result of the quake's impact. Liquefaction also occurred as Christchurch is built on an alluvial plain.

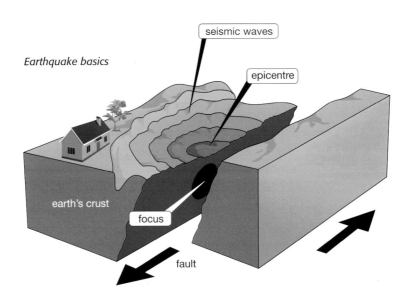

Earthquake basics

seismic waves

epicentre

earth's crust

focus

fault

FOLDING AND FAULTING 2007 QUESTION 3 PART B

*Examine the impact of **folding** and **faulting** on the landscape. In your answer refer to **one** landform in **each** case. (30 marks)*

MARKING SCHEME

Folding
Named landform: **2 marks**
Discussion: **7 (6) SRPs**

Faulting
Named landform: **2 marks**
Discussion: **6 (7) SRPs**

– *Credit relevant labelled diagrams*
– *Give credit for one named example of each landform*

FORMATION OF FOLD MOUNTAINS

The fold mountains I have studied are the Himalayan mountains. These were created by the convergence of the Indo–Australian and Eurasian plates. The first stage in the formation of fold mountains involves the accumulation of vast amounts of organic and inorganic sediment in horizontal layers on ancient sea floors. Over time the plates on either side of the sediment zone move towards one another. The convergence of these plates happens as a result of convection currents.

Convection currents (thermal convection) occur in the mantle of the earth, below the lithosphere. The high temperatures in the mantle result in the creation of liquid molten material. As the liquefied rock rises by thermal convection, it makes its way towards the earth's crust. The molten material cools as the temperature falls, which causes the molten material to slip sideways. As further cooling occurs, the material descends into the hot mantle, and the cycle starts again. As these currents slip sideways, they pull the overriding lithosphere through a process known as slab pull; this eventually resulted in the convergence of the Indian and Eurasian plates.

As the Indian plate was forced northwards due to slab pull, an ancient sea was gradually closed and sediments on the sea floor were compressed and compacted. When the Indian plate converged with the Eurasian plate, compressional forces pushed the rocks and sediments on the boundaries of the plates upwards, forming fold mountains. Marine fossils from the ancient sea can still be found on the mountain-tops. The Indian plate, which began its northwards movement around 70 million years ago, continues to push against the Eurasian plate today.

The landform associated with faulting that I have studied is the Great African Rift Valley, which extends from Ethiopia to Tanzania. The Rift Valley is created because of the divergence of the African plate, a process that is causing the stretching and rifting of the continental crust. Rifting occurs due to the movement of convection currents in the mantle. As tensional force created by the movement of convectional currents is applied to the earth's crust, the crust experiences a surface area increase, resulting in the formation of normal faults. When a series of normal faults occur parallel to one another, the fault in the centre will become displaced and down faulting can occur, resulting in the creation of a rift valley. Rift valleys are also known as grabens.

An associated landform caused by faulting is a block or a horst mountain; these are associated with the uplift of land or down faulting on either side of a crustal block, e.g. Black Forest Mountains, Germany, and Ox Mountains, Ireland.

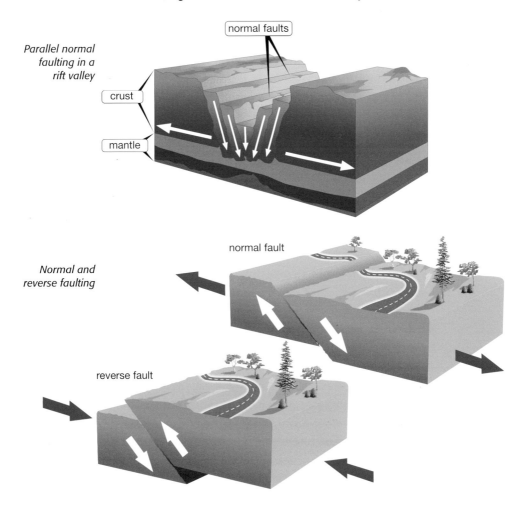

Parallel normal faulting in a rift valley

Normal and reverse faulting

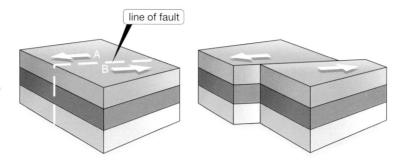

Tear faulting

Faulting processes are associated with all types of plate boundaries: normal faults occur at diverging, reverse faults at converging and tear faults at passive plate boundaries. The global distribution of faults is directly related to plate movement.

FOLDING AND FAULTING 2010 QUESTION 2 PART B

Explain how the study of plate tectonics has helped us to understand the global distribution of fold mountains. (30 marks)

MARKING SCHEME ✓

Reference to global distribution: **2 marks + 2 marks**
Two named fold mountains: **2 marks + 2 marks**
Plate tectonics examined: **11 SRPs**
– *Maximum of 6 SPRs if examination is of plate tectonics with no reference to fold mountains*
– *Give credit to relevant information on diagrams*

CREATION OF FOLD MOUNTAINS

An understanding of plate tectonics is critical to our understanding of the global distribution of fold mountains. Fold mountains are created when continental plates converge. Caledonian fold mountains in the north-west of Ireland, for example, were created by the convergence of the American and Eurasian plates 400 million years ago. The fold mountains of the Munster Ridge and Valley region were created as a result of the convergence of the Eurasian and African plates 250 million years ago. Folding can also occur when continental and oceanic plates meet. The Andes in South America were created by the collision of the Nazca and South American plates.

HIMALAYAS

The most famous fold mountains that I have studied are the Himalayan mountains. These were created by the convergence of the Indian–Australian and the Eurasian plates.

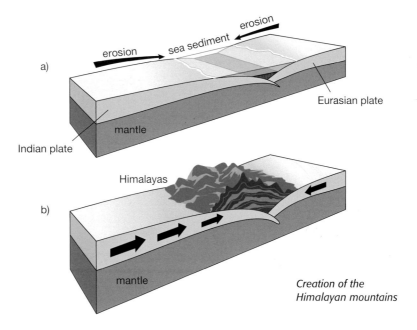

a)

erosion   sea sediment   erosion

Eurasian plate

mantle

Indian plate

b)

Himalayas

mantle

Creation of the Himalayan mountains

HIMALAYAS   The first stage in the formation of fold mountains involves the accumulation of organic and inorganic sediment (denudation of the continental crust) on ancient sea floors. In time the plates on either side of the sediment zone move towards one another. The convergence of these plates happens as a result of convection currents.

Convection currents (thermal convection) occur in the mantle of the earth, which is located below the lithosphere. The high temperatures in the mantle create liquid molten material, and as the liquefied rock rises by thermal convection, it makes its way towards the earth's crust. As this occurs, the molten material cools due to a decrease in temperature, and this causes the molten rock to slip sideways. As further cooling occurs, the material descends into the hot mantle, and the cycle starts again. As these currents slip sideways, they pull the over-riding lithosphere along in a process known as slab pull.

The Indian plate was forced northwards due to slab pull, and an ancient sea was gradually closed and sediments on the sea floor compressed and compacted. When the Indian plate converged with the Eurasian plate, the compression caused the rocks and sediments on the boundaries of the plates to be pushed upwards, forming fold mountains. Marine fossils can still be found on the mountain-tops. The Indian plate, which began its northwards movement around 70 million years ago, continues to be pushed against the Eurasian plate today.

THE ROCK CYCLE 2006 QUESTION 1 PART B

*With reference to any **one** rock type, explain how it was formed and how it can produce a distinctive landscape.* (30 marks)

MARKING SCHEME

Formation of rock type, rock type identified: **2 marks**
Formation: **5 SRPs**
Overall coherence: **3 marks graded**

Distinctive landscape/naming landscape: **2 marks graded**
Formation: **5 SRPs**
Overall coherence: **3 marks graded**

LIMESTONE

A rock type I have studied is limestone, which is an organic sedimentary rock. This type of rock is generally composed of the fossil remains of plants and animals which accumulated on the floors of shallow seas. Irish limestone was formed 300–350 million years ago and is composed of calcium carbonate and sea shells which collected in warm tropical waters. At this stage, Ireland was located just on the equator and most of the country was under water. Collections of marine shells, hard skeletal bones and corals accumulated in low-lying coastal areas. Over time these components experienced compaction and cementation.

- Compaction: particles in the lower sediments are pushed together under the weight of overlaying sediments. Water and air are eventually removed.
- Cementation: the cementing agents (silica and calcium carbonate) are carried in solution by water and deposited in the pore spaces between rocks and particles and over time bind these into solid rock.

These processes, when combined, are known as lithification. All limestone originating from this period is referred to as carboniferous. Limestone is the most common rock type in Ireland and can be found throughout the midlands and in the Burren in Co. Clare. Limestone is used as a building material, as decorative flagstones and in the manufacture of cement and lime for fertilisers.

THE BURREN

Limestone has created a distinctive karst environment in the Burren in Co. Clare. The Burren is distinctive because of its surface and subterranean features. Surface features include limestone pavements, clints, grikes and swallow holes or sluggas. These features were formed by chemical weathering, i.e. carbonation, which changes calcium carbonate into soluble calcium bicarbonate. Grikes are grooves in the limestone; clints are ridges; and swallow holes are large cylindrical depressions (e.g. Poll na gColm). Subterranean features can be found in large cave structure or caverns. Distinctive limestone landforms have been formed in these caves, including stalagmites, stalactites and limestone curtains. These are formed by the solidification of the soluble calcium bicarbonate.

The Burren is a highly distinctive physical landscape related to rock formation and weathering over time.

Karst environment in the Burren in Co. Clare

THE ROCK CYCLE **2008 QUESTION 3 PART B**

*Explain, with reference to an example you have studied, the formation of **one** rock type and how it produces a distinctive landscape.* (30 marks)

 MARKING SCHEME ✔

(I) Examine its formation for 14: **16 marks**
(II) Examine its production of a distinctive landscape for 16: **14 marks**

	ROCK FORMATION	DISTINCTIVE LANDSCAPE
Identification:	**2 marks**	**2 marks**
Named example:	**2 marks**	**2 marks**
Examination:	**5 (6) SRPs**	**6 (5) SRPs**

– *Examination of distinctive landscape must follow on from rock formation*
– *Credit relevant labelled diagrams to a maximum of 2 SRPs*
– *Question is not tied to Ireland*

GRANITE

Granite is an igneous intrusive plutonic rock. It was formed due to the slow cooling of molten magma deep within the earth's crust. It has large crystals due to slow cooling, and the key mineral components are quartz (colourless or transparent), feldspar (a reflective, flat mineral) and mica (composed of either black or white crystals). The percentages of these minerals vary, resulting in the creation of granites of varying colours, ranging from black/grey to red/pink. Granite is a hard, heavy rock which is resistant to denudation. Granite has economic potential and is quarried and used as an ornamental rock, for counter tops, table tops and headstones.

LEINSTER BATHOLITH

A plutonic landform I have studied is the Leinster batholith, which is located in the Dublin/Wicklow mountains. This plutonic structure was created approximately 400 million years ago, when the American and Eurasian plates collided during the Caledonian folding period. As this occurred, liquid molten material forced its way upwards into the layers of sedimentary rocks. This magma was unable to break through the crust, and it cooled and collected in a large area deep within the crust. As the ages passed, the magma cooled slowly to create a batholith, which is composed primarily of granite. During cooling, the overlying sedimentary rock experienced metamorphism as sandstone was transformed into quartzite and shale into slate. Over time, the overlying sedimentary rock was weathered and eroded. Today, parts of the batholith have been exposed to reveal quartzite, slate and granite.

a)

Formation of a batholith

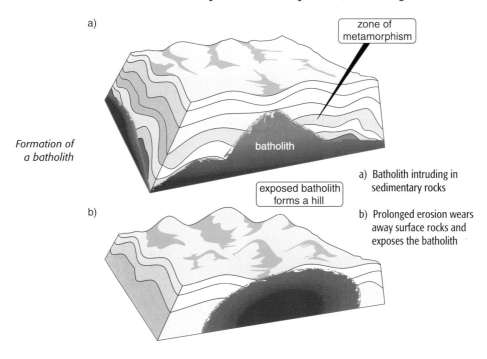

zone of metamorphism

batholith

exposed batholith forms a hill

b)

a) Batholith intruding in sedimentary rocks

b) Prolonged erosion wears away surface rocks and exposes the batholith

THE ROCK CYCLE 2009 QUESTION 2 PART B

 Examine, with reference to examples from Ireland, the formation of sedimentary rocks. (30 marks)

 MARKING SCHEME ✓

Name two sedimentary rocks: **2 marks + 2 marks**
Name two associated Irish locations: **2 marks + 2 marks**
Examination: **11 SRPs**
– *Give credit for 1 SRP for diagram without annotation*
– *Give credit for extra labelling in diagram from examination SRPs*
– *Allow treatment of up to three rocks in examination*
– *At least 3 SRPs for treatment of second sedimentary rock*
– *If description only: 2 SRPs maximum*

FORMATION

Sedimentary rocks are formed from material derived from the breakdown of pre-existing rocks and organic matter. They are normally formed on or near the earth's surface. There are two types of sedimentary rock: inorganic, formed by erosion and weathering of older rocks; and organic, created from once-living organisms.

All sedimentary rocks have the common characteristic of layering or stratification. The line separating one layer from the other is known as the bedding plane. Sediments are converted into rock by compaction and cementation due to the presence of silica and calcium carbonate. In compaction, the particles in the lower sediments are pushed together under the weight of overlying sediments. Water and air are eventually removed. In cementation, the cementing agents (silica and calcium carbonate) are carried in solution by water and deposited in the pore spaces between rocks and particles; over time these particles are bound into solid rock. These combined processes are known as lithification.

Example 1: Old Red Sandstone
Sediments were laid down 350–400 million years ago when Ireland was located just south of the equator. During this period, the huge Caledonian fold mountains of Galway, Mayo and Donegal were eroded by weathering and erosional processes. The sediments were transported by rivers through the processes of suspension, saltation and traction, and were deposited in lowland areas. Over time, these deposits of sand, gravel and pebbles were compacted and cemented to create solid rock. Due to chemical weathering, the iron

particles in the rock rusted to give the sandstone a red colour. Old red sandstone is common in Munster, including the ridge and valley region. Sandstone is quarried in many locations in the province. It is used in the construction industry, for road construction, and in the implementation of coastal management programmes.

compaction and cementation

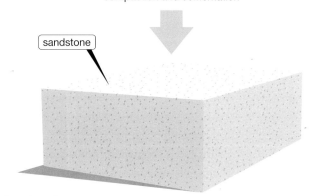

sandstone

Formation of sandstone

Example 2: Shale

This is composed of silt and clay which was deposited as fine sediments in enclosed shallow bays or estuaries. The thin stratified layers were later compressed and compacted. Economic use of shale is limited because it is brittle, but it can contain some crude oil deposits. Shale can be found in many parts of Ireland, including the Dublin/Wicklow mountains and the west Clare coastline. If shale experiences metamorphism, it is transformed into slate.

THE ROCK CYCLE 2010 QUESTION 1 PART C

Examine, with reference to examples from Ireland, the formation of metamorphic rocks. (30 marks)

MARKING SCHEME ✔

Name two metamorphic rocks: **2 marks + 2 marks**
Name two associated Irish locations: **2 marks + 2 marks**
Examination: **11 SRPs**
– *Give credit for labelling in diagram for examination*
– *Give credit for 1 SRP for diagram without annotation*
– *Give credit for third named metamorphic rock*
– *Max 2 SRPs if description only*

The tectonic forces which cause earthquakes, folding, faulting and volcanoes can also cause changes in rocks. This change is known as metamorphism and is brought about by heat and/or pressure. There are two types of metamorphic rock found in Ireland: foliated, which has a distinct layered structure; and non-foliated, which has a very dense or granular structure.

SLATE   Slate is a foliated metamorphic rock. Slate is fine-grained and occurs in a variety of colours, and it splits easily into thin sheets. It is created by the

Slate – a foliated metamorphic rock

dynamic metamorphism of shale. In shale, minerals are arranged in random order, but due to dynamic metamorphism the minerals are compressed and aligned in parallel lines, which allows for easy cleavage (splitting). Slate has been used for roofing, table tops, blackboards and stairways, but today it has been largely replaced by synthetic products. Examples of slate in Ireland can be found in Killaloe, Co. Clare, and Valentia Island, Co. Kerry.

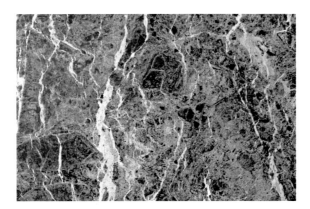

Marble – a non-foliated metamorphic rock

MARBLE   Marble, a non-foliated metamorphic rock, is a coarse crystalline rock formed by metamorphism of limestone or chalk. Pure limestone produces a white marble (like Carrara marble in Tuscany, Italy), but impurities commonly produce red, pink, yellow, green and black marble. Connemara marble is green, Cork marble is red, Kilkenny marble is black, and Rathlin Island marble is white. The economic uses of marble include building stone for interior columns of churches and museums, and interior floors in Mediterranean houses.

QUARTZITE   Quartzite (metamorphism of sandstone) is another non-foliated metamorphic rock. This solid quartz rock is produced by the cementing of sand grains with crystalline quartz. It is smooth, finely textured, hard and glassy in appearance. It is normally light in colour but can have tints of grey, red or purple. Irish examples of quartzite can be found on Mount Errigal and Slieve League in Donegal, Great and Little Sugar Loaf in Co. Wicklow and Croagh Patrick in Co. Mayo. Quartzite is used for road surfacing.

HUMAN INTERACTION WITH THE ROCK CYCLE
2006 QUESTION 1 PART C

*Examine how humans interact with the rock cycle in the case of **one** of the following: mining, quarrying, oil/gas exploration, geothermal energy production.* (30 marks)

MARKING SCHEME ✓

Interaction identified: **2 marks**
Discussion: **11 SRPs**
Overall coherence: **6 marks graded**
– A second interaction may be credited from the SRPs

– Amalgamate all relevant discussion points
– Credit examples/locations to a maximum of 2 SRPs
– Accept positive or negative aspects of the interaction

Quarrying is the extraction of rocks from the earth's surface for use in construction or manufacturing. The quarrying industry in Ireland was worth nearly €3 billion in 2007/08. The majority of quarrying in Ireland is related to demand from the construction industry, including housing and road infrastructure developments. Key quarrying companies include Roadstone in Co. Offaly, Readymix in Co. Clare and J. A. Woods in Co. Cork. The industry has experienced significant contraction due to the collapse of the construction sector since 2008 and a reduction in government investment in capital building programmes.

METHODS   Three main types of quarrying methods are used in Ireland:

1. Plug and feather quarrying, using steel bars which split the rock. This method is very effective on rocks with distinct bedding planes or cleavage, such as limestone and slate.
2. Blast quarrying, using explosives. This is used on harder rock structures or where material is required for road construction.
3. Shear quarrying, which uses steel discs to cut material from the rock face.

In Co. Clare, there are many limestone quarries where the rock is extracted and used in the manufacture of cement and lime for agricultural use. Sandstone is quarried extensively in the Munster region, while marble is extracted from sites in Galway, Kilkenny and Cork.

Quarrying in Ireland

Exploitation of, and human interaction with, the rock cycle in Ireland has resulted in significant economic returns for the country and helps create employment. But quarrying activities can also raise issues of environmental concern: the disposal of waste material; the possible run-off of waste into rivers, lakes and streams; and dust and noise pollution. However, if sustainable management policies are implemented, these concerns can be kept to a minimum.

HUMAN INTERACTION WITH THE ROCK CYCLE
2007 QUESTION 2 PART C

*Referring to any **one** of the following, examine how humans interact with the rock cycle:*
- *Mining*
- *Quarrying*
- *Oil/gas exploration*
- *Geothermal energy production.* (30 marks)

MARKING SCHEME

Interaction identified: **2 marks**
Discussion: **14 SRPs**
– Give credit for up to three examples

Oil and gas reservoirs occur in rocks in Ireland. Most oil and gas originates from the anaerobic decay of organic matter (algae, plankton and plant material) in the sea, lakes and rivers. The decomposing material is transformed by burial and compaction. As the material subsides, it experiences increasing temperatures which transform it into insoluble matter known as kerogen.

Kerogen can, over time, be transformed into hydrocarbons due to heat and pressure. Hydrocarbons are less dense than rock, so they migrate through pore spaces, joints, cracks and faults. When they encounter coarse-grained rock, they begin to accumulate, creating reservoirs.

GAS FIELDS The Kinsale gas field was discovered in 1971 and began production in 1978, but its gas reservoirs are relatively shallow, and resources are expected to be depleted in the next eight to ten years. The Corrib gas field off the coast of Mayo, discovered by Shell, has significant reserves, but there have

Gas rig in the Kinsale gas field

been problems related to transportation to land, refining and storage.

More recently, exploration companies have become interested in mapping and surveying the Dublin coastline in order to establish the extent of oil and gas reserves that may be located in the Irish Sea.

BENEFITS   The potential benefits of an internal hydrocarbon energy resource for Ireland are significant: they include lower energy costs, positive impact on the balance of trade and a reduction in the economic and political risk of being a net importer of energy. However, due to a lack of these resources, we currently import nearly 87 per cent of our total energy requirements, with oil being the most important, followed by coal and gas. This dependency on imports represents a significant economic risk.

HUMAN INTERACTION WITH THE ROCK CYCLE
2009 QUESTION 2 PART C

*Discuss, with reference to **one** of the following, how humans interact with the rock cycle:*
- *Mining*
- *Extraction of building material*
- *Oil/gas exploration*
- *Geothermal energy production.* (30 marks)

MARKING SCHEME ✓

Interaction identified: **2 marks**
Discussion: **14 SRPs**
– Give credit for up to two examples of location

LISHEEN MINES   Lisheen Mines, located in Co. Tipperary, is a source of lead and zinc ores, which are extracted and exported through Cork port. The deposits were identified in 1990, and in 1997 full planning permission for the construction of the mine was granted by the Irish state. In December 1999 the first shipment of ores left Cork port, and by 2008, 2.8 million tonnes of ore were exported.

As an extractive industry, mining can result in environmental damage. Particular concerns include dust and noise pollution, possible destabilisation of natural slopes, and the safe disposal of waste.

In Lisheen Mines, activities are closely monitored by the Environmental Protection Agency. The mining company has been granted an integrated pollution control licence, which can be withdrawn if its activities fail to comply with designated environmental standards. The mines also have an independently certified management system (ISO 14001) to oversee all its operations. The preservation of local water supplies is a critical component of its environmental management system. The mine operates a five-step approach to water management, including water separation, recycling, treatment, efficiency and the monitoring of discharge prior to release into the Drish and Rossestown rivers. Water used for processing has to comply with salmonid and human consumption regulations before it is released. A tailing management system is also in operation, with 50 per cent of material disposed of in underground sites and the remainder in a tailing management facility which is closely monitored. Monitoring of air and noise pollution is also undertaken on a continual basis.

ENVIRONMENTAL IMPACT

The mining operation provides direct employment for 372 people, 70 per cent of whom are from the local hinterland, which has a very positive impact on this rural area. Lisheen Mines is an example of how economic activities can be undertaken in a sustainable manner. Other mines in Ireland include Tara Mines, Co. Meath, Silvermines, Co. Tipperary, and Tynagh Mines, Co. Galway.

Lisheen Mines in Co. Tipperary

HUMAN INTERACTION WITH THE ROCK CYCLE
2010 QUESTION 2 PART C

*Humans interact with the rock cycle in many ways. Discuss this with reference to any **one** human interaction you have studied. (30 marks)*

GEOTHERMAL ENERGY

Geothermal energy involves the use of heat, which is produced from volcanic activity on or beneath the earth's crust. A key region associated with geothermal energy is Iceland. Iceland is located on the divergent North American and Eurasian plates, and it is also a hot spot location, so Iceland experiences significant volcanic activity. When liquid molten magma rises close to the earth's surface, high temperatures occur at relatively shallow depths. This results in the heating of groundwater, and in some cases groundwater temperatures rise above boiling point. This geothermally heated water can then be used to produce geothermal energy. Wells are underground, and the geothermally heated water is pumped to the surface. When it reaches the surface, it turns into steam, which is used to drive turbines and generate electricity. In Iceland, three geothermal power plants provide 17 per cent of the country's electricity requirements (2004 figures). These plants are cost effective and environmentally friendly.

Reykjavik, the capital of Iceland, is entirely heated by geothermal energy. The city is one of the cleanest in the world as there are little or no fossil fuel emissions. After the heated groundwater is used to produce geothermal energy, the cooler water is pumped through underground pipes in greenhouses, thereby enabling flowers and salad crops and vegetables to be produced year round.

Geothermal energy power plant in Iceland

LANDFORM DEVELOPMENT: SURFACE PROCESSES – RIVER, MARINE AND GLACIATION 2006 QUESTION 2 PART B

 *With the aid of a labelled diagram, examine the processes that have led to the formation of any **one** Irish landform of your choice.* (30 marks)

MARKING SCHEME ✓

Landform identified: **2 marks**
Irish example: **2 marks**
Labelled diagram: **4 marks graded**
Examination: **8 SRPs**
Overall coherence: **6 marks graded**
- *Open to other processes (fluvial/glacial/mass movement)*
- *Diagram must have labelling for full marks*
- *Extra (sequential) labelled diagrams can be credited from SRPs*
- *New information from extra labelling/explanation on diagram can be credited from SRPs*
- *Named process without explanation may be awarded an SRP once. Other named processes will require some explanation*

 Feature: Beach

Irish example: Kilkee, Co. Clare

A beach is a feature of marine deposition created by the action of low-energy constructive waves, whereby the swash is greater than the backwash. A beach is a depositional feature associated with an advancing coastline. The advancing

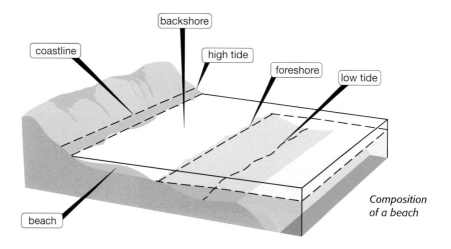

coastline
backshore
high tide
foreshore
low tide
beach

Composition of a beach

waves carry sediments of different sizes by: solution (material dissolved in water); suspension (material carried in suspended motion); traction (material dragged along the sea floor); and saltation ('hip-hop' movement of material along the marine bed). When the energy of these waves is reduced and the longshore drift is interrupted, the sediments are deposited between the low tide and high tide marks.

A beach has two distinct areas: the backshore and the foreshore. The foreshore has a gentle gradient and is composed of small sediments such as sand, silt and pebbles. The backshore has a steeper gradient and contains larger material; it also contains the storm beach. The foreshore is exposed at low tide, while the backshore is only covered at high tide or by storm waves.

A beach can therefore be defined as an accumulation of wave-deposited material between the low and high tide marks.

LANDFORM DEVELOPMENT: SURFACE PROCESSES – RIVER, MARINE AND GLACIATION 2008 QUESTION 1 PART B

*Examine, with the aid of a labelled diagram or diagrams, the processes that have led to the formation of any **one** Irish landform of your choice.* (30 marks)

MARKING SCHEME ✓

Landform identified: **2 marks**
One named process: **2 marks**
Irish example: **2 marks**
Labelled diagram: **4 marks graded**
Examination: **10 SRPs**
 – *Give credit for 1 SRP for diagram without annotation*
 – *Give credit for extra labelling in diagram from examination SRPs*
 – *Feature or process can be starting point*
 – *If description only: 5 SRPs maximum*

Feature: Meander
Irish example: Lower Stage of the River Corrib, Co. Galway
A meander is a feature of both erosion and deposition and is usually associated with the mature or old age stage of a river system. In a straight-flowing river, the energy of the river is concentrated in the centre. However, as a river

Formation of a meander

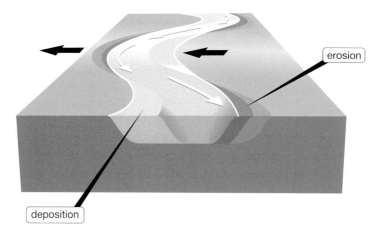

begins to migrate across its flood plain in the mature and old age stage, the energy is diverted to the outside bend, and erosion of the river bank occurs.

PROCESSES OF EROSION

The main processes of erosion are:

- hydraulic action: the force of moving water
- abrasion: the use of the load as a tool of erosion
- attrition: the rounding and smoothing of the load due to constant friction and motion
- solution: the chemical reaction of water on certain rocks – most effective on soft rock (e.g. carbonation on limestone).

As the river comes into contact with the outside bend, it begins to erode the river bank laterally, through hydraulic action and abrasion. This results in undercutting at the waterline, which weakens the bank's structure. Eventually an overhang is created, and this material will collapse under the power of gravity, causing a more pronounced bend to be created.

On the inside bend, the energy of the river is reduced, and the river reaches its over-competence level and begins to deposit the heavier material on the river bed. This material, which was transported by traction and saltation, is composed of pebbles, stones, sand grains and some silt. As deposition continues on the bed of the inside bend, the river becomes shallower. Eventually, a point bar of gravel and pebble deposition is created. This process of erosion on the outside bank and deposition on the inside bank will continue until the river takes on a very distinctive meandering pattern across its flood plain.

LANDFORM DEVELOPMENT: SURFACE PROCESSES – RIVER, MARINE AND GLACIATION 2009 QUESTION 1 PART C

*Examine, with the aid of a labelled diagram/diagrams, the processes which have shaped **one** Irish landform of your choice.* (30 marks)

MARKING SCHEME ✓

Landform identified: **2 marks**
One named process: **2 marks**
Irish example: **2 marks**
Labelled diagram: **4 marks graded**
Examination: **10 SRPs**
– *Give credit for 1 SRP for diagram without annotation*
– *Give credit for extra labelling in diagram from examination SRPs*
– *Feature or process can be starting point*
– *If description only: 2 SRPs maximum*

a

FLOOD PLAIN

A flood plain (for example the Shannon system) is a feature of river deposition, associated with the mature and old age stages of a river system. The ability of a river to transport material is influenced by the energy of the river system, which is primarily influenced by its volume and velocity. In the mature stage of a river system, the river transports material by:

- solution: material in a dissolved form
- suspension: the transportation of material in suspended motion
- saltation: the 'hip-hop' movement of material along the river bed
- traction: the dragging of heavier material along the river bed.

RIVER TRANSPORTATION

However, during a period of heavy and prolonged rainfall, the volume of the river may increase significantly. This may cause the level of the river to rise. If the level of the river rises over the banks of the river, water will flow into the surrounding low-lying area. While this continues, the velocity of the river's flow is reduced, and this causes the river to reach its over-competence level, thus causing the river to deposit some of its load. The heavier material is deposited closest to the flooded river bank, while the lightest material is deposited in the surrounding low-lying area. As the volume of the river drops, the river returns to its natural bed, leaving behind a layer of deposition on the river bank and surrounding low-lying ground. This cycle of flooding, deposition and retreat can continue indefinitely, creating a flood plain. The material deposited by the river, made up of sand, silt and gravels, is known as alluvium. It can be rich in mineral matter and may increase the fertility of the flood plain.

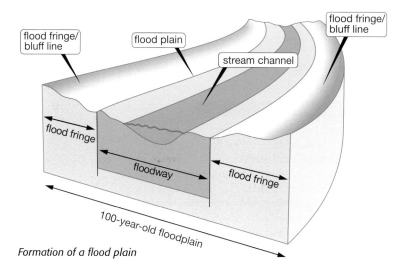

flood fringe/ bluff line

flood plain

flood fringe/ bluff line

stream channel

flood fringe

floodway

flood fringe

100-year-old floodplain

Formation of a flood plain

LANDFORM DEVELOPMENT: SURFACE PROCESSES – RIVER, MARINE AND GLACIATION 2010 QUESTION 1 PART B

Answer (i) or (ii)
(i) Examine, with the aid of a labelled diagram or diagrams, the processes that have led to the formation of any **one** *Irish landform of erosion* **or** *deposition of your choice.* **Or**
(ii) Describe and explain **one** *mass movement process that you have studied.* (30 marks)

SEE LATER ANSWER ON MASS MOVEMENT – PAGE 57

MARKING SCHEME ✓

Landform identified: **2 marks**
Named process: **2 marks**
Irish example: **2 marks**
Labelled diagram: **2 marks + 2 marks**
Examination: **10 SRPs: 2 marks**
- *Give credit for labelling in diagram from examination*
- *Feature or process can be starting point*
- *Maximum of 2 SRPs if description only*

ANSWER **A**

Feature: Cirque

Irish example: Devil's Punch Bowl, Co. Kerry

A cirque is a feature of glacial erosion. It forms in a natural hollow in an upland area. During a period of glaciation, snow accumulates faster than it melts (or ablates). This snow collects in natural hollows, and over time, due to weight and compaction, the snow is transformed into firn or névé ice. Eventually, when all the air is removed, the ice turns blue in colour. As a result of compaction and freeze-thaw action, the natural hollow increases in size. During a period of slightly higher temperatures, the snow melts, and meltwater begins to accumulate in the natural hollow. This causes the glacial ice to move, a process known as rotational slip. As this happens, the hollow increases in size as a result of two processes of glacial erosion: abrasion and plucking. Abrasion happens as the glacier begins to rotate on a pivotal point at the base of the hollow. This movement creates friction and heat, increasing the amount of meltwater on the glacier's side and floor.

Pulled by gravity, the glacier begins to slide out of the hollow, plucking protruding rocks from the hollow's sides and floor. A steep wall is created at the back of the hollow due to freeze-thaw action and abrasion. The glacier eventually moves away from the hollow, leaving behind a highly distinctive feature, which has three steep sides and a narrow lip, leading into a U-shaped valley. In some cases the cirque may fill up with water, and the feature is then referred to as a tarn lake.

Formation of a cirque

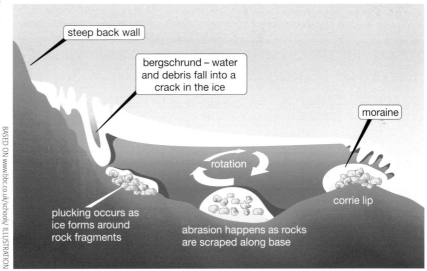

BASED ON www.bbc.co.uk/schools/ILLUSTRATION

ANSWER **B**

Feature: Sand Dunes

Irish example: Curracloe Beach, Co. Wexford

Marine sand dunes are features of deposition which can form at the back of beaches. At low tide, the foreshore and backshore of beaches are exposed. This causes the surface sand grains to dry out. These loose grains can then be transported by the wind, and if a natural hollow occurs at the back of the beach, the wind-transported sand grains begin to accumulate there. If a mound of sand is formed over time, this will eventually be colonised by marram grass. Marram grass is a unique form of marine vegetation, with long intertwined roots which bind loose sand grains together. The grass also has large frond-like leaves which trap wind-blown sand grains.

Sand dunes can grow up to 30m in height. However, they are very fragile structures and can be damaged by human activities, including walking, horse-riding, motor-bike scrambling and sand-boarding. Sand dunes are recognised as unique physical landforms and are classified as Special Areas of Conservation (SAC) under EU environmental legislation. Many coastal county councils are now restricting public access to these landforms in order to prevent damage to the marram grass. In the absence of marram grass, the dunes will become unstable, and the loose sand will be dispersed by the prevailing winds. This will result in the loss of a unique physical landform which is an important habitat for marine fauna and flora.

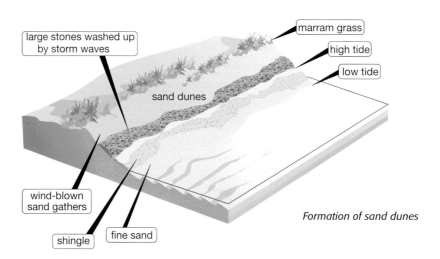

Formation of sand dunes

ISOSTATIC PROCESSES 2009 QUESTION 3 PART B

Isostatic processes involve adjustments to the balance between land and sea. Discuss how these processes have shaped the Irish landscape over time. (30 marks)

MARKING SCHEME ✓

Name one feature: **2 marks**
Name one Irish example: **2 marks**
Discussion: **13 SRPs**
- *Accept river features of rejuvenation and coastal features*
- *Allow reference to one more named feature as SRPs*
- *Give credit for 1 SRP for diagram without annotation*
- *Give credit for extra labelling on diagram from discussion SRPs*

The presence of wave-cut platforms and beaches which are above present high tide marks, as well as fjords and rias, suggests that changes in sea levels have occurred over time. These changes are a result of isostatic processes.

ISOSTATIC MOVEMENT

Isostatic movement can occur as a result of the presence of a heavy load on the earth's crust, such as an ice cap, a large glacial lake or a mountain range. This weight/load can cause the lithosphere to sink a little into the asthenosphere. If the ice cap melts or the lake dries up or the mountain range erodes, the weight will be removed, and over thousands of years the lithosphere will gradually rise up again. This movement is known as isostatic rebound. The movement of the crust in response to the addition or removal of weight can result in sea level changes, creating coastlines of emergence and coastlines of submergence.

Features of emergence are caused by a fall in sea level or a rise in land level. These features include raised beaches, raised wave-cut platforms, raised caves, raised sea arches and raised coastal plains. Irish examples of raised beaches can be seen in Courtmacsherry in Co. Cork and the Ards Peninsula in Co. Down.

Features of submergence, which occur as a result of a rise in sea level or a fall in land level, include rias, fjords and drowned drumlins which now form islands. Irish examples include: rias – south-west coastline from Dingle Bay to Waterford harbour; fjord – Killary harbour, Co. Mayo; drowned drumlins – Clew Bay, Co. Mayo.

RIVER REJUVENATION

A change in sea level can also be seen in river rejuvenation. This can occur in the old age stage of a river, if there is a drop in the base level – the lowest point of entry of a river into the sea. This can happen due to a fall in sea level or a rise in land level. When this occurs the river is forced to attain a new graded profile.

Thus in the old age stage the river begins to erode vertically into its river bed in order to reach the new sea level. The river takes on characteristics associated with the youthful stage and is thus said to be rejuvenated. Irish rivers which have experienced rejuvenation include the Barrow, Nore, Suir and Shannon.

Features associated with rejuvenation:

- Knick point: this marks the point of a sudden change in gradient as the river begins to erode vertically. This point can include a waterfall, which can retreat upstream due to headward erosion.
- Paired terraces: as the river erodes vertically it cuts into the river bed, leaving the former valley floor above river level.
- Incised meanders: as the river erodes vertically, former meanders become incised or entrenched in the valley floor.

Isostatic movement

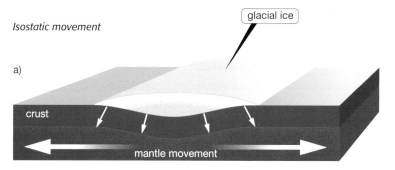

a)

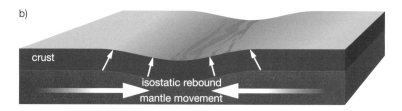

b)

c)

LANDFORM DEVELOPMENT
2007 QUESTION 2 PART B

*With the aid of a labelled diagram, examine the processes that have led to the formation of any **one** Irish landform of your choice.* (30 marks)

MARKING SCHEME

Landform identified: **2 marks**
One named process: **2 marks**
Irish example: **2 marks**
Labelled diagram: **6 marks (graded)**
Examination: **9 SRPs**
– *Give credit for extra labelling in diagram from examination of SRPs*
– *If description only: 3 SRPs maximum*

FORMATION OF FOLD MOUNTAINS

The landform I have studied is the Munster ridge and valley region, which was formed by folding associated with the convergence of tectonic plates. This folded mountain area stretches from west Waterford across Cork and into Kerry.

These mountains were created during the Armorican period of folding (named after a region in south-west France), which created old fold mountains. This folding movement occurred 250 million years ago, due to the collision of the Eurasian and African plates. Plates move as a result of convection currents in the mantle, which occur as molten liquid is heated from the core and rises

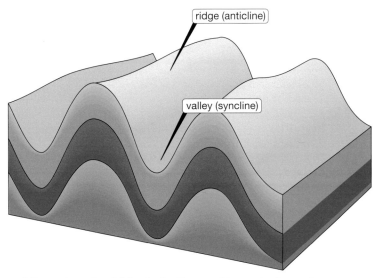

ridge (anticline)

valley (syncline)

Anticline and syncline folding in the Munster ridge and valley region

upwards. As it reaches the lithosphere, it begins to cool, becomes denser and slips sideways. This causes the over-riding crustal plates to move very slowly through a process known as slab pull.

MUNSTER RIDGE AND VALLEY

In the creation of the Munster ridge and valley region, two different sedimentary rocks were involved: old red sandstone (laid down 350–400 million years ago) and limestone (300–350 million years ago). As the plates moved together, pressure was exerted from the south, and the horizontal rock layers were compressed and folded into huge anticlines (ridges) and synclines (valleys). This resulted in the creation of a series of parallel ridges, including the Comeraghs, Knockmealdowns, Macgillycuddy's Reeks and the Galtees, and valleys which have an east–west trend. The valleys contain shale and limestone and today form the pathways of the rivers Blackwater, Lee and Bandon.

Since formation, denudation of the mountains has occurred and the softer limestone has been removed, exposing the underlying old red sandstone.

HUMAN INTERACTION WITH SURFACE PROCESSES

2006 QUESTION 2 PART C

*Examine how human processes can have an impact on the operation of **one** of the following natural processes:*
- *Mass movement processes*
- *River processes*
- *Coastal processes.* (30 marks)

MARKING SCHEME ✓

Impact/human process identified: **2 marks**
Discussion: **11 SRPs**
Overall coherence: **6 marks graded**
- *If all human processes but no natural processes (or vice versa), overall coherence: 0 marks*
- *Up to two examples can be credited from the SRPs*
- *A second (but not a third) impact/process may be credited from the SRPs*
- *Amalgamate all relevant discussion points*

Some coastal areas experience high levels of erosion, and increasing rates are related to rising sea levels and the more unpredictable weather conditions (tropical storms, high winds and Atlantic storms) which have been linked to global warming and climate change. The erosion of coastlines has a negative impact on settlements, road infrastructure and agricultural land. The main processes of marine erosion are hydraulic action, abrasion, attrition, compression and decompression of air, and solution. In an effort to reduce coastal erosion, some local authorities have implemented coastal management practices using: groynes (wooden or stone structures which jut into the sea at right angles); hydrodynamic walls (curved sea walls which deflect wave energy); and coastal rock embankments and elongated piers or jetties, which deflect and reduce wave energy.

EXAMPLES   In Salthill in Co. Galway, an important seaside resort used by both locals and tourists, the local authorities have erected groynes and coastal rock embankments. These measures have reduced erosion of the coastline. The groynes have helped increase the deposition of wave-transported material, thus enhancing the recreational potential of this coastal area. These groynes and coastal boulders have been designed to facilitate access to the coastal area and are now used by anglers and walkers, and seating is provided for the general public. Work undertaken by the local authority provides an excellent example of how coastal management policies can reduce the negative impact of natural physical processes while enhancing the recreational potential of scenic areas. Well-developed management strategies such as these are an example of sustainable management policies. Other examples of coastal areas where local authorities have implemented erosion control strategies include Lahinch in Co. Clare and Youghal in Co. Cork.

Wooden groynes which reduce the energy of waves and encourage deposition

HUMAN INTERACTION WITH SURFACE PROCESSES 2007 QUESTION 3 PART C

*Discuss how **one** of the following could impact on the landscape:*
- *Deforestation (SEE ANSWERS IN CHAPTERS 9 AND 10 ALSO)*
- *Coastal management*
- *Flood control.* (30 marks)

MARKING SCHEME ✓

Impact identified: **2 marks**
Discussion: **14 SRPs**
Overall coherence: **6 marks graded**
– *Give credit for up to three examples*

FLOOD CONTROL

In Ireland, river flooding has resulted in significant damage to houses, businesses, infrastructure and agricultural land. In November 2009, very high rainfall levels resulted in land saturation and the build-up of huge volumes of water in many of our main rivers, including the Shannon, Bandon and Lee. In some areas, including the Shannon and Lee, flood prevention measures – including the use of ESB dams – were used to try to control floodwaters. However, in the case of the river Lee and Cork city, the dam was unable to withstand rapidly rising water levels, and on the evening of Thursday, 24 November, the ESB was forced to open the flood gates and release a huge amount of water in a short space of time. The city's newly installed drainage system was unable to cope, and the western side of the city experienced severe flooding, resulting in the destruction of property, the displacement of people from their homes and the disruption of water supplies as the filtration system and pumping system were both damaged. Engineers examining the causes and consequences of the flooding of Cork city highlighted the problem of building on flood plains; the

Inniscarra Dam on the river Lee

JOHN HERRIOTT

lack of coordination between a variety of agencies responsible for the control of water levels; and the possibility that Ireland will experience more winter rainfall as climatic conditions appear to be changing.

In other areas of the country, local authorities have implemented a variety of measures to reduce flooding by rivers. In Mallow, flood walls are used to try to control water flow on the Blackwater; and in Clonmel, raised river embankments similar to levees have been built to control the levels of the river Suir. A global example of flood control management is the levees on the Mississippi River; however, even these could not withstand the rising water levels experienced by the city of New Orleans in August 2005.

HUMAN INTERACTION WITH SURFACE PROCESSES **2008 QUESTION 1 PART C**

*With reference to examples you have studied, describe and account for one way in which humans attempt to influence or control natural processes. In your answer refer to **one** of the following:*
- *Fluvial processes*
- *Marine processes*
- *Mass movement.* (30 marks)

MARKING SCHEME

Influence/control identified: **2 marks**
Named example: **2 marks**
Reference to natural processes: **2 marks**
Discussion: **12 SRPs**
– *Mere discussion without tie into influence/control: maximum of 6 SRPs*
– *Credit second example from discussion*
– *Examples not tied to Ireland*
– *Amalgamate all relevant discussion*

MASS MOVEMENT

Mass movement, also known as mass wasting, is the movement of loose material as a result of gravity. The material is usually derived from the weathering of bedrock. Mass movement does not require any transporting agent.

The rate of mass movement is influenced by: gradient of slope; slope material; water content; vegetational cover; tectonic activity (earthquakes or volcanoes); and human activities including overgrazing, deforestation, road construction, construction of wind farms, quarrying and mining.

Mass movement can be slow and can take place over a long period of time or it can be very quick, resulting in significant damage.

CONTROL METHODS People have attempted to control mass movement processes by increasing vegetation cover, particularly in upland areas. In Ireland, many of the upland slopes of the BMW region have experienced soil erosion, due to overgrazing by close-cropping animals such as sheep and goats. In an attempt to reduce the mass movement of soil and rock material in these fragile areas, farmers have been encouraged to reduce their stocking density of animals and to increase the percentage of land under forestry. The state forestry board, Coillte, which is responsible for promoting forestry production in Ireland, has provided grants, incentives and educational programmes for farmers to encourage them to increase forestry cover in upland areas.

In areas where road construction has destabilised or steepened natural slopes, local authorities use wire meshing, vegetation cover and rock embankments to stabilise slopes. Examples include the Kinsale roundabout in Cork and the Cork/Mallow road. In the Costa del Sol in Spain, the new motorway linking Malaga to Cadiz has steepened many natural slopes, and the authorities have responded by inserting steel rods and concrete structures to reduce the danger of mass movement of material.

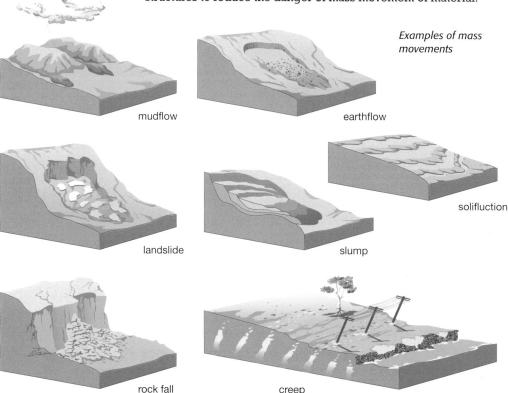

Examples of mass movements

mudflow

earthflow

landslide

slump

solifluction

rock fall

creep

HUMAN INTERACTION WITH SURFACE PROCESSES 2009 QUESTION 3 PART C

*Examine, with reference to **one** of the following, how human activities can impact on surface processes:*
- *Mass movement processes*
- *River processes*
- *Coastal processes.* (30 marks)

MARKING SCHEME ✓

Impact identified: **2 marks**
Named example: **2 marks**
Reference to natural processes: **2 marks**
Discussion: **12 SRPs**
– *Mere discussion without reference to impact: maximum of 6 SRPs*
– *Credit second example from discussion*
– *Examples not tied to Ireland*
– *Amalgamate all relevant discussion*

RIVERS AND DAM CONSTRUCTION

ARDNACRUSHA

The construction of dams on rivers interferes with the natural processes of river erosion, transportation and deposition. In Ireland, dams have been constructed to harness river energy as a source of hydroelectric power.

The most significant river system to be used for hydroelectric power (HEP) is the Shannon system. Work on the HEP potential of the Shannon began in the early 1920s. By 1929 a huge dam had been built at Ardnacrusha in Co. Clare, and a dam at Parteen was also built to control water flow and water levels on the Shannon system. In order to harness the HEP potential of the Shannon, the ESB had to create a storage basin area upstream of the dam, and a large section of the river Shannon downstream of Killaloe in Co. Clare was deliberatedly flooded. The levels of the Shannon and its three major lakes – Allen, Ree and Derg – had to be kept at artificially high levels in order to provide enough water to generate electricity. This resulted in the flooding of some agricultural land, and farmers in the affected areas received compensation from the ESB. The construction of the dam also affected the migratory path of spawning fish, including salmon and eels. A fish pass was built to surmount this problem.

PROBLEMS

The construction of dams can interfere with human settlement patterns, agricultural practices, native fauna and flora and natural processes of river erosion, transportation and deposition. The storage of water behind these dams can be an issue of concern, particularly during periods of prolonged and heavy rainfall (for example, Cork city and Limerick city in November 2009).

WEATHERING (CHEMICAL AND PHYSICAL)
2010 QUESTION 3 PART C

*With reference to the Irish landscape, examine the processes which have influenced the development of any **one** underground landform in a karst region.* (30 marks)

MARKING SCHEME ✓

Named process: **2 marks**
Underground landform identified: **2 marks**
Irish example: **2 marks**
Discussion: **12 SRPs**
– *Maximum of 2 SRPs if discussion only*
– *Give credit for labelling on diagrams from discussion*
– *Credit 1 SRP for diagram without annotation*

WEATHERING

FEATURES

Karst is the term given to limestone areas which have been exposed to weathering (for example the Burren in Co. Clare). Limestone is a soft rock which is porous and well jointed with distinctive bedding planes. The rock is very susceptible to chemical weathering, in particular carbonation. Karst development may be initiated either by the uplift of a limestone surface or its exposure by denudation.

Limestone is normally well jointed (has cracks), which means that rainwater falling on the rock flows along the cracks rather than percolating through the

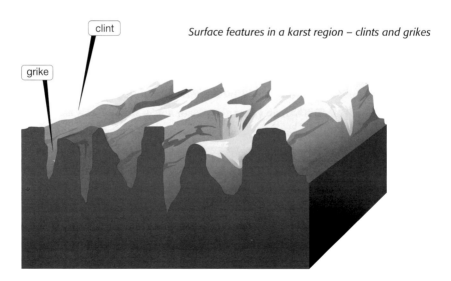

clint

grike

Surface features in a karst region – clints and grikes

surface. The rainwater forms a weak carbonic acid, and when limestone (calcium carbonate) is mixed with water it changes to soluble calcium bicarbonate. Chemical weathering is concentrated along the joints, which become enlarged in a pattern of furrows (grikes) with ridges (clints) between them. These are normally found in parallel sets and at right angles to the bedding plane.

Subterranean features can also be found in large cave structures or caverns. As the water slowly flows through joints, bedding planes and fissures, it gradually dissolves the limestone. These pathways slowly become enlarged into a network of underground passages, with particularly large cavities developing where fissures intersect. These features include caves and dripstones.

- Caves: as running water passes through limestone, it enlarges fissures (cracks) until caves or caverns are formed.
- *DRIPSTONES* • Dripstones: just as calcium carbonate is taken into solution as calcium bicarbonate, the reaction can be reversed if the levels of carbon dioxide decrease due to evaporation. As water drips into caves, some evaporation may take place, causing CO_2 levels to decrease. At this stage, the water is no longer able to hold all the soluble calcium bicarbonate, and it is left to solidify as calcium carbonate on the ceiling or as it reaches the ground.

Carbonation on limestone

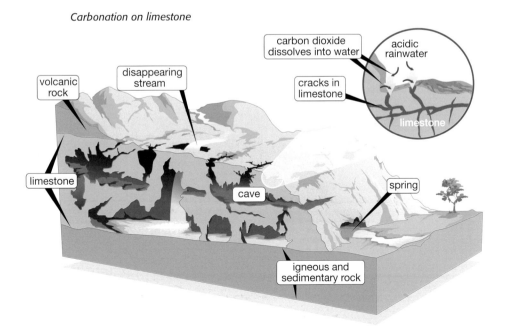

There are a number of different types of dripstone:

- Stalactites: the seepage of water through the ceiling and the evaporation of CO_2 causes calcium carbonate to develop into stone 'icicles' which grow downwards from the ceiling. Each drop of water leaves a deposit. At the outside of the icicle deposition is heaviest, and a hard ring develops and gradually grows to form a tube. Over time, the centre may solidify to form a solid stalactite.
- Stalagmites are formed at the floor of the cave. The calcium carbonate deposition solidifies to form a dome structure which increases in height.
- Columns occur when stalactites and stalagmites join together.
- Curtains occur when water flows through a small fissure rather than a hole. The calcium carbonate solidifies as a curtain dripstone.

All these features can be seen in the Aillwee caves in the Burren and in Crag Cave in Co. Kerry.

Underground features in a karst environment

REGIONAL GEOGRAPHY

2

CONCEPT OF A REGION **2007 QUESTION 5 PART A**

*A region is an area that has one or more characteristics that distinguish it from other areas. Describe the key characteristics of a **climate** region or a **geomorphological** region of your choice.* (20 marks)

MARKING SCHEME

Region named: **4 marks**
Description/explanation: **8 SRPs**

ANSWER **A**

GEOMORPHOLOGICAL REGION: CALEDONIAN FOLD MOUNTAINS

A distinctive physical region I have studied is the Caledonian fold mountains in the north-west of Ireland.

These fold mountains were created approximately 400 million years ago as the North American and Eurasian plates collided. These plates were on either side of an ancient sea known as Iapetus.

Due to the presence of convection currents in the mantle, the plates on either side of the sea floor began to converge. Ocean floor sediments were compressed and uplifted to form the Caledonian fold mountains of the north-west of Ireland, Scotland and Scandinavia.

Since formation, these mountains have experienced weathering and erosion. Sediments were transported to lowland areas; some were compressed and cemented to form old red sandstone, which was formed 350-400 million years ago. Over time, too, the erosion and weathering of the mountains results in isostatic change as weight is removed from the earth's crust.

Today, however, the mountains of the north-west, including Derryveagh, Blue Stacks and the Nephin Range, are distinctive physical features that enhance the scenic landscape of the region.

ANSWER **B**

CLIMATE REGION: INDIA

A distinctive climate region I have studied is India.

Contrary to popular belief, 'monsoon' does not mean 'rainy season'; rather it refers to a wind system that exhibits a significant seasonal reversal in direction. In general, during the winter these winds blow off the continent, thus creating a dry winter monsoon; while in summer warm moisture-laden winds blow from the sea to the land.

Due to the presence of the Himalayan mountains, India has a unique monsoon climate which can be divided into three distinctive seasons.

1. Cool, dry season from mid-December to late February. Light offshore winds from a high pressure system over the north-west of India produce clear skies with average temperatures of 15°C in the north and 30°C in the south. There is very little rainfall.

2. Hot, dry season from March to the end of May. Daytime temperatures can reach 40°C, with dry north-westerly winds. During May the winds change to a southerly direction, resulting in humid conditions but with limited rainfall.

4. Hot, wet season from June to December. South-westerly winds bring heavy rainfall, especially during July.

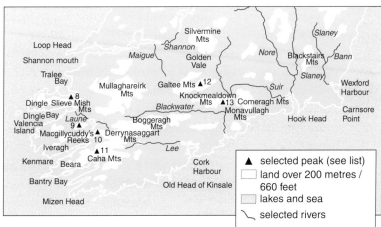

Munster ridge and valley region

CULTURAL REGIONS 2006 QUESTION 5 PART C

'Culture is an important factor in defining some regions.'
*Examine the above statement with reference to **any** region*
you have studied. (30 marks)

> **MARKING SCHEME** ✓

Aspect of culture named: **2 marks**
Naming region: **2 marks**
Examination: **10 SRPs**
Overall coherence: **6 marks graded**
– *A second (but not a third) aspect may be credited from the SRPs*
– *Amalgamate all relevant discussion points*

The distinctive cultural language region I have studied is the Gaeltacht in Ireland. This region is composed of parts of Donegal, Mayo, Galway, Kerry, Cork, Meath and Waterford, and within these areas Irish is still spoken as a community language. Many Gaeltacht regions have Irish colleges and summer schools where students and visitors can become immersed in the language and culture.

The Irish language is part of the Celtic branch of Indo-European languages, which also includes Scots Gaelic, Welsh, Cornish and Breton. The preservation of the Irish language has been regarded by successive Irish governments as critically important. In the Irish educational system, the Irish language is strongly supported from primary to secondary and into third level. This has resulted in the preservation of the language, with nearly 40 per cent of the total population claiming to have some ability to speak and understand Irish. In 2007 Irish was recognised as an official language of the EU.

The 2006 census of population indicated that about 92,000 people live in Gaeltacht areas. These areas receive significant supports from government, which attempt – through economic assistance – to preserve a unique culture and identity. The government agency Údarás na Gaeltachta is responsible for the economic, social and cultural development of these areas, and grants and incentives are available for the establishment of employment opportunities in order to reduce out-migration and encourage population growth. Raidío na Gaeltachta was established in 1972, and the television channel TG4 began broadcasting in 1996, while Seachtain na Gaeilge has became an annual event that encourages all to promote and engage with the language. Some national newspapers also provide an Irish supplement, e.g. *Fóinse* in the *Irish Independent*, which further raises the profile of the language. Further evidence of the increasing profile of the language was evident in the 2011 general election campaign, when the three main party leaders debated in Irish.

Language is an important component of cultural identity, and when passed on from generation to generation assists the preservation of traditions and community identity.

Gaeltacht regions in Ireland

CULTURAL REGIONS **2007 QUESTION 5 PART C**

*Account for the development of cultural differences in a **continental/sub-continental** region that you have studied.* (30 marks)

Kashmir is a distinctive cultural region based on religious differences.

ORIGINS

In 1947, the Indian sub-continent became independent from British colonial administration. The newly independent sub-continent began to divide into different countries: India, Pakistan and (later) Bangladesh. The divisions were driven mainly by religious difference.

The region of Kashmir lies on the border between Pakistan and India. With independence, this region began to experience significant cultural tension, based on religious differences between the Hindu and Islamic populations. Kashmir has a 75 per cent Islamic population, who sought the support of Pakistan. The remainder of the population are Hindus, who sought the support of India. Over time, significant internal tensions developed which resulted in civil conflict. Three wars occurred, resulting in loss of life and destruction of property. The United Nations (UN) intervened and brokered a ceasefire between the conflicting groups. The UN also established a line of control which divided Kashmir into two different zones of administration: the south is administered by India and the north by Pakistan.

IMPLICATIONS

The changing boundary in Kashmir has significant negative implications for the resident populations. Cultural division based on religious differences has increased over time. The country is now divided into two distinctive religious divisions. In the north of the country, which is administered by Pakistan, the majority are Muslims; in the south, which is administered by India, the majority are Hindus. Tension between these groups has historically been high, but levels have increased with the new boundary, and the situation has been exacerbated by the struggle for control of the region by India and Pakistan. These countries view Kashmir as an area of political and economic importance, and Pakistan is extremely concerned about India's control of the river Indus, as water is a key resource in this area. Tension has also increased due to a growth of Islamic fundamentalism in the area. Furthermore, both India and Pakistan have developed nuclear capabilities, and the region remains highly volatile.

Kashmir – political and cultural division

CULTURAL REGIONS 2008 QUESTION 5 PART C

*Describe and explain the importance of culture in defining regions in a **continental/sub-continental** region you have studied.* (30 marks)

MARKING SCHEME ✓

Aspect of culture identified: **2 marks**
Region named: **2 marks**
Naming region: **2 marks**

Examination: **13 SRPs**
– *Mere description/explanation only: 6 SRPs maximum*
– *Discussion without reference to appropriate region: 0 marks*
– *Other aspects of culture may be credited from the SRPs*

India is a subcontinental region with a population of over one billion and an annual population growth of 1.3 per cent. It is the seventh largest country in the world (it is one-third the size of the United States) and the second most populous (population density is 386 persons per sq km). It gained independence from Britain in 1947. The significant cultural diversity of India is related to migration by Indo-European settlers, the spread of Islam through trading routes and migration, and British colonialism.

LANGUAGES

India has 18 official languages, and up to 1,600 minor languages and dialects. The official language, Hindi, is spoken by 41 per cent of the population. English is spoken by the educated and business class and is the most important language for business, commercial and political purposes. Since independence, language divisions in the country have led to conflict and disunity, as language is considered a strong expression of culture.

RELIGION

The dominant religion in India is Hinduism, which was introduced by migrants from areas including south and west Africa, South East Asia and Indonesia. It is based on a caste system – a multi-layered social structure. The top layer includes priests and professionals, while the bottom layer comprises the 'unclean' and 'untouchables'. The layers are decided by heredity, so movement between levels is impossible, especially in rural areas. Some change is occurring in urban areas but is very slow.

Minority religions in India include Buddhism, Islam, Sikhism and Christianity. Buddhism was initially established in the sixth century BC. Its followers are mainly located in the south and north-east of India.

Islam developed in the country during the tenth century. There are an estimated 200 million Muslims in India, with the greatest concentration in the northern states. The spread of Islam to India is associated with the establishment of trade routes and migration from the Arabian region. All members of Islam are considered equal and there is no caste system.

Sikhism appeared in the fifteenth century. A combination of Hinduism and Islam, it does not have a caste system and is popular in the Punjab region in the north-west.

Christianity was introduced during British colonial times; numbers are small and have no distinct geographic distribution.

After independence in 1947, the Indian sub-continent began to split on religious grounds, and two states were created: India (Hindu) and Pakistan (Islamic). However, drawing the political boundary was difficult, and many minorities were left in each country. This led to dreadful violence and the eventual migration of up to 15 million people.

India – distinctive physical regions

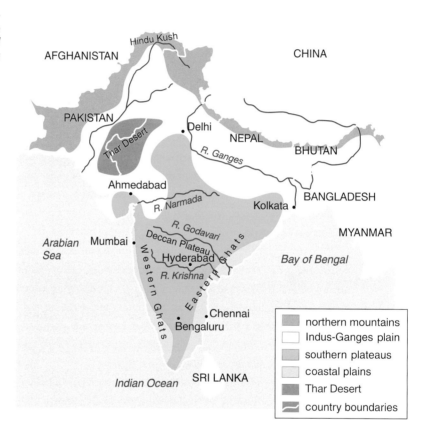

CULTURAL REGIONS 2010 QUESTION 4 PART C

*Describe and explain the importance of culture in defining **any** region studied by you.* (30 marks)

MARKING SCHEME ✓

Region named: **2 marks**
Aspect of culture identified: **2 marks**
Explanation: **13 SRPs**
– *Other aspects of culture may be credited from the SRPs*
– *Accept a broad definition of culture*

A cultural region I have studied is Northern Ireland, which was established by the Government of Ireland Act 1920. Its population is distinctive in terms of religion, economic ethos, political affiliations and ethnic links.

RELIGION Religion is very important in defining cultural regions, and religious beliefs have an important role to play in cultural differentiation. Northern Ireland is mostly composed of two different religious groups. The majority are Protestants whose roots can be traced to the Scottish and English planters of the mid-1600s who were granted land in Northern Ireland under British colonial rule. The second religious group is the Catholic minority, and their roots can be traced back to the displaced population of the Plantations.

In general, Catholics are nationalist in outlook and want Northern Ireland to be politically independent from Britain: this has resulted in the development of a strong republican/nationalist tradition. In contrast, the Protestant population is mostly unionist or loyalist in outlook and wishes to retain strong links to Britain and the British Crown. Since the 'Troubles', which began in 1968, tension between the majority, Protestant, and minority, Catholic populations increased. In Belfast and Derry distinct religious boundaries have developed – for example the Falls Road (Catholic) and the Shankill Road (Protestant), and the Waterside (Protestant) and Bogside (Catholic) – and these differences are clearly seen in the iconography of the streets. These religious tensions have hugely negative economic and socio-cultural effects.

There was no political interaction between Northern Ireland and the Irish

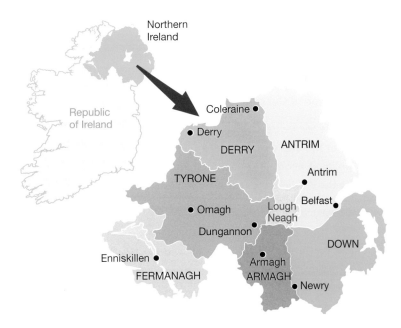

[government until the 1960s, but dialogue was discontinued when the Troubles] began.

GOOD FRIDAY AGREEMENT

A major breakthrough was achieved with the signing of the Belfast Agreement (Good Friday Agreement) in 1998. This resulted in the establishment of a three-strand agreement:

Strand 1: the establishment of the Northern Ireland assembly, which is composed of 108 democratically elected members.

Strand 2: the establishment of north–south ministerial bodies which discuss areas of mutual interest, e.g. tourism, agriculture, and waterways. The key objective is to establish cross-border co-operation.

Strand 3: allows for the creation of British–Irish inter-governmental conferences to encourage dialogue and mutual co-operation.

The key objective of the Good Friday Agreement is to improve relations between all sectors rather than dwell on differences. Its success can be clearly seen in the political, cultural and economic progress of the region.

REGIONAL BOUNDARIES
2006 SAMPLE PAPER **QUESTION 6 PART C**

*Explain with reference to **one** example the causes and consequences of change in the boundaries of a region over time.* (30 marks)

Germany is an example of a region which has experienced a change in boundaries over time.

Division of Germany

Cause of change

BERLIN WALL

After the end of World War II, Germany was divided into east and west. The political, economic and social divide between east and west was symbolised by the Berlin Wall, which was constructed in 1962.

Consequence of change

CAPITALISM AND COMMUNISM

The west became a democratic country underpinned by capitalism's free market forces, while the east fell under the control of the USSR, which introduced a communist system of centralised planning, exerting state control over all aspects of life. West Germany's postwar economic recovery was rapid and it became a founding member of the EU in 1957. By contrast, east Germany

*Germany
– East and West*

KEY

West Germany

East Germany

experienced poor economic growth under the communist system, which placed great emphasis on the development of heavy industries that used large amounts of raw materials, energy and labour. Agriculture was developed on the basis of collectivisation, which offered farmers little incentive to increase output or to update methods of production. Overall, the economy showed slow growth rates, and consumer income was limited. The service sector remained very much underdeveloped as a result, with the exception of employment opportunities within state institutions.

Reunification

Cause

A NEW GERMANY   In 1989, the communist government in east Germany collapsed. The Berlin Wall was taken down, and in 1990 the map of Germany was redrawn as west and east were united in a single democratic system.

Consequences

Despite sharing similar cultural traits, language and religion, the unification of Germany has not been simple. East Germans' expectations were very high, especially regarding economic prosperity, but their economy and workers found it difficult to be competitive in a free-market economy. Hundreds of thousands of former east Germans migrated to western Germany in search of better-paid jobs, but their poor skills and lack of adaptability made it difficult for them to gain well-paid positions in the modern, technologically advanced economy that characterises west Germany. Increasing cultural tension developed between Turkish workers in western Germany and the newly mobile east German workforce. Meanwhile, due to the significant out-migration of its younger population, the former east Germany began to experience population decline, and with an ageing society is becoming more and more dependent on government support.

Despite these difficulties Germany has regained its economic dominance within the EU, and with strict fiscal management policies its economy has now begun to show strong signs of growth.

URBAN REGIONS **2006 QUESTION 4 PART C**

*'The boundaries of city regions have expanded over time.'
Discuss this statement with reference to **one** example you
have studied. (30 marks)*

MARKING SCHEME ✔

Named example: **2 marks**
Reference to time: **1 SRP**
Discussion: **10 SRPs**
Overall coherence: **6 marks graded**
– Discussion can refer to describe/explain/discuss
– If two examples discussed, mark both and credit the better one
– If a theoretical answer (no example given), overall coherence: 0 marks

The city region I have studied is Paris, which is located in the Paris Basin. The city covers an area of 100km in diameter and has a population of ten million. An old historic city, it has experienced significant growth over time. As a primate city, Paris dominates all other French cities in terms of population density and economic activities. The growth of the city has been influenced by a number of factors, including its site and situation.

LOCATION

Paris is located on the bridging point of two rivers, the Marne and the Seine, which means that it is a key nodal site and trading route. It is the centre of France's national and international transport systems, including road, rail, river and air: its airports are Orly to the south, the centrally located Charles de Gaulle, and Beauvais, 75km to the north, which is used by low-cost airlines.

ECONOMIC IMPORTANCE

It is a core economic region and has a well-developed primary base in the Paris Basin, and the city has become a key market centre for agricultural outputs. It has a diversified secondary sector which offers significant employment opportunities. Over time, industry has expanded outwards from the inner city to the suburbs.

Seventy per cent of all service-based employment in France is centred on the Paris region. Paris is the seat of government and administration, and this has resulted in the establishment of a significant civil service. The city and surrounding hinterland is also a well-developed educational centre and is noted as a financial services centre, with employment opportunities in banking, commerce and business consultancy. It has become a key centre of immigration, and the resulting population growth has led to the development of five new satellite towns, including Evry and Marne-la-Vallée.

Paris Basin – key urban centres and transport network

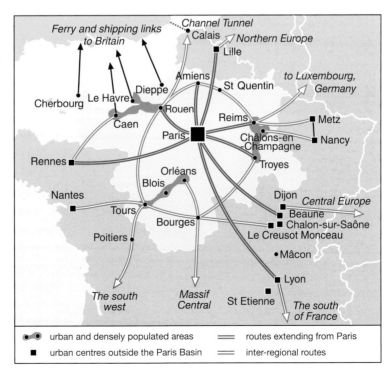

- ●●● urban and densely populated areas
- ■ urban centres outside the Paris Basin
- ═ routes extending from Paris
- ═ inter-regional routes

URBAN REGIONS 2007 QUESTION 6 PART B

*Examine the growth of an urban area in a **European region – not Ireland** – of your choice.* (30 marks)

MARKING SCHEME ✓

Region named: **2 marks**
Urban area named: **2 marks**
Examination: **13 SRPs**
– Discussion without link to an urban area: 7 SRPs maximum
– Mere description only: 7 SRPs maximum

The city region I have studied is the Randstad in The Netherlands. The Randstad is the most urbanised area in western Europe, and is made up of a number of key cities: Amsterdam, Utrecht, Rotterdam, The Hague and Haarlem. The region contains 7.2 million people (46 per cent of the Dutch population) in only 22 per cent of the country's total land area.

EMPLOYMENT

The Randstad has experienced significant growth since the 1850s. The region has high employment growth rates, and an unemployment rate of only 3.9 per cent in 2005. Its labour force is well educated – the region has eight universities and 18 colleges of higher education.

Randstad

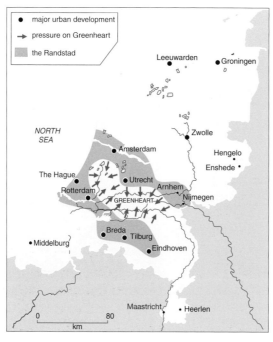

The Randstad is a core economic region with a diversified employment base: 84 per cent of the population is employed in services, 13 per cent in industry and 3 per cent in agriculture. Key services include financial, business and creative industries (advertising, the arts and publishing). Financial services are prominent in Amsterdam, information and communication technologies in Utrecht, and insurance and telecommunications in The Hague.

TOURISM   The Randstad is also a noted tourist destination, and Amsterdam is ranked tenth among the best European cities for conferences and exhibitions. The nodality of the region has also resulted in significant growth in key modes of transport, including the port of Rotterdam, which is ranked eighth in the world in terms of container transport. The Randstad has a well-developed canal network, and the new freight railway that links Rotterdam to Germany has further enhanced its economic potential and growth. Schiphol Airport is one of the busiest in Europe and is an important hub for continental and intra-European flights.

PLANNING   Due to its long history of growth, the Randstad has a well-established urban
POLICY   planning policy. This policy aims to limit urban sprawl and protect the Greenheart area. The Greenheart in the centre of the region is very important in terms of horticultural activity. The area is a world leader in greenhouse cultivation of high value outputs. Horticulture accounts for 5 per cent of GDP, and 90 per cent of flowers are produced for the export market.

The Greenheart is also an important zone for recreation, and planning policies have attempted to preserve and protect this area from urban sprawl. Planners allow the construction of high-density buildings in designated areas in the Randstad, but try to maintain buffer zones or green belt areas to reduce congestion. However, critical problems exist, especially in terms of traffic congestion, pressure on freshwater supplies, and noise and air pollution.

URBAN REGIONS **2008 QUESTION 4 PART C**

*Describe and explain the growth of **one** major urban area in a continental/sub-continental region you have studied. (30 marks)*

MARKING SCHEME   ✓

Region named: **2 marks**
Urban area named: **2 marks**
Examination: **13 SRPs**
– Do not accept Irish or European regions
– Discussion without reference to appropriate region: 0 marks
– Mere description/explanation: maximum of 6 SRPs

The sub-continental region I have studied is India, and the urban area I have studied is Kolkata. India is a developing economy, and its current rate of urbanisation is approximately 28 per cent. According to experts, the rate of urbanisation in developing countries is expanding rapidly, and it is estimated that by 2030 almost 60 per cent of people in developing countries will live in

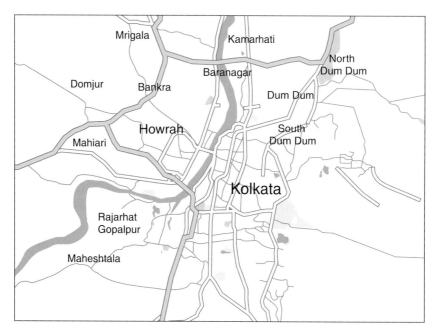

Map of Kolkata

cities. Kolkata has a population of over 12 million and a population density of 25,000 per square kilometre.

This level of growth will lead to serious problems, especially in terms of pressure on both physical infrastructure – including roads, transport, housing, water supply and waste disposal – and social infrastructure, including health, education, employment opportunities and recreational facilities.

CAUSES OF URBANISATION

Increasing rates of urbanisation in Indian cities are related to two critical issues: rural-to-urban migration and high fertility rates which leads to high levels of natural increase.

Rural-to-urban migration is influenced by a variety of push and pull factors. Push factors include lack of employment opportunities in rural areas, low living standards, poverty and lack of access to services such as health and education. Additionally, migration from rural areas may also occur as people try to improve their social and economic conditions by migrating to areas where the caste system is less rigid. Migrants move to urban areas with the expectation of a better way of life; however, this expectation may not be fulfilled.

POVERTY

Many of India's large cities, including Delhi and Kolkata, are unable to cope with increasing population numbers. In Kolkata, poverty is a critical problem, and it has been exacerbated by increasing rates of urbanisation. Many residents do not have access to adequate food, shelter, clothing or clean water.

Thirty per cent of the population live in slums known as *bustees* and survive by collecting waste food and material in landfill sites, and by begging on the streets. Sanitation and access to clean water is limited, and diseases such as cholera and typhoid are common. Infant mortality rates are high. Access to medical and health facilities is limited. An estimated 500,000 people live on the streets of the city. India is still a developing country, and the government does not have adequate economic resources to address the significant economic and social challenges posed by increasing levels of urbanisation.

URBAN REGIONS **2009 QUESTION 6 PART B**

 *Examine the development of **one** urban area in a **European region (not Ireland)** that you have studied.* (30 marks)

 MARKING SCHEME

Region named: **2 marks**
Urban area named: **2 marks**
Examination: **13 SRPs**
– *Do not accept Irish or continental/sub-continental regions*
– *Discussion without reference to named or clearly inferred urban area: 0 marks*
– *Mere description: maximum of 6 SRPs*
– *An urban area can be a city, a specific part of a named city, or areas such as Randstad*

 The urban region I have studied is Paris.

Paris is a primate city and is characterised by significant urban sprawl. The city is located in the centre of the Paris Basin and covers an area of 100km in diameter with a population of ten million.

LOCATION   Paris is located on a very advantageous site for the development of an urban centre. Its location at the meeting point of two rivers, the Marne and the Seine, has allowed the city to develop as an important bridging point. It is also an historic trading, administrative and defensive centre. Its situation has also aided the growth and expansion of the city. Paris is centrally located on the lowland fertile plain of the Paris Basin, which is well drained by the Seine, Marne and Oise, and has become a focal point of routeways and trade. This has allowed the city to become the centre of France's national and international transport systems, including road, rail, river and air. There are three major airports: the centrally located Charles de Gaulle, Orly airport to the south, and Beauvais airport 75km to the north, which is used by low-cost airlines.

ECONOMIC IMPORTANCE

Paris, the capital of France, is the centre of national government, administration, finance and an international business/trade centre. Seventy per cent of all service-based employment in France is centered on the Paris region. In addition, it is a well-developed educational centre and a noted financial services centre, with employment opportunities in banking, commerce and business consultancy. Its importance in fashion, culture and tourism provides a variety of service-based employment opportunities. The area is a nodal centre of transport and communications and has become a key centre of immigration; the resulting population growth has led to the development of five new satellite towns.

The Paris Basin is the most fertile agricultural region in France, and the city developed as a key market centre for its output.

Paris and its surrounding hinterland is the industrial heartland of the French economy because of its location, well-developed primary base, large internal market, excellent transport and communications, and significant labour force, which has a long industrial tradition and is skilled and adaptive. The region has a diversified secondary economic base ranging from cars to chemicals and textiles to footwear.

All these factors have influenced the growth of Paris over time.

Paris Basin – key urban centres and transport network

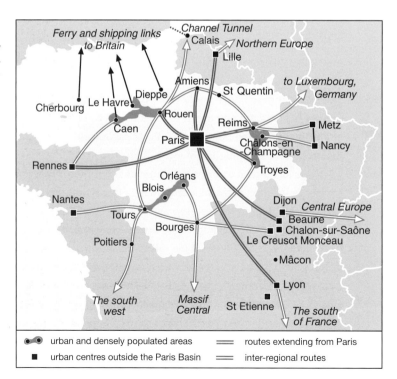

URBAN REGIONS 2010 QUESTION 5 PART B

 *Examine the development of **one** urban area in any **Irish region** studied by you.* (30 marks)

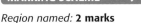
MARKING SCHEME ✓

Region named: **2 marks**
Urban area named: **2 marks**
Examination: **13 SRPs**
− *Do not accept European or continental/sub-continental regions*
− *Discussion without reference to a named or clearly inferred urban area: 0 marks*
− *Development can be positive or negative*

 Dublin is a primate city located in the Southern and Eastern region and has experienced significant growth since the 1960s. Its daily urban system now extends to cover an 80km commuting zone.

The expansion of Dublin is related to:

CAUSES OF EXPANSION

• Its position as the nodal point of the country's transport network (road, rail, sea and air).
• Its being the centre of employment opportunities due in particular to a significant increase in service-based employment which has occurred over time. The city is a key area for financial services and research and development (R&D).
• Rising land values, which encouraged outward growth.
• Its growth in the recent past as a key area of in-migration for the newly mobile eastern European workforce.

NEW TOWNS

Expansion from the 1960s onward resulted in the establishment of three new towns: Blanchardstown, Clondalkin and Tallaght. However, over time these became part of the urban area as land values increased and people moved further out, thus extending the commuting zone.

PROBLEMS

This kind of expansion has resulted in a number of critical socio-cultural, economic and environmental problems.

• The high cost of residential housing, resulting from an expanding population and the building boom associated with the 'Celtic Tiger' economy. In addition, there is a large amount of older housing, particularly in the inner city, which requires renovation and upgrading.
• Increasing population pressure on green belt and recreational space.

- High levels of traffic congestion.
- Environmental concerns – pollution, in particular air (smog) and noise pollution, as well as scenic degradation. Population growth is placing huge pressure on fresh water supplies, and the local authorities are now considering the possibility of bringing water from the Shannon system to alleviate water shortages in Dublin.
- Decline of the inner city population, related to the growth of the suburbs. The inner city also has poor housing stock and high values which makes housing very expensive.
- Urban sprawl intensifies all the problems above.
- The central role of Dublin has inhibited growth in other Irish cities, creating a significant regional imbalance in terms of population distribution and economic activity.

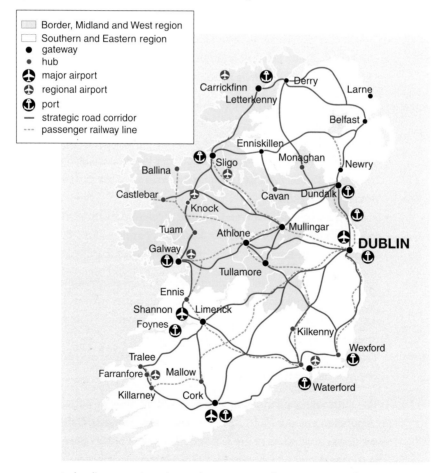

Ireland's economic regions, urban centres and transport networks

ECONOMIC REGIONS 1: CORE REGIONS
2010 QUESTION 6 PART B

Regions can be defined by many factors including:
- *Economic*
- *Human*
- *Physical.*

*Explain how any **one** of the above factors has defined an **Irish region** studied by you.* (30 marks)

MARKING SCHEME ✓

Region named: **2 marks**
Examination: **14 SRPs**
– *Do not accept European or continental/sub-continental regions*
– *Maximum of 2 SRPs for mere listing of aspects of factor (heading) chosen*

An economic core region I have studied in Ireland is the greater Dublin area (GDA). This region's economic development has been encouraged by a variety of physical and socio-economic characteristics. The GDA is dominated by Dublin city, which has a population of 1.2 million, is a primate city and is the centre of political and economic decision-making.

AGRICULTURE The region has a well-developed primary sector which includes intensive productive agriculture that has been positively influenced by the physical landscape and proximity to an expanding high-value market. The soils of the GDA are predominately brown earths. These soils are deep, with high levels of inherent fertility, and are suitable for intensive livestock rearing, dairying and beef, and also cereal and market gardening production. The climate of the region, with adequate rainfall levels and average temperatures in winter of 3–6°C and in summer of 15°C, ensures a long growing season. The region is noted for the growth of barley and wheat, high-quality dairy and beef output, and high-value market gardening goods, including new potatoes, salad vegetables and fruit. Agricultural incomes in the region are significantly above national averages, and farmers are young and well educated. The emphasis is on scientific methods of production and high-value, high-quality output. Agriculture in the region has all the attributes associated with a core agricultural region.

SECONDARY ECONOMIC ACTIVITIES The development of secondary sector activities has also been positively influenced by both physical factors and socio-economic conditions.

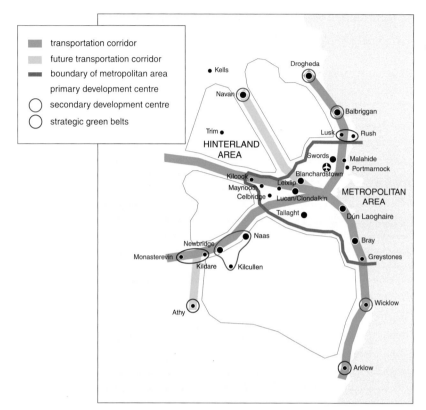

The greater Dublin area (GDA)

Legend:
- transportation corridor
- future transportation corridor
- boundary of metropolitan area
- primary development centre
- secondary development centre
- strategic green belts

Historically, the region's central location, its well-developed portal area and proximity to Britain for importing raw materials and exporting finished goods has encouraged the development of manufacturing activity. Key industries included brewing and distilling, food processing and textile manufacturing. In the more recent past, the region has become a key location for more high-tech industries, including electronics, computers and pharmaceuticals. Many industrial estates and business parks have developed in key locations, including Leixlip, Finglas and Tallaght. Key multinational companies in the region include IBM, Microsoft and Intel. The availability of a well-educated, flexible and innovative workforce and well-developed transport and communications networks have been critical to the growth and expansion of the secondary base of the GDA economy.

TERTIARY SECTOR   In the GDA, the expansion of the tertiary sector has been critical to its economic success. Dublin is the political, administrative and financial centre of the Irish economy, and the region has high employment opportunities in these areas. The development of the International Financial Services Centre (IFSC) during the 1990s allowed for the expansion of internationally traded services, and Dublin became a leading location for many multinational financial service companies. The GDA is also a nodal point for the country's transport and communication networks, and the expansion of this sector has resulted in a significant growth in employment. In addition, the tourist industry is well developed and adds significantly to the economic vitality and growth of the region.

The GDA is an example of a core economic region which has developed and expanded over time as a result of a range of physical and socio-economic conditions.

ECONOMIC REGIONS 2: PERIPHERAL REGIONS
2010 QUESTION 6 PART B

Regions can be defined by many factors including:
* *Economic*
* *Human*
* *Physical.*

*Explain how any **one** of the above factors has defined an **Irish** region studied by you.* (30 marks)

MARKING SCHEME

Region named: **2 marks**
Examination: **14 SRPs**
– *Do not accept European or continental/sub-continental regions*
– *Maximum of 2 SRPs for mere listing of aspects of factor (heading) chosen*

An example of a peripheral economic region in Ireland is the Western region, which includes the counties of Mayo, Galway and Roscommon. The economic development of this region has been negatively affected by a variety of physical and socio-economic attributes.

LANDSCAPE   The physical landscape is mainly rugged upland areas, which have a negative influence on soil structure, transport networks and population density and distribution. The soils of the region are dominated by shallow infertile gleys and acidic peat. Many upland areas experience soil erosion and mass movement in the form of soil creep and rock falls.

AGRICULTURE   Agriculture tends to be extensive in nature, with an emphasis on sheep, dairying and beef. Farms are generally small-scale and fragmented, and farmers are older and more conservative than their counterparts in the rest of

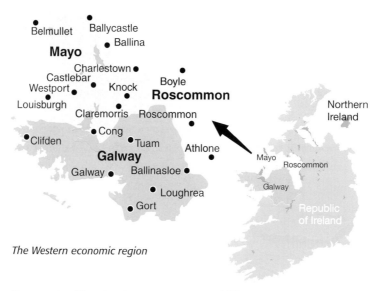

The Western economic region

the country. Farming is seen as a way of life rather than an economic activity, and many farmers are dependent on support from the Common Agricultural Policy (CAP). Climatic conditions hinder the growth of cereals and root crops, and pasture is the main component of the agricultural economy, but growth rates are lower than those in the south and east of the country.

FISHING Fishing is an important component of the economy of the Western region, but because of the restrictions imposed by the Common Fisheries Policy – the total allowable catch (TAC) system – many small-scale fishermen are finding it increasingly difficult to remain economically viable.

SECONDARY ACTIVITIES The development of secondary sector activities in the Western region was traditionally hampered by its isolated geographic location, poorly developed transport links, poor internal market and the lack of an educated, skilled workforce. In order to stimulate secondary sector activities, the Irish government established two agencies, Údarás na Gaeltachta and the Industrial Development Authority. These agencies have transformed the secondary sector of the region, and Galway in particular has become a key location for many multinational high-tech companies, including Ingerscoll Rand (engineering), ADC (electronics, computers), Nortel (telecommunications) and Boston Scientific (medical health care manufacturing). Despite the growth in secondary sector activities, however, the region still requires constant support from national government in order to compete with the Southern and Eastern region. During the most recent economic downturn, unemployment levels in the region have risen significantly, and emigration is now becoming the only option for many people.

TERTIARY
ACTIVITIES   The tertiary sector has been positively affected by the growth of tourism in recent decades, Galway in particular experiencing significant growth in tourist numbers. Development of the region's tourist potential remains hampered by the seasonality of the industry and by the area's underdeveloped transport network, though there have been some improvements in transport: the Galway to Dublin motorway, the upgrading of the Galway–Dublin rail line and the development of Ireland West Airport in Knock. Investment in transport has been made possible by significant capital transfers from the EU through the European Regional Development Fund, but further investment is needed.

Educational opportunities in the region have grown over time, and NUIG and GMIT are critical in terms of providing third-level educational opportunities for the younger population of this region.

The Western region remains a peripheral economic region which will require continuing economic assistance from national government.

ECONOMIC ACTIVITIES IN REGIONS: 1 PRIMARY ACTIVITIES 2006 QUESTION 4 PART B

*Examine some of the factors that have influenced the development of **one** economic activity in a non-Irish region that you have studied.*
(30 marks)

 MARKING SCHEME ✓

Economic activity named: **2 marks**
Region named: **2 marks**
Examination: **10 SRPs**
Overall coherence: **6 marks graded**
– *Credit naming factors (to a maximum of two) from the SRPs*
– *Amalgamate all relevant discussion for SRPs, but do not credit naming a third factor*
– *Accept European or continental/sub-continental region*
– *Accept any economic activity (primary/secondary/tertiary)*
– *If only one factor identified, overall coherence: 0 marks*
– *If no link to economic activity, overall coherence: 0 marks*

    The economic activity I have studied is agriculture in the Paris Basin.

FACTOR 1: PHYSICAL
LANDSCAPE

This region occupies a quarter of France. Most of the region is covered by limon soil – wind-blown soil deposited during and after the last Ice Age. This soil is fine-grained and rich in mineral material. Clay deposition occurs in the east and south of the region. This soil is highly suitable for arable farming. Up

Paris Basin – key urban centres and transport network

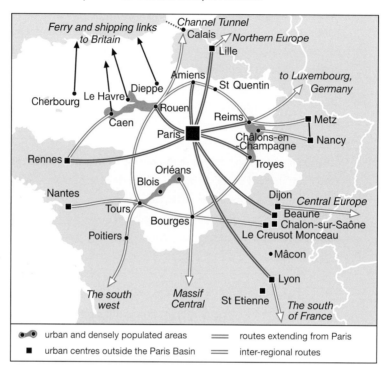

to 80 per cent of agricultural land use in the Paris Basin is devoted to cereals: wheat is the main crop in Île de France and Picardy; maize and barley are also produced; and sugar beet is grown as a rotation crop. On the eastern slopes of the basin, viticulture is also important. Both dairying and market gardening are concentrated in the Paris hinterland. This is related to significant demand from the Paris urban market of ten million people. Overall the region is very suitable for arable farming, and mechanisation is widely used.

FACTOR 2: CLIMATIC CONDITIONS

The region is influenced by two climatic types. The coastal area has a maritime climate, with south-westerly winds providing adequate rainfall throughout the year, and temperatures are mild during the winter and warm in summer. The inland area experiences a transitional maritime/continental climate, with annual precipitation of 1,000mm (at the coast) and 600mm (inland). Temperatures in Paris average 2°C in January and 20°C in July. Climate, relief and soil fertility have encouraged intensive agriculture based on scientific methods, farms are large, and farmers are progressive and well educated. Income levels from farming are high, and the region has all the characteristics of a core intensive agricultural centre which is positively affected by both physical and socio-economic characteristics.

ECONOMIC ACTIVITIES IN REGIONS 1: PRIMARY ACTIVITIES 2006 QUESTION 5 PART A

*Examine the development of primary activities in **one non-Irish** European region of your choice.* (20 marks)

MARKING SCHEME ✓

Region named: **2 marks**
Two primary activities named: **2 marks**
Examination: **5 SRPs**
Overall coherence: **4 marks graded**
– *If no region named, overall coherence: 0 marks.*
– *Do not accept Irish/continental/sub-continental regions*

AGRICULTURE

The non-Irish European region I have studied is the south of Italy. The two key primary activities in this region are agriculture and forestry.

Agriculture is the most important primary activity in the south of Italy, but its development has been handicapped by both physical factors and socio-economic conditions.

About 85 per cent of the region is upland and mountainous, which has inhibited the development of soils and has resulted in significant soil erosion.

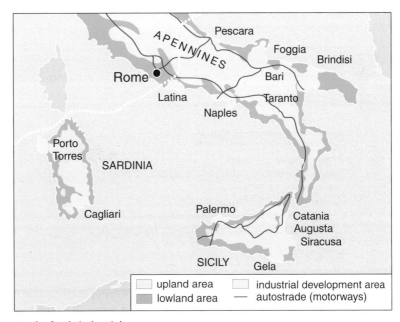

South of Italy industrial zones

The climate is a harsh Mediterranean one, and many areas experience drought conditions in the summer months. In addition, the traditional landholding systems of *latifundia* (large lowland estates owned by absentee landlords) and *minifundia* (small upland farming units which have experienced significant subdivision and have become economically unviable) have resulted in extensive farming practices throughout the region.

FORESTRY   In the past, the upland areas were covered by extensive forests of hardwoods and softwoods. The vegetation of the Apennines is similar to that of central Europe. Dense clusters of chestnut, cypress and oak occupied the lower slopes, and at higher elevations there were extensive patches of pine and fir. However, forestry was not managed sustainably, and extensive deforestation occurred. Today, forest areas are limited, and the forestry industry is not highly significant. The deforestation of the south of Italy's timber resources in the past is a prime example of the consequences of unsustainable management policies.

Forestry can be an important renewable resource, as long as adequate replanting policies are implemented; and the benefits of forestry can be significant both economically and environmentally. The deforestation of the uplands in the south of Italy has increased soil erosion and has had a negative effect on the biodiversity of the region.

ECONOMIC ACTIVITIES IN REGIONS 1: PRIMARY ACTIVITIES 2007 QUESTION 4 PART C

*Examine the development of primary activities in a **continental/sub-continental** region of your choice.* (30 marks)

MARKING SCHEME ✓

Region named: **2 marks**
Two primary activities identified: **2 marks + 2 marks**
Examination: **12 SRPs**
Overall coherence: **4 marks graded**
– *Do not accept Irish or European regions*
– *Discussion without link to a region: 6 SRPs maximum*

The sub-continental region I have studied is India. The two key primary activities I will deal with are agriculture and fishing.

The Indus-Ganges plain, which gets its name from the rivers Ganges and
AGRICULTURE Indus, is a rich, fertile land encompassing most of northern and eastern India.

The soil is rich in silt, making the plain one of the most intensely farmed areas of the world. Farming on the Indus-Ganges plain primarily consists of rice and wheat grown in rotation. Other crops include maize, sugar cane and cotton. However, farming in the region is labour-intensive, and all planting, weeding and harvesting is done by hand. Farm plots are small and subdivision is common as a result of the growing population. The main source of rainfall is the south-west monsoon, which supplies over 80 per cent of India's annual rainfall and is crucial for India's agricultural system. If the monsoon is late, young crops suffer and irrigation systems can be affected. Low-intensity rain can negatively affect crop productivity, especially rice; and poor yields can in turn result in hunger and possible famine (as happened in 1987). Very high-intensity rain can cause flooding and destroy crops (July-August 2009).

FISHING Commercial fish production in India has increased more than five-fold since independence in 1947. Fishing is now a key economic activity for many coastal states. The development of the industry has been encouraged by government investment, which has focused on expanding inland fish farming, modernising

India – distinctive physical regions

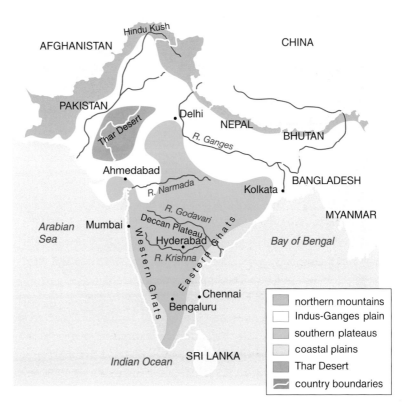

coastal fishing ports and encouraging exports of deep sea fish. The government has also invested in improving fishing methods, ice production, fish processing, storage and marketing.

The value of fish and processed fish rose from less than 1 per cent of total exports in 1960 to 3 per cent by 1993. Key species include mackerel, sardines, shark, ray, tuna and mullet. India's Exclusive Economic Zone extends 279km into the Indian Ocean and includes almost two million square kilometres of rich fishing grounds. By the mid-1980s, only 33 per cent of that area had been exploited. Potential annual catch in this zone is estimated at 4.5 million tonnes. In 1990, India had 1.7 million full-time fishermen, 1.3 million part-time fishermen and 2.3 million people indirectly employed in fishing activities. The main fishing ports include Kerala, Chennai and Mumbai. India is now one of the largest seafood-exporting nations, and shrimp, lobster tails and shark fins are key commodities for the huge Japanese market. Exports from the fishing industry are valued at nearly $2 billion.

ECONOMIC ACTIVITIES IN REGIONS 1: PRIMARY ACTIVITIES 2007 QUESTION 6 PART C

*Examine **two** factors that have influenced the development of primary activities in any **Irish region** you have studied. (30 marks)*

MARKING SCHEME

Region named: **2 marks**
Two primary activities identified: **2 marks + 2 marks**
Two factors named: **2 marks + 2 marks**
Examination: **10 SRPs**
– Discussion without link to a region: 4 SRPs maximum
– Discussion of one factor only: 4 SRPs maximum

The region I have studied is the Border, Midlands and West (BMW) region in Ireland. Two important primary activities in this region are agriculture and fishing.

Climate and soils are two critical factors influencing the development
AGRICULTURE of agriculture. The BMW region experiences a cool temperate oceanic climate with mild winters and significant rainfall throughout the year, averaging between 2,500mm in the uplands and 1,500mm in the lowlands. Average summer temperatures rarely exceed 15°C. These conditions restrict

agricultural activities, especially growing cereals (wheat and barley) and tillage. Pasture is the most important vegetation, and dairying, beef rearing, and sheep are important components of agricultural activity.

A significant proportion of the BMW is upland (averaging above 300m); this has resulted in the formation of shallow infertile soils which are exposed to soil erosion and the leaching of important minerals during periods of heavy rainfall. Thus, the upland areas are associated with extensive grazing of sheep. However, overstocking has occurred, and this has increased the problem of soil erosion in uplands.

In the lowlands the soil structure has been negatively affected by significant areas of acidic peatlands, and soil waterlogging and gleisation are also problems. In addition, the soils of the BMW have limited horizon development, and the humus layer is not as rich in organic material as the brown earth soils of the south and east.

The combination of climate and soil structure has inhibited the development of agriculture in the region, and only 14 per cent of the farms are considered economically viable. Agriculture accounts for 15 per cent of total employment in the region, the average age of farmers is 54 years compared to 52 years for the state, average farm size is 26.5 hectares (state 32.9 hectares) and average income is €7,772 (state €11,042). In addition, many farmers are dependent on CAP support to remain economically viable.

FISHING
The BMW region has significant natural advantages for the development of its commercial fishing industry:

- A sheltered indented coastline from Donegal to Galway has many deep-water natural harbours, including Killybegs, Rossaveal and Galway.
- A shallow extensive continental shelf encourages the growth of plankton – a food source for fish. These shallow waters also make fish harvesting easier.
- The North Atlantic Drift keeps Irish ports ice-free during the winter and encourages the growth of plankton.

The coastal communities of Donegal, Mayo and Galway have sought to exploit the economic potential of Ireland's fishing resources, but their efforts have been thwarted by a lack of government support and by restrictions imposed by the EU under the Common Fisheries Policy, introduced in 1983 to conserve and manage this important renewable resource. Fish stocks have continued to decline, so restrictions on fish catches have been implemented, including the total allowable catch (TAC) system; regulations on net sizes; restrictions on access to spawning grounds; and a reduction in the number of fishing days per year.

This policy has had significant implications for the Irish fishing industry, especially in terms of quotas (TAC). Ireland owns 16 per cent of EU waters, yet only 11 per cent of TAC, and only 20 per cent of the value of fish caught in the Irish Fishing Box are landed by Irish-registered boats. Spanish boats are allowed access to the Irish Box, and this is not aiding the development of the industry. Mackerel, herring and cod are the most important species for the Irish fishing fleet, but now these species are under threat due to declining stocks as a result of overfishing. Further restrictions are being introduced to protect these endangered species. These restrictions are aimed at protecting an important natural resource from unsustainable management practices; however, they are also having a devastating impact on the number of fishermen and the economic viability of the industry for many coastal communities in the BMW region.

Ireland's Border, Midlands and West region (BMW)

ECONOMIC ACTIVITIES IN REGIONS 1: PRIMARY ACTIVITIES 2008 QUESTION 6 PART B

*Examine the development of primary economic activities in **an Irish region** that you have studied.* (30 marks)

MARKING SCHEME

Region named: **2 marks**
Two named primary activities: **2 marks + 2 marks**
Examination: **12 SRPs**
– *Do not accept European or continental/sub-continental regions*
– *Discussion without reference to appropriate region: 0 marks*
– *Up to two examples can be credited from SRPs*
– *Mere description only: maximum of 6 SRPs*

The Irish region I have studied is the Southern and Eastern region, and the two key primary activities in this region are agriculture and forestry.

AGRICULTURE

Agriculture in the Southern and Eastern region has been positively influenced by both physical and socio-economic conditions. The physical landscape of key areas in the south and east facilitates the development of large-scale agricultural units which use a lot of mechanisation and very little direct labour (for example, dairying in the Golden Vale and beef rearing in Meath and Kildare). Soils in the south and east are generally inherently fertile, and key soil types include brown earths and gleys. Brown earths in particular are ideal for arable farming, and the Southern and Eastern region is noted for its cereals, tillage and market gardening.

Some farmers in the Southern and Eastern region earn up to 50 per cent more than farmers in the BMW; they are also younger and are more likely to view farming as an economic activity rather than a way of life. Agricultural activity in the Southern and Eastern region has all the characteristics associated with a core agricultural region: high levels of mechanisation, large field sizes, consolidated holdings, specialised activities, high incomes, scientific methods of production and young educated farmers.

FORESTRY

Because of large-scale deforestation in the past, Ireland has very little land under forestry – just 10 per cent of total land use in 2010. However, the Southern and Eastern region, especially in the upland areas of Dublin/Wicklow and Cork/Kerry, is highly suitable for forestry production. Climate conditions are not extreme, and the region can produce timber three to four times faster than Sweden. The state forestry board, Coillte (established in 1989), has had a positive impact on afforestation policies, and the availability of forestry grants from the EU has increased annual planting rates in Ireland from 10,000 hectares in 1989 to 30,000 by 2009. Key species include Sitka spruce and Scots pine, and in the recent past greater emphasis has been placed on the planting of native deciduous trees. Wicklow and Waterford have the highest rates of forestry in the Southern and Eastern region, while Dublin has the lowest levels. This reflects the demands on land in terms of high levels of urbanisation and land values.

Ireland's Southern and Eastern region

ECONOMIC ACTIVITIES IN REGIONS 1: PRIMARY ACTIVITIES **2009 QUESTION 4 PART B**

Describe and explain any **two** *physical factors that have influenced the development of agriculture in an* **Irish region** *that you have studied.* (30 marks)

The region I have studied is the BMW in Ireland. Two important factors influencing the development of agriculture in the region are climate and soils.

CLIMATE

The region experiences a cool temperate oceanic climate with mild winters and significant rainfall throughout the year, averaging 2,500mm in the uplands and 1,500mm in the lowlands. Average winter temperatures range from 3°C to 5°C, and frost in coastal areas is unusual due to the presence of the North Atlantic Drift. Average summer temperatures rarely exceed 15°C, though they can sometimes reach mid to high 20s. The climate is one of non-extremes; however, these climatic conditions restrict some agricultural activities, especially growing cereals (wheat and barley) and tillage. Summer temperatures are not high enough to ripen cereal crops, while high rainfall means that soils are wet and colder than those in the south and east. Pasture is the most important vegetation, and dairying, beef rearing, and sheep are important components of agricultural activity. However, pasture productivity is lower in the BMW than in the Southern and Eastern region, and this is related to lower average temperatures during the growing season and waterlogging of lowlands due to high rainfall.

SOILS

A significant area of the BMW is upland, averaging above 300m. This has resulted in the formation of shallow infertile soils, which are exposed to soil erosion and experience the leaching of important minerals during periods of heavy rainfall. The upland areas are associated with extensive grazing of sheep and goats; but overstocking has exacerbated the problem of soil erosion in uplands. In the lowlands, the soil structure has been negatively affected by significant areas of acidic peatlands, and waterlogging and gleisation of soils is a problem. In addition, the soils of the BMW have limited horizon development, and the humus layer is poorer in organic material than the brown earth soils of the south and east.

The combination of climate and soil structure has inhibited the development of agriculture in the region, and only 14 per cent of the farms are considered economically viable. Agriculture accounts for 15 per cent of total employment in the region, the average age of farmers is 54 years compared to 52 years for the state, average farm size is 26.5 hectares (state 32.9 hectares) and average income is €7,772 (state €11,042). In addition, many farmers are dependent on CAP support to remain economically viable.

ECONOMIC ACTIVITIES IN REGIONS 1: PRIMARY ACTIVITIES 2010 QUESTION 5 PART C

*Describe and explain **two** factors that influence the development of agriculture in a **non-European continental/sub-continental region** that you have studied.* (30 marks)

See answer to 2007 Question 4 Part C on page 94

ECONOMIC ACTIVITIES IN REGIONS 2: SECONDARY ACTIVITIES 2007 QUESTION 5 PART B

*Examine the development of secondary economic activities in an **Irish region** that you have studied.* (30 marks)

MARKING SCHEME

Region named: **2 marks**
Two named secondary activities: **2 marks + 2 marks**
Examination: **12 SRPs**
– *Do not accept European or continental/sub-continental regions*
– *Discussion without link to a region: 6 SRPs maximum*

The region I have studied is the Border, Midlands and West (BMW) region.

BACKGROUND   The key secondary activities in this region are computer/electronics and medical health care devices. Industries that have been attracted to the BMW region include Boston Scientific (medical health care devices), which is located in Galway city and employs 2,200 people, and ADC, a software company, also in Galway city. The development of these sectors of economic activity is directly related to the government policy of attracting multinational companies. This policy was initiated in the 1960s as Ireland began to develop a free market economy and began a policy of 'industrialisation by invitation'.

FACTORS   A number of factors have helped the BMW region attract these MNCs.

- Membership of the EU (since 1973), which has allowed companies access to an internal market of approximately 500 million and a market with no internal tariff and trade barriers.
- Improved infrastructure in the region, which has reduced geographical isolation, cut transport costs and increased access to EU markets. These improvements have been significantly aided by investment provided by the EU. Improvements in road and rail infrastructure include the upgrading of the M6, which now links Galway city to Dublin (with a journey time of only two hours); the upgrading of the Ennis/Galway road network; and improvements to the Galway–Sligo–Letterkenny route. Provisions are in place to upgrade the Western Rail Corridor.
- A well-educated English-speaking workforce. The spread of third-level educational centres has been important in increasing the skill levels of the BMW workforce; examples include Galway–Mayo Institute of Technology and Letterkenny Institute of Technology.
- Proactive government policy, including tax incentives, the building of advance factories and the provision of training programmes.

ECONOMIC ACTIVITIES IN REGIONS 2: SECONDARY ACTIVITIES 2008 QUESTION 4 PART B

*Examine the factors that influence the development of **one** economic activity in **a European region (not Ireland)** that you have studied. (30 marks)*

 MARKING SCHEME ✓

Named economic activity: **2 marks**
Two factors identified: **2 marks + 2 marks**
Region named: **2 marks**
Examination: **11 SRPs**
– *Do not accept Irish or continental/sub-continental regions*
– *Discussion without reference to appropriate region: 0 marks*
– *Mere description: maximum of 5 SRPs*
– *Give credit for examples: maximum of 2 SRPs*

The economic activity I have studied is the secondary sector in the south of Italy. Two key aspects influencing its development are historical factors and government policy.

The development of secondary sector economic activities in southern Italy

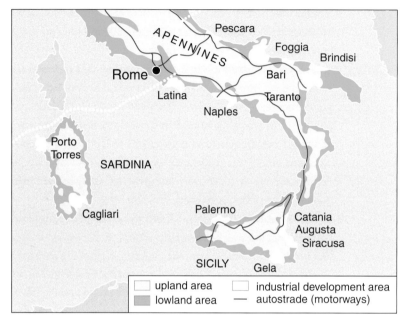

South of Italy industrial zones

HISTORICAL FACTORS

has been historically hindered by a lack of native energy sources and native raw materials. Prior to World War II, industrialisation was heavily dependent on access and proximity to a native energy source. At this stage, the key energy source in western Europe was coal, and heavy resource-orientated industries, including iron and steel, developed in key coalfield locations, including the Ruhr, the British midlands and the Saar. The south of Italy did not have its own supply of coal and importation costs were high, which meant that the region was largely bypassed by the Industrial Revolution. The region's lack of raw materials also hindered its industrial development: proximity to raw materials was essential for industrial development in the pre-World War II period. The south of Italy also experienced high transport costs due to its poorly developed infrastructure. Additionally, it had a low-income internal market and was geographically isolated from the core urban and industrial market of the north Italian plain. Finally, the region's labour force was unskilled in secondary activities, and high levels of out-migration occurred throughout the early and mid-1900s.

GOVERNMENT POLICY

During the early 1960s and until the mid-1980s, the Italian government adopted a regional policy known as 'Cassa per il Mezzogiorno' (Fund for the South) to try to promote industrialisation and secondary activities. During the post-World War II period, the factors influencing industrial location had

ECONOMIC ACTIVITIES IN REGIONS 3: TERTIARY ACTIVITIES 2006 QUESTION 6 PART C

Account for the development of tertiary activities in **one non-Irish European region** *of your choice.* (30 marks)

MARKING SCHEME ✓

Two activities identified: **2 marks each**
Naming region: **2 marks**
Discussion: **9 SRPs**
Overall coherence: **6 marks graded**
– *Discussion on tertiary activities without link to region: overall coherence: 0 marks*
– *Discussion on one activity only: overall coherence: 0 marks*

The non-Irish European region I have studied is the south of Italy. Two key sectors of the tertiary environment in this region are tourism and transport.

TOURISM

The south of Italy has a number of critical competitive advantages with regard to the development of a tourist industry. It has a varied physical landscape, including mountainous areas (e.g. the Apennines) and low-lying coastal zones with numerous sandy beaches and sheltered bays (e.g. the Amalfi coastline). The region also has some highly scenic areas associated with both active and dormant volcanoes, including Etna and Vesuvius. In addition, it has a wide variety of native species of fauna and flora, and its natural environment has not been seriously affected by human activities. Its rich culture of historic settlement dates back to the Greeks and Romans and encompasses Arab settlers and traders. Many remnants of these historic settlements can be seen in the landscape.

In terms of climate, the south of Italy experiences high summer temperatures, with an average of 14 to 16 hours of sunshine per day, and limited rainfall. In addition, an increase in disposable incomes and annual paid leave has had a positive impact on tourist numbers. The tourist potential of the region has also been positively affected by infrastructural developments, including the *autostrade* and airports at Bari, Palermo and Naples.

The region is an attractive destination for domestic tourists, many of whom come from the north Italian plain, and also for international tourists. In 2006, the region attracted over 12 million tourists, of whom nine million were domestic.

TRANSPORT

The development of a modern transport network has been crucially important to the economic development of the south of Italy. Initial government investment concentrated on developing the road network: the Autostrada del Sole, part of the Cassa plan, links the south of Italy to the prosperous north Italian plain. In addition, the government has invested in deepwater ports, including Taranto and ports in Sicily, which facilitate the import of raw materials and energy and the export of finished products. Furthermore, investment has been provided by the government to develop a number of key airports, including Bari, Naples and Palermo. Air transport is an important component

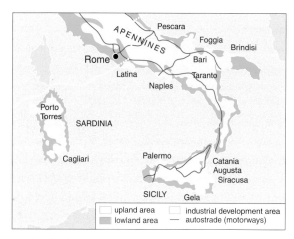

of the tertiary sector as it facilitates the transport of high-value, low-weight goods and increases the tourist and business potential of a region.

Despite these investments, however, the south of Italy remains an under-developed rural area, and continuous investment in transport infrastructure will be required to reduce the geographic isolation of this Objective 1 region (Convergence region).

South of Italy – autostrade and ports

ECONOMIC ACTIVITIES IN REGIONS 3: TERTIARY ACTIVITIES **2007 QUESTION 4 PART B**

*Examine the development of any **one** of the following economic processes in **a European region – not Ireland –** of your choice.*
- *Industry*
    (SEE ANSWERS TO SECONDARY ACTIVITIES – 2008 QUESTION 4 PART B, PAGE 103 AND 2010 QUESTION 6 PART C, PAGE 107)
- *Tourism.* (30 marks)

MARKING SCHEME   ✓

Region named: **2 marks**
Discussion: **14 SRPs**
- *Do not accept Irish or continental/sub-continental regions*
- *Discussion without link to a region: 8 SRPs maximum*
- *Give credit for up to three examples*

TOURISM

The non-Irish European region I have studied is southern Italy. The economic activity that I will deal with is tourism.

Southern Italy enjoys a number of significant competitive advantages for the development of a tourist industry. Its varied physical landscape includes mountainous areas and low-lying coastal zones with sandy beaches and sheltered bays (e.g. the Amalfi coastline). Tectonic activity in the region means that there are some very scenic areas of volcanic activity, including Mount Etna and Mount Vesuvius. It has a wide range of native species of fauna and flora, and its natural environment has not been seriously eroded by human activities. It has a rich culture of historic settlement dating from the Greeks through the Romans to Arab settlers and traders. The remains of these historic settlements are still evident in the landscape.

The climate is also perfect for tourism, with high summer temperatures and limited rainfall.

In addition, an increase in disposable consumer incomes and annual paid leave has had a positive impact on tourist numbers. The tourist potential of the region has been positively affected by the development of the *autostrade* and airports. The region had an estimated 12 million visitors in 2006, which helped create employment: direct (hotels and transport); indirect (restaurants, food production and the wine industry); and induced (craft goods, etc.). The additional spending power that tourists bring to the south of Italy increases local incomes and provides a boost to the wider economy.

FACTORS

The development of the south of Italy's tourist potential has been positively affected by:

- higher incomes among consumers
- increased annual paid holidays and shorter working hours
- improvements in accessibility related to developments in transport
- greater competition, resulting in lower costs
- package holidays
- increased education among consumers.

Tourism as an economic activity can result in significant economic, environmental and socio-cultural advantages for destination economies. However, in the absence of sustainable management policies, tourism can also have significant negative impacts on destination areas.

ECONOMIC ACTIVITIES IN REGIONS 3: TERTIARY ACTIVITIES **2008 QUESTION 4 PART B**

*Examine the factors that influence the development of **one** economic activity in **a European region (not Ireland)** that you have studied. (30 marks)*

MARKING SCHEME

Named economic activity: **2 marks**
Two factors identified: **2 marks + 2 marks**
Region named: **2 marks**
Examination: **11 SRPs**
– *Do not accept Irish or continental/sub-continental regions*
– *Discussion without reference to appropriate region: 0 marks*
– *Mere description: maximum 5 SRPs*
– *Give credit for examples: maximum 2 SRPs*

The economic activity I have studied is tourism in the urban region of Paris. Two critical factors have influenced the development of tourism: the attractions of the region and changing consumer characteristics.

TOURIST ATTRACTIONS
    Tourism in the Paris region is well developed, and it is an important area of economic activity in terms of employment creation and exchequer earnings. Paris is well endowed with tourist attractions, particularly historical and cultural sites and events. Key cultural attractions include the Arc de Triomphe and a wide variety of museums and art galleries, including the Louvre. The tourist potential of the city has been enhanced by the establishment of the Disneyland resort and the development of the French theme park Parc Asterix. Paris and its surrounding hinterland is a noted centre for high-quality foods and cuisine. It has also promoted its viticulture industry as a key tourist attraction. Many vineyards in the region are open to the public, offering wine tours and wine tasting. The city and region is also one of the fashion capitals of Europe.

    Since it is a popular destination for weekend and city breaks, the number of tourists visiting the region has grown significantly over the years. This increase has been helped by the development of the Channel Tunnel, the availability of high-speed rail networks and the use of the region's airports by low-cost airlines (e.g. Ryanair's flights to Beauvais). In 2003, an estimated 28.8 million tourists visited the city.

CONSUMERS
    The tourist industry of Paris and its hinterland has been positively affected by changing consumer characteristics, including:

Paris Basin – key urban centres and transport network

- higher incomes, resulting in a greater consumer spend for tourism-related activities, e.g. city breaks, cultural and historic tours
- longer annual paid holidays and shorter working hours, especially for consumers in high-income core economies, e.g. Germany, northern Italy and the Low Countries
- improvements in accessibility related to developments in transport which allow consumers greater flexibility in terms of when they travel and how long they stay
- greater competition among tourist providers, which has resulted in lower costs for consumers, particularly for transport (Eurostar and the Channel Tunnel), accommodation and activities
- the growth of internet package holidays, which has increased the marketability and accessibility of Paris as a destination area
- increased education among consumers regarding the attractions and facilities of Paris as a tourist destination.

ECONOMIC ACTIVITIES IN REGIONS 3: TERTIARY ACTIVITIES 2008 QUESTION 5 PART B

*Examine the development of tertiary economic activities in **an Irish region** that you have studied.* (30 marks)

MARKING SCHEME ✓

Region named: **2 marks**
Two named tertiary activities: **2 marks + 2 marks**
Examination: **12 SRPs**
– *Do not accept European or continental/sub-continental regions*
– *Do not accept Ireland (the whole of) as a region*
– *Discussion without reference to appropriate region: 0 marks*

TRANSPORT

The Irish region I have studied is the Southern and Eastern region. The key tertiary activities in this region are transport and tourism.

The development of transport networks is the lifeline of any economic system. Historically, the transport network in the south and east of Ireland was undeveloped, with the exception of the ports of Cork, Waterford and Dublin. These ports had been important to the British Empire and were the best developed transport facilities in the country up to independence and beyond.

The development of a modern transport infrastructure in the region did not occur until Ireland joined the EU in 1973. As a member of the EU, the Irish government received significant capital transfers from the Common Regional Policy. Some of this capital has been invested in upgrading the transport infrastructure of the Southern and Eastern region. Improved transport infrastructure in the region has reduced geographic isolation, reduced transport costs and increased access to key EU markets.

Ireland's Southern and Eastern region

Significant investment has been made in building motorways, including the M6 linking Dublin to Galway, and the M7, which links Dublin to Limerick, and a large number of bypasses, which have improved the accessibility of cities and towns in the region. There has also been investment in rail infrastructure, including the upgrading of main lines and the purchase of new rolling stock. It is now easier to travel by rail from Dublin to Cork, Cork to Limerick and Cork to Killarney. Airports have also been upgraded, and new terminals have been built at Cork and Dublin. All these improvements have been aided by EU investment and are part of the National Spatial Strategy (introduced in 2002) and the Transport 21 programme. The creation of hubs (including Mallow, Tralee and Kilkenny) and gateways (including Cork, Limerick and Waterford) and the linking of these hubs and gateways with upgraded and new road corridors has improved the transport efficiency of the region.

TOURISM   The Southern and Eastern region has significant tourist potential because of its physical landscape and cultural/historical attractions. The region's coastline, which extends from Clare, through Kerry, Cork, Waterford, Wexford and Wicklow to Dublin, boasts many spectacular features of both erosion and deposition. Inland areas include the Munster ridge and valley region, the Dublin/Wicklow mountains, the rivers Shannon, Lee, Blackwater and Liffey, and many inland lakes, which are a rich source of recreational and tourist potential. Top-quality golfcourses, horse riding, angling and walking trails are also available for visitors seeking an activity-based holiday.

The historical/cultural history of the region is rich and varied, ranging from a large variety of pre-Christian, Christian and Norman settlements to museums which preserve a rich account of Irish society and history down through the ages. The accessibility of the region in terms of ports, airports, rail and roads has enhanced its tourist potential. Seventy-five per cent of total tourist revenue, which was estimated at €4.9 billion in 2007, is spent in the Southern and Eastern region. The sector is a key source of employment opportunity and has a positive multiplier effect on the wider economy.

ECONOMIC ACTIVITIES IN REGIONS 3: TERTIARY ACTIVITIES 2009 QUESTION 5 PART C

*Account for the development of **one** tertiary economic activity in any **one continental/sub-continental region** that you have studied.* (30 marks)

> **MARKING SCHEME** ✓
>
> *Region named:* **2 marks**
> *Named tertiary activity:* **2 marks**
> *Examination:* **13 SRPs**
> – *Do not accept Irish or European regions*
> – *Discussion without reference to appropriate region: 0 marks*
> – *If more than one tertiary activity is given, mark both separately and accept the best*
> – *Allow up to 3 SRPs for specific examples or locations related to named activity*

The sub-continental region I have studied is India, and an important tertiary activity in this region is transport. India's transport sector is large and varied, and it caters for a population of 1.1 billion. In 1997, the transport sector contributed 4.4 per cent to the nation's GDP, with road transportation contributing the greatest share.

TRANSPORT   Transport is the lifeline of any economy, and connectivity between India's urban and rural areas is essential for economic growth. Since the early 1990s, India's expanding economy has experienced a 10 per cent increase in demand for transport infrastructure and services. However, the sector has not been able to keep pace with rising demand. Major improvements in the sector are therefore required to support the country's continued economic growth and to reduce poverty in both rural and urban areas.

ROADS   The main modes of transport in India are road, rail and ports. Roads are the

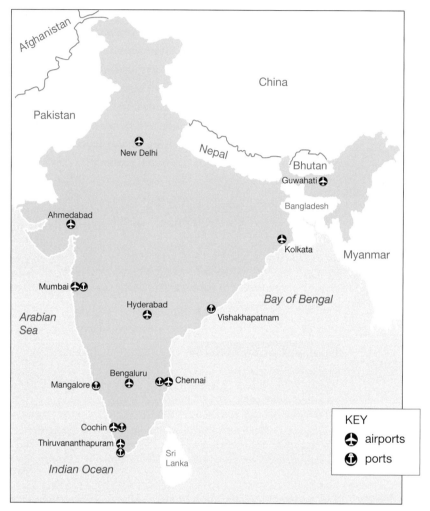

India's ports and airports

most important mode of transport as they carry almost 90 per cent of the country's passenger traffic and 65 per cent of its cargo. The density of India's highway network – 0.66km of highway per square kilometre of land – is similar to that of the United States (0.65) and much greater than China's (0.16). However, most highways in India are narrow and congested, with poor surface quality, and 40 per cent of India's villages do not have access to all-weather roads.

RAIL   India's railway system is the largest railway network in Asia and the fourth most heavily used system in the world. It carries an estimated 14 million passengers a day and is one of the world's largest employers. Until recently, the railways played a leading role in carrying passengers and cargo across India's vast country. However, with the introduction of tariff policies, including a tax on cargo to subsidise passenger travel, the movement of freight is increasingly shifting from railways to roads.

PORTS India has 12 major and 185 minor and intermediate ports along its vast coastline: examples include Mumbai, Chennai and Kolkata. These ports serve the country's growing foreign trade in petroleum products, iron ore and coal, as well as the import and export of container goods. The development of India's ports can be traced back to British colonialism. Inland water transportation remains largely undeveloped despite India's 14,000km of navigable rivers and canals.

Overall, transport infrastructure in India is more developed in the centre and south-western parts of the country, which is related to population distribution and physical landscape. The continual development of India's transport infrastructure remains a critical economic challenge facing the Indian government.

ECONOMIC ACTIVITIES IN REGIONS 3: TERTIARY ACTIVITIES 2010 QUESTION 4 PART B

*Examine the factors that influence the development of **one** tertiary economic activity in **a European region (not in Ireland)** that you have studied.* (30 marks)

MARKING SCHEME ✓

Named tertiary economic activity: **2 marks**
Two factors identified: **2 marks + 2 marks**
Region named: **2 marks**
Examination: **11 x SRPs**
– *Do not accept Irish or continental/sub-continental regions*
– *Discussion without reference to named or clearly inferred region: 0 marks*
– *All further factors require discussion*

The non-Irish European region I have studied is Scania in Sweden. The economic activity I will deal with is tourism.

Scania has a number of critical competitive advantages in developing a tourist industry. It has a well-developed transport network, including road, rail and air transport, which has made the region more accessible; for example, TOURIST ATTRACTIONS the Øresund bridge is a 16km-long tunnel and bridge linking Malmö with

Copenhagen. The region has a wide variety of native species of fauna (deer, elks and hares) and flora, and over 1000km of marked walking trails. There are a number of important rivers and large lakes, which are highly scenic, and are centres for the development of an important angling tourism industry. Malmö has many parks, gardens and restaurants, and is a city of huge cultural diversity, with over 170 different nationalities. The region experiences a cool temperate oceanic climate with warm summers (average water temperatures at beach locations are 19°C) and mild winters.

CONSUMERS Over time, the development of Scania's tourism potential has been positively affected by:

- higher incomes
- longer annual paid holidays and shorter working hours
- better accessibility due to developments in transport
- greater competition between travel companies, resulting in lower cost
- package holidays
- increased education among consumers.

Tourism has a positive impact on employment creation: direct (hotels, transport), indirect (food production) and induced (craft goods, etc.). An estimated 60,000 people are employed in tourism and related activities.

Tourism as an economic activity can bring significant economic, environmental and socio-cultural advantages to destination economies. However, without sustainable management policies, tourism can also have significant negative impacts.

ECONOMIC & ENVIRONMENTAL CHALLENGES
2006 SAMPLE PAPER **QUESTION 4 PART C**

*Examine **one** of the economic challenges facing a **non-European** region of your choice.* (30 marks)

The non-European region I have studied is India. A critical economic challenge facing this country is the rapid rate of urbanisation.

India is a developing economy, and its current rate of urbanisation is approximately 28 per cent, but according to experts the rates of urbanisation *URBANISATION* in developing countries are expanding rapidly, and by 2030 almost 60 per cent of people in developing countries will live in cities. This level of growth will lead to serious problems, especially pressure on physical infrastructure, including roads, transport, housing, water supply and waste disposal; and social infrastructure, including health, education, employment opportunities and recreational facilities.

Increasing rates of urbanisation in Indian cities are related to two critical issues: rural-to-urban migration; and a high fertility rate leading to high levels of natural increase.

MIGRATION Rural-to-urban migration is influenced by a variety of push and pull factors. Push factors include lack of employment opportunities in rural areas, low living standards, poverty, and lack of access to services, e.g. health and education. Additionally, people may try to improve their social and economic conditions by migrating to areas where the caste system is less rigid. Migrants move to urban areas with the expectation of a better way of life; however, this expectation may not be fulfilled.

CITIES Many of India's large cities, including Delhi and Kolkata, are unable to cope with their growing populations. In Kolkata, poverty is a critical problem, and it has been exacerbated by increasing rates of urbanisation. Many residents do not have access to adequate food, shelter, clothing or clean water. Thirty per cent of the population live in slums known as *bustees* and survive by collecting waste food and material in landfill sites and by begging on the streets. Sanitation and access to clean water are limited, and diseases such as cholera and typhoid are common. Infant mortality rates are high. Access to medical and health facilities is limited. An estimated 500,000 people are living on the streets of Kolkata. Because India is still a developing economy, the government does not have adequate economic resources to address the significant economic challenges posed by increasing levels of urbanisation.

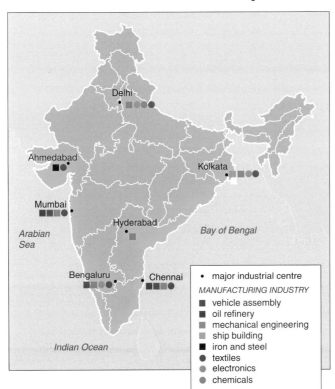

India's major industrial centres

REGIONAL GEOGRAPHY

HUMAN PROCESSES/ACTIVITIES
2006 QUESTION 5 PART B

*Describe how any **two** of the following have influenced human activities in a **continental/sub-continental** region that you have studied:*
- *Climate*
- *Soil*
- *Relief*
- *Drainage.* (30 marks)

> **MARKING SCHEME** ✓
>
> Two processes with 15 marks for each. For each process...
> *One or more activities named:* **2 marks + 2 marks**
> *Examination:* **5 SRPs**
> *Overall coherence:* **3 marks graded**

CLIMATE

The sub-continental region I have studied is India. Agriculture is a key human activity in India, and about 60 per cent of the population is involved in this sector.

Climate has a significant influence on agricultural activities. The presence of the Himalayan mountains means that India has a unique monsoon climate which has three distinct seasons.

- Cool, dry season: mid-December to late February. Light offshore winds from high pressure over the north-west of India produce clear skies with average temperatures of 15°C in the north and 30°C in the south. There is very little rainfall.
- Hot, dry season: March to the end of May. Daytime temperatures can reach 40°C, with dry north-westerly winds. During May, the winds change to a southerly direction, resulting in humid conditions but with limited rainfall.
- Hot, wet season: June to December. South-westerly winds bring heavy rainfall, especially during July.

The timing and intensity of the monsoon rains are critical. Delays in arrival can affect the timing of crop planting and irrigation systems. Low intensity can reduce crop productivity, especially rice. Poor yields can result in hunger and possible famine (as in 1987). Very high intensity causes flooding and can destroy crops (July–August 2009).

120 LEAVING CERTIFICATE GEOGRAPHY: *MODEL ANSWERS*

SOIL Soil also has an important role to play in agricultural activity and productivity. In the Indus-Ganges plain, the soil is rich in silt, making the plain one of the most intensely farmed areas of the world. The soil's composition means that it is inherently fertile, drains easily and is particularly suited to tilling and harrowing. It has a rich organic layer, and the development of humus is aided by a variety of living organisms. Farming on the Indus-Ganges plain primarily consists of rice and wheat grown in rotation. Other crops include maize, sugar cane and cotton.

In other areas of India (e.g. the Thar Desert), the soil structure is unable to support intensive agricultural activity. In the Thar Desert, the low-lying loams are heavy and may have a hard pan of clay, calcium carbonate or gypsum, caused by calcification. This occurs as nutrients that were leached from the surface are drawn back up by capillary action: this results in a hard pan which is nearly impermeable and restricts the growth of plants with long root structures. What little vegetation there is consists of sparse grass and shrub. Farming populations in the Thar Desert are nomadic, moving animals from one *tobas* (water hole) to the next and grazing animals on available vegetation.

Soils of India

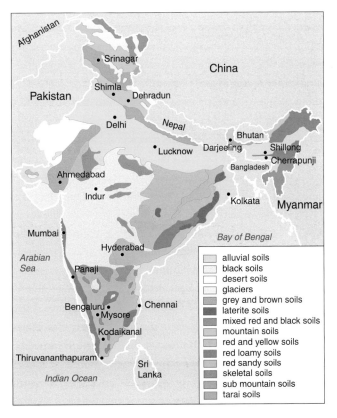

HUMAN PROCESSES/ACTIVITIES
2009 QUESTION 4 PART C

*Examine how the distribution of population in **a European region (not Ireland)** that you have studied has been influenced by the region's level of economic development.* (30 marks)

MARKING SCHEME

Named region: **2 marks**
Reference to distribution of population: **2 marks**
Reference to associated economic development: **2 marks**
Discussion: **12 SRPs**
– *Do not accept Irish or continental/sub-continental regions*
– *Discussion without link to a named region: 0 marks*
– *Maximum of 6 SRPs for discussion without reference to distribution*
– *Maximum of 6 SRPs for discussion without reference to economic development*

Italy has experienced change in population distribution related to changing patterns and levels of economic development.

SOUTH–NORTH MIGRATION

During the 1960s, the south of Italy was characterised by significant out-migration, resulting in a population decline, as people migrated to the north Italian plain (NIP). Between 1951 and 1971, over four million people left the south (out-migration) due to a combination of push and pull factors, the main destination being the urbanised north. Until the 1970s, the south was too underdeveloped to encourage population growth, while the population of the NIP expanded due to in-migration and natural increase. However, in the 1980s, traditional industries in the NIP – including textiles, iron and steel, shipbuilding and vehicle manufacturing – began to shed labour as a result of rationalisation and restructuring, and population growth levels declined.

CASSA PER IL MEZZOGIORNO

During the same period, economic development in the south was increasing as the proactive government regional policy known as Cassa per il Mezzogiorno encouraged economic changes and expansion in key areas of the economy, including agriculture, industry and tourism. This created an increase in job opportunities, particularly in secondary and tertiary activities, resulting in a decrease in out-migration and a slight increase in population.

The distribution of population in the south of Italy also experienced change as populations in the upland areas were encouraged to relocate to the more fertile low-lying coastal zones. In addition, industrial growth centres were established by the Italian government in order to promote economic development and employment opportunities in coastal locations. An example of this is the industrial triangle of Bari, Brindisi and Taranto, which became a key centre for oil refining, petro-chemicals and iron and steel works. This resulted in a redistribution of population and an increase in population density in the coastal lowlands.

Over time, as economic conditions improved, Italy became an attractive destination for foreign migrant workers, especially from Africa, Asia, Albania and the former Yugoslavia. Many of these migrants are illegal (50,000 per year) and enter through the less patrolled southern coastline.

Map of Italy

EUROPEAN UNION 2006 QUESTION 6 PART B

*Examine the impact of European Union expansion on Ireland's economy **and/or** culture.* (30 marks)

Ireland joined the EU in 1973 along with Britain and Denmark, bringing the number of member states to nine. In 1973, Ireland was a rural, underdeveloped economy which was over-dependent on agriculture and had limited secondary and tertiary employment opportunities. Membership of the EU has been critically important to Ireland's economic growth, and the expansion of the EU over time has had a positive impact on trade and productivity and output levels in all sectors of the Irish economy.

1980s   During the 1980s, the EU expanded in a southerly direction as Greece, Spain and Portugal joined. These countries were classified as rural, underdeveloped economies and, along with Ireland, they were given Objective 1 status under the EU Common Regional Policy (CRP), which meant that they received significant capital transfers to aid their economic development. In 1988, the CRP was strengthened and reformed, and Ireland, Spain, Greece and Portugal received more capital assistance from the EU in the form of Cohesion Funds. Ireland received £3.9 billion (€4.95 billion) from the CRP during the period 1989–93 and an additional £6.9 billion (€8.76 billion) from 1994 to 1999. This money was invested in key areas of infrastructural improvement, agriculture, fishing, tourism and education, and resulted in a significant expansion of Ireland's economic sectors and employment levels.

1990s   In 1995, the EU expanded in a northerly direction as Sweden, Finland and Austria joined. These countries were well developed economically with high levels of GDP, and they increased the trading potential of the community. Ireland's trading patterns benefited from this expansion and also from the creation of the single market, which facilitated the free movement of goods, capital, labour and services. Ireland's trade with the EU has grown significantly over time. In 1972, Ireland was importing 17 per cent of its total imports from

a) **THE EU IN 1973**

original six members
new member states

b) **THE EU IN 1986**

EU 9
three new member states

c) **THE EU IN 1995**

EU 12
three new member states

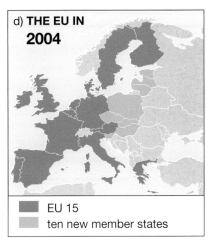

d) **THE EU IN 2004**

EU 15
ten new member states

e) **THE EU IN 2007**

EU 25
two new member states

EU expansion 1973–2007

EU countries (excluding the UK), and by 2005 this figure had increased to 26 per cent. However, the greatest change has occurred in our export relationship with the EU. In 1972, Ireland exported 16 per cent of its total exports to the EU (excluding the UK); this figure had increased to 46 per cent by 2005. The establishment of MNCs in Ireland has been strongly linked to our EU membership, and expansion of the EU has had a positive impact on our industrial economy, particularly in key sectors of chemicals and electronics.

2000s   Further expansion of the EU in 2004 (ten new members) and 2007 (two new members) resulted in an expansion of the internal market from 350 million to 500 million. Between 1995 and 2007, the population of the EU increased by 29 per cent. This expanding internal market is critical as it means that Ireland has a greater export potential, and it also enables us to source alternative markets for the importation of raw materials and energy.

The flow of labour from this expanded community has also positively impacted on the growth of the Irish economy as a large number of migrant labourers from new member states entered the Irish economy from the late 1990s onwards. The number of work permits granted to non-Irish migrant workers increased from 6,000 in 1999 to nearly 50,000 in 2003.

Expansion of the EU has, however, put pressure on the availability of Structural Funds, because many of the new member countries have low levels of economic development, and their economies suffer from structural difficulties such as over-dependence on primary activities and traditional, declining industries. These countries need significant support in the form of capital transfers from the CRP, and this has meant that less funding is available for Ireland. Furthermore, the entry of lower wage-cost economies may have implications for MNCs in Ireland, as some may relocate to these cheaper labour markets: for example, Dell Computers has relocated production from Limerick to Poland.

The expansion of the EU presents Ireland with opportunities and potential problems. However, on balance, membership has resulted in very positive benefits to the Irish economy and society.

EUROPEAN UNION **2008 QUESTION 6 PART C**

Examine the economic and/or cultural impacts of expansion on any **one member state of the EU**. (30 marks)

MARKING SCHEME

Impact identified: **2 marks**
Named example: **2 marks**
Examination: **13 SRPs**
– *Discussion without reference to appropriate region: 0 marks*
– *Discussion without reference to expansion: maximum of 6 SRPs*
– *Other impacts may be credited from SRPs*

I will examine the economic implications for Ireland of EU enlargement.

Ireland joined the EU in 1973, along with Britain and Denmark, bringing the total membership to nine. In 1973, Ireland was viewed as an underdeveloped rural economy which was over-dependent on agriculture, had few urban centres and limited employment opportunities in secondary and tertiary activities. The country was to receive significant monetary aid from the EU in order to improve its economic potential. The Common Agricultural Policy (CAP) was highly significant for Ireland: it helped transform the agricultural economy from a labour-intensive conservative system to a modern capital-intensive specialised sector. The prosperity of the core countries of the EU during the 1970s and 1980s ensured that member states that were over-dependent on agriculture received significant capital assistance to develop their agricultural base.

CAP

Ireland also benefited from capital transfers from the Common Regional Policy (CRP), which was established in 1975.

CRP

In 1981, Greece became a member, followed by Spain and Portugal in 1986. Together with Ireland, these countries were assigned Objective 1 status and received financial assistance from the reformed CRP and the newly created Structural Funds. During the period 1975 to 2006, Ireland received €16.5 billion from the CRP.

A further enlargement of the EU occurred in 1995 with the entry of Finland, Sweden and Austria. These countries had a high level of economic development and were thus net contributors to the EU budget, while Ireland remained a net beneficiary. The size of the EU market was now 380 million, and with the establishment of the Single European Market, barriers to trade were removed, allowing for the free movement of goods, capital, labour and services.

This had positive implications for the Irish economy, which had at this stage developed into a key exporter of manufactured goods and services. In addition, Ireland became an increasingly attractive location for multinational companies (MNCs), which had access to the growing and expanding internal EU market.

In 2004, the EU expanded again as ten eastern European countries joined, increasing the internal market to approximately 430 million. However, these new member states had low levels of economic development and high unemployment rates, were heavily dependent on agriculture and required significant financial assistance from the CRP. Thus capital transfers to Ireland began to decline as a result of the expansion of the EU and the significant economic growth in the Irish economy during this period. In 2007, Bulgaria and Romania joined the EU, bringing total membership to 27 and the internal market to an estimated 500 million people.

TRADE WITH THE EU

During the period 1972 to 2005, the pattern of Ireland's trade with the EU underwent significant change. In 1972, 17 per cent of Ireland's total imports came from the EU; by 2005, this figure had increased to 26 per cent, thus reducing our traditional dependence on Britain. The pattern of exports also changed: in 1972, 16 per cent of total exports went to the EU; this figure grew to 46 per cent by 2005. This diversification and growth is of critical importance to the Irish economy, and enlargement of the EU over time has encouraged expansion of the Irish export economy.

MNCs are a crucial component of the Irish industrial sector, and expansion of the EU has allowed these industries access to a growing free internal market. A negative aspect of expansion is the reduction of financial support for the Irish economy, but this was counteracted by increased levels of economic growth in all sectors until 2008.

The expansion of the EU has resulted in positive economic benefits to Ireland since the country joined in 1973.

EUROPEAN UNION **2009 QUESTION 5 PART B**

*Describe and explain **two** impacts on Ireland of the enlargement of the European Union.* (30 marks)

MARKING SCHEME ✓

Impacts identified: **2 + 2 marks**
Examination: **13 SRPs** (7/6 SRPs for each impact)

Impact 1: Market

Ireland joined the EU in 1973, with Denmark and Great Britain, bringing the total number of members to nine. Membership of the EU has been critical for Ireland's economic development, and access to a large internal market has benefited primary, secondary and tertiary economic activities. The enlargement of the EU since 1973 has allowed Ireland to access an expanding market. Further enlargement occurred in the 1980s as Greece, Spain and Portugal joined and membership increased to 12. In the 1990s, three more countries joined: Sweden, Austria and Finland. These countries had high levels of economic development and strengthened the economic power of the EU. Ireland's trade in both primary and secondary products grew, aided by the establishment of the Single European Market, which allows for the free movement of goods, capital, labour and services.

Further expansion occurred in 2004 (ten new members) and 2007 (two new members). Today, membership of the EU is 27, and Ireland has access to an internal market of nearly 500 million. As our economy is export-led, membership of this large and expanding market is crucial for our economic survival, and it is a key attraction for the establishment of multinational companies in Ireland.

Impact 2: Cultural Diversity

Ireland's membership of the EU has exposed the country to greater cultural diversity, which has benefited both society and the economy. In particular, the more recent enlargement of the EU to include many eastern European countries has had a significant impact on cultural diversity here. The free movement of labour and the growth of the Irish economy during the late 1990s and into the 2000s meant that Ireland became an important destination for labour migrating from eastern Europe. This has encouraged cultural diversity, which can be clearly seen in the foods available, entertainment, cultural festivals, retail outlets and a wide variety of international restaurants. This diversity is concentrated in the key urban centres of Dublin, Cork, Limerick and Galway, where strong ethnic communities from many eastern European countries now live.

PATTERNS & PROCESSES IN ECONOMIC ACTIVITIES

MEASURING DEVELOPMENT: COLONISATION/ DECOLONISATION AND GLOBALISATION

2008 QUESTION 7 PART B

Examine the impact of colonisation on a developing economy you have studied and on its adjustment to globalisation. (30 marks)

MARKING SCHEME ✓

Impact identified: **2 marks**
Named developing economy: **2 marks**
Examination: **13 SRPs**
– *Discussion without reference to colonisation/adjustment to globalisation: maximum 6 SRPs*
– *Discussion without reference to named developing economy: maximum 6 SRPs*

India is one developing country that has been affected by colonialism – the domination of areas by powerful countries, primarily for economic gain.

Policy of Mercantilism
Under the British Empire, raw materials from India were used to fuel the industrial development of this colonial power. As a result, cash crops (e.g. tea,

coffee, jute, spices and rubber) took over from traditional food crops and caused significant changes in native agricultural activities. Large plantations based on large-scale operations saw land removed from peasant ownership. They were also established in the most fertile areas, which impacted negatively on food production for local consumption.

India's industrial output was restricted so that it would not compete with colonial production. Until 1800, India had well-developed craft manufacturing industries, especially textiles, a good labour force and access to raw materials. Under British administration, these industries declined to allow British products to access the large Indian market and to enable Britain to exploit its raw materials.

Infrastructural developments were restricted to the building of ports (e.g. Mumbai, Kolkata and Chennai) and railways that facilitated the transportation of goods and their export to Britain.

Over time, India's trade became dependent on Britain. India produced raw materials and cash crops, while Britain became a key economic power in the production and sale of finished goods to the developed and developing world. Taxes were also placed on the domestic Indian population, payable to the British Empire. Under colonialism, the economy, raw materials and labour of India were exploited by Britain.

Globalisation

Globalisation means that events and actions taking place in one part of the world have implications for communities and economies in other parts of the world. After achieving independence in 1947, India was very slow to adjust to an open global economy. Initial efforts to expand its economic base concentrated on agricultural development and the promotion of secondary activities in a closed market economy. However, a significant change in government policy occurred in the 1980s when trade barriers were removed and India entered the open market global economy. This policy has allowed many multinational companies (MNCs) to establish manufacturing and office functions in India. It has now become a key country for global manufacturing. The globalisation of the Indian economy has led to a greater diversity of production, and the country is noted for its textiles, chemicals, food products, steel, transportation equipment, cement, mining, petroleum, machinery and software outputs. Key US companies which have established operations in India include IBM and Dell; and the Finnish company Nokia also has a large presence. In addition, India has expanded its number of trading partners. This policy has reduced its historical dependence on Britain.

MEASURING DEVELOPMENT: COLONISATION/ DECOLONISATION AND GLOBALISATION

2010 QUESTION 7 PART C

Explain the effects of globalisation on the economy of a developing country that you have studied. (30 marks)

MARKING SCHEME ✓

Named developing country: **2 marks**
Effects identified: **2 marks + 2 marks**
Examination: **12 SRPs**
– *Maximum of 2 SRPs without reference to globalisation*
– *Maximum of 2 SRPs for discussion without reference to named developing country*
– *Accept positive/negative effects of globalisation*
– *Credit a third effect from within examination*

A developing country I have studied that has been affected by globalisation is India.

GLOBALISATION
Globalisation means that events and actions taking place in one part of the world have implications for communities and economies in other parts of the world. India gained its independence from Britain in 1947, and until the mid-1980s it adopted a policy of imposing tariff and trade barriers and a closed market system. However, during the 1980s the Indian government decided to develop an open market economy, and this policy allowed it to be affected by the process of globalisation.

MNCs
The greatest impact of globalisation on India's economy and society can be seen in the locating of multinational companies (MNCs) there. India is a highly attractive location for MNCs because it has a huge workforce, and many workers in urban areas are well educated and speak English. The workforce is also relatively cheap, and is flexible, with limited union activity. MNCs in India have transformed employment opportunities, particularly in urban areas, and India's economic development in the future is strongly linked to continued investment from such companies. BMW is investing $23 million in a new assembly plant to build its 3 and 5 Series cars, Cisco plans to invest $1.1 billion in the next three years in a research and development centre in Bengaluru (formerly Bangalore), and Nokia is spending $100–150 million to expand production facilities.

The globalisation of the Indian economy has led to a greater diversity of production, and the country is noted for textiles, chemicals, food products, steel, transportation equipment, cement, mining, petroleum, machinery and software outputs. These products have become part of the global economy, and the role of transport development has been important in allowing India to become an important player in the global economy. Further evidence of the impact of globalisation on India's economy can be seen in its diverse trading partners, which include the USA, China, the United Arab Emirates, the UK, Hong Kong and Germany. Globalisation – particularly in the form of information transfer – may also be responsible for the erosion of the caste system in urban areas.

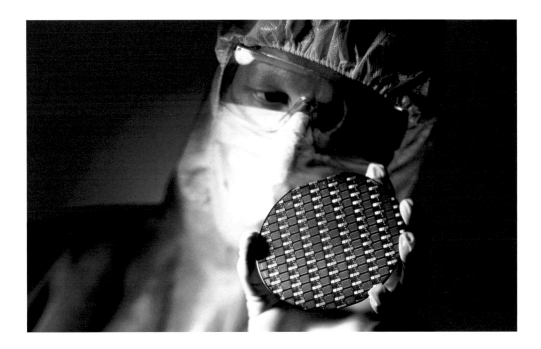

MULTINATIONAL COMPANIES (MNCs)
2006 SAMPLE PAPER QUESTION 8 PART C

 *Ireland has experienced both success and failure as a location for multinational companies. Explain **one** reason why Ireland continues to be a favoured location for MNCs and also **one** reason why some MNCs have left Ireland to move to other locations.* (30 marks)

 A critical factor in attracting MNCs to Ireland is proactive government policy. The Irish government provided tax incentives in the form of tax-free profits (this is no longer allowed under EU competition laws) and low corporation tax,

GOVERNMENT POLICY

currently 12.5 per cent. The government also established the Industrial Development Authority (IDA) to target MNCs, and to do so they pursued a policy of building advance factories and emphasised the availability of a well-educated, English-speaking workforce. The spread of third-level education centres, including institutes of technology and universities, has been important in increasing the skill levels of the Irish workforce. Government investment in education expanded significantly from the late 1980s onwards and has given Ireland a competitive advantage in expanding employment opportunities in MNCs.

MNCs that established operations in Ireland include Apple Computers in Cork and Boston Scientific in Galway and Cork.

CHANGING ECONOMY

Despite Ireland's success in attracting MNCs, some of these companies have not remained in the country, and one reason for this is changing economic variables: labour costs, energy costs, transport costs, global economic recession and changes in taxation. Since the mid-1990s, wage levels in Ireland – both the minimum wage and wages for highly skilled and educated workers – have increased significantly. This increase has had a negative impact on some MNCs, which have relocated manufacturing operations to cheaper labour markets. A pertinent example is the relocation of Dell Computers from Limerick to Poland.

Energy and transport costs in Ireland have also increased substantially during the last ten years, and this is reducing the economic returns for some MNCs, resulting in closures and relocation. The global economic downturn has also had an impact: in response to lower global consumer demand, some MNCs have restructured their operations, resulting in employment loss and relocation (for example Element Six in Shannon, Co. Clare).

The global nature of MNCs means that they are able to relocate as economic circumstances change. Ireland is now considered to be an expensive location for some MNCs, and they are responding to this by moving to more profitable regions. Since the onset of recession in 2008, however, Ireland has reduced its costs so as to compete more effectively in the global economy.

MULTINATIONAL COMPANIES (MNCs)
2007 QUESTION 8 PART C

*In the case of **one** multinational company (MNC) that you have studied, examine the global nature of its activities.* (30 marks)

APPLE INC.

Apple Inc., formerly known as Apple Computers, is an MNC I have studied.

The mobility of Apple Inc. operations has been enhanced as a result of improvements in global transport networks and developments in telecommunications, particularly the phone, fax and internet. Apple Inc. is an American MNC that designs and manufactures consumer electronics, computer software and commercial servers. Well-known products include the iPod and iPhone. Apple Inc. currently employs 35,000 workers worldwide, has annual sales of $42.91 billion and operates 284 retail stores in ten different countries.

CORK

The company was established in the Silicon Valley in California in 1976. Apple established its first manufacturing plant outside the USA in Cork in 1980, which at its peak employed 1,000 people. However, during the global economic recession of the mid-1990s, Apple undertook a restructuring of its global manufacturing plants, and employment numbers in the Cork plant were reduced to 450. In 1998, it established a customer call centre in Cork, which employs about 300 people. It has since expanded the Cork base in key areas, including customer services, software testing, finance, logistics and a new e-commerce division, and currently employs about 1,000 people there.

ASIA

Many of Apple's manufacturing plants are now located in Asia, including China; this allows the company to take advantage of cheaper labour costs in the global periphery or developing economies. The company outsources manufacturing activities to other organisations, including Foxconn and Inventec. In 2006, Apple Inc. was accused of promoting the exploitation of workers in China as part of its manufacture of the iPod in outsourced manufacturing units. It was reported that workers were employed in sweatshop conditions, that the average working week was in excess of 60 hours, that many workers were under age and that living conditions in units provided by the outsourcing company were poor. Apple responded by undertaking an internal enquiry and now maintains that all people employed in the manufacture of Apple products are paid a fair wage and that working conditions and accommodation are monitored.

Globally, Apple Inc. has substantial manufacturing, sales, marketing and support organisations worldwide. Cupertino in the Silicon Valley, California, remains the global headquarters of the organisation and is the key centre for research and development and product design. This top tier of the organisation utilises a highly educated, skilled and flexible workforce, and wage levels are high. Some of Apple's engineering operations have located in Paris and Tokyo in the more recent past.

MULTINATIONAL COMPANIES (MNCs)
2008 QUESTION 8 PART B

*With reference to **one** multinational company (MNC) which you have studied, examine how its distribution is influenced by global factors.* (30 marks)

MARKING SCHEME ✓

Naming MNC: **2 marks**
Naming two global factors: **2 marks + 2 marks**
Examination: **12 SRPs**
– Discussion without link to a named MNC: maximum of 6 SRPs
– Discussion with no obvious reference to global nature: maximum of 6 SRPs

NIKE

The MNC I have studied that has developed a global approach to production and marketing is the clothing and footwear giant Nike. The ability of Nike to develop a global network is directly related to improvements in global transport networks and developments in telecommunications, including phone, fax and internet. These improvements have allowed many MNCs to expand operations into a number of different countries.

Nike's headquarters is in Oregon in the USA; it has annual sales of $10 billion and directly employs 16,000 people in management, design and marketing. In its headquarters, the company employs a highly skilled, high-wage workforce, with an emphasis on research and development of clothing and footwear products. This labour force is at the cutting edge of design and is the think-tank of Nike industries. The headquarters is the centre of decision-making for the company and controls and monitors all Nike operations throughout the globe.

OUTSOURCING

Nike has outsourced many of its production activities to other companies, which employ about half a million people. The company has developed a global system of clothing and footwear production and sales, which is designed to take advantage of differences in labour costs and skill levels in different parts of the world.

From the early 1970s to the 1980s, the company operated production activities in core economies including the USA, Ireland and Britain. However, due to rising labour costs and increased union activity, the company relocated these manufacturing units to cheaper labour markets, particularly in South East Asia (South Korea and Taiwan, and more recently Indonesia, Thailand and China), where production activities are outsourced to over 30 different companies.

During the 1990s, Nike was investigated due to concerns over potential exploitation of labour in these developing countries. Significant media coverage was given to the claims that Nike goods were manufactured in sweatshop conditions. In an effort to reduce negative media attention, Nike joined the Fair Labor Association, which guarantees basic minimum wages and decent working conditions.

Nike is an example of an MNC which has adopted a global approach to attain economic advantages related to the supply and cost of labour in the global periphery.

MULTINATIONAL COMPANIES (MNCS)
2009 QUESTION 8 PART B

*Examine the mobility of modern economic activities, referring to **one** multinational company (MNC) that you have studied.* (30 marks)

 MARKING SCHEME

Naming MNC: **2 marks**
Naming two mobility factors: **2 marks + 2 marks**
Examination: **12 SRPs**
- *Discussion without link to a named MNC: maximum of 6 SRPs*
- *Discussion with no obvious reference to mobility of modern economic activities: maximum of 6 SRPs*
- *Give credit for three locations as SRPs from examination*
- *Locations must refer to at least two countries*

The factors influencing industrial location have changed over time. Modern global industries have more flexibility in terms of locational choice than older industries had. Traditional industries, including iron and steel, were resource orientated: their location was strongly linked to access to energy, raw materials, large supplies of labour and of course the market. However, following World War II, a greater variety of energy sources and raw materials, and improvements in transport and communications, gave industries more choice about where they set up. The increased role of national governments in influencing industrial location also facilitated a greater geographic distribution of manufacturing activities. National governments use proactive policies to attract industry, offering tax incentives, grants and the availability of a large and adaptable labour force, and they invest in transport infrastructure, which reduces geographic isolation. The mobility of industrial location can be clearly seen by studying the global operation of MNCs.

The MNC I have studied is Dell Computers.

DELL'S HQ   Dell's headquarters is in Austin, Texas, and the company has world sales of $35.5 billion and employs about 39,000 workers. The company has developed a global system of production and sales of computer systems. This system seeks to take advantage of differences in labour costs and skill levels throughout the world. In its headquarters, the company employs a highly skilled, high-wage workforce with an emphasis on research and development; this think-tank is at the cutting edge of computer technology. Dell's headquarters is the centre of decision-making for the company and controls and monitors all Dell operations throughout the globe.

REGIONAL OPERATIONS   The company has also developed a regional approach to manufacturing and marketing, and this can be clearly seen in its decision to establish its European regional centre in Ireland.

Dell Ireland was established in Limerick in 1991 and expanded rapidly to employ 3,300 workers at its peak. Until recently, it was the production centre for Europe, the Middle East and Africa, and in addition the company opened a sales centre, call centre and central administration unit in Dublin, at one point employing 1,200 people. Dell chose to locate in Ireland for several reasons:

- the availability of a highly skilled and educated workforce
- proximity to the University of Limerick and its pool of graduates from computer and engineering courses
- good telecommunications in the mid-west region
- good access to key European markets by both port and air
- the absence of tariff and trade barriers for goods manufactured in the EU
- significant government grants and incentives
- proximity to other established computer companies, e.g. Intel, Microsoft and Apple.

However, changing economic circumstances have led Dell to relocate from Limerick to Poland.

The third component of the global nature of Dell was the establishment of a call centre in India and the sourcing of raw materials and basic production line manufacturing activities in South East Asia. Ninety per cent of raw materials and components used by Dell in Limerick were imported from factories in the global assembly line economy, with 52 per cent coming from the Far East.

ECONOMIC ACTIVITIES: SECONDARY
2006 SAMPLE PAPER **QUESTION 9 PART C**

*Analyse **one** of the major factors – apart from energy – which have influenced the location of a manufacturing industry which you have studied.* (30 marks)

A manufacturing industry I have studied is medical health care devices. One medical health care company that has been attracted to the BMW region is Boston Scientific, which is located in Galway city and employs 2,200 people.

GOVERNMENT
POLICY

The development of this sector is directly related to proactive government policy, including the attraction to Ireland of multinational companies, investment in education and investment in transport.

The policy – 'industrialisation by invitation' – of attracting multinational companies (MNCs) was initiated in the 1960s as Ireland began to develop a free market economy. In order to attract MNCs, the Irish government provided tax incentives in the form of tax-free profits (no longer allowed under EU competition laws) and a low level of corporation tax, currently 12.5 per cent. In addition, the government established the IDA to target MNCs, and they pursued a policy of building advance factories and emphasising the availability of a well-educated English-speaking workforce. The spread of third-level educational centres (institutes of technology and universities) has helped increase the skills of the Irish workforce. Government investment in education expanded significantly from the late 1980s onwards and has generated a critical competitive advantage in expanding employment opportunities in health/medical care industries.

Ireland has a small domestic market, but as a member of the EU since 1973, companies which have manufacturing bases in Ireland have access to a market of about 500 million people with no internal tariff and trade barriers between them.

INFRASTRUCTURE

The Irish government, aided by Structural Funds from the EU, has invested in the country's transport infrastructure, both within the country and also in ports and airports, to increase our connectivity to mainland western Europe. This investment has reduced Ireland's geographic isolation, reduced transport costs and increased access to EU markets. In the BMW region, these improvements include the upgrading of the Galway–Dublin railway line and work on the Galway city road network, which now has an extensive new access corridor based on the western ring road. Upgrading has also occurred on the Galway, Mayo, Sligo and Donegal road infrastructure and the Galway, Ennis, Limerick and Galway, Loughrea, Athlone corridor. The creation of hubs (including Mallow, Tralee and Kilkenny) and gateways (including Cork, Limerick and Waterford) in the Southern and Eastern region, and the linking of these by upgraded and new road corridors, has increased the transport efficiency of the region. These improvements have been a significant part of the National Spatial Strategy which was introduced in 2002. Transport is the lifeline of any expanding economy, and investment has resulted in increased economic growth, particularly in secondary and tertiary activities.

In short, it is clear that proactive government policy has been critical in encouraging the development of the medical health care industry in Ireland.

ECONOMIC ACTIVITIES: SECONDARY
2006 QUESTION 7 PART C

*Examine any **two** of the major factors that have influenced the location of a secondary economic activity that you have studied.* (30 marks)

MARKING SCHEME ✓

Two factors named: **2 marks**
Economic activity named: **2 marks**
Discussion: **10 SRPs**
Overall coherence: **4 marks graded**
– *Answer very clearly confined to secondary activity*
– *Accept one example or location as an SRP*

The secondary economic activity I have studied is the computer industry in Ireland. The key factors influencing the development of this sector are labour and market. Computer manufacturing companies which have located in Ireland include Apple in Cork, Dell in Limerick (now relocated to Poland) and IBM in Dublin.

LABOUR   The availability of a well-educated, English-speaking workforce has been a critical factor in the development of the computer industry in Ireland. Companies have established their production and marketing European regional headquarters in the country, employing skilled, educated, flexible and innovative workers who are capable of meeting the demands of the modern global economy. A crucial component of this workforce is its high levels of education in computer technology and engineering. There has been significant investment in third-level education in Ireland, particularly since the mid-1980s. Institutes of technology have been established and investment has been made in our universities. This investment has come from national government and also from EU Structural Funds. Ireland's well-educated workforce has proved very attractive, especially for many American MNCs.

MARKET   Ireland has a small domestic market, but our membership of the European Union has been an important factor in encouraging the growth of computer design and manufacturing. As a member of the EU, goods manufactured in Ireland can access a 500 million-strong internal market which has no internal tariff or trade barriers. The EU market is affluent, with consumers enjoying high standards of living and significant disposable income. As a developed economy, it is an important market, in terms of both numbers and spending power.

Significant investment has also been made in Ireland's transport infrastructure, and this has improved our access to markets. Transport is a cost of production, and any improvement in infrastructure represents a significant saving to the computer industry. Portal development, particularly in Dublin, Cork and Waterford, has increased our access to the critical EU market. Some computer components are high value-to-weight outputs, which means that air transport to the EU market can be used.

ECONOMIC ACTIVITIES: SECONDARY
2007 QUESTION 7 PART B

*Examine the influence of any **two** of the factors listed on the location of one secondary economic activity that you have studied.*
- *Transport*
- *Labour*
- *Energy*
- *Environment*
- *Raw materials*
- *Capital*
- *Market.* (30 marks)

See earlier answers on Apple (page 137), Nike (page 138) and Dell (page 139) and 2006 Sample Paper Question 9 Part C (page 141).

ECONOMIC ACTIVITIES: TERTIARY
2007 QUESTION 9 PART B

*Examine the development of transport/communication **or** financial services in developed economies, referring to examples you have studied.* (30 marks)

MARKING SCHEME ✓

Named examples: **2 marks + 2 marks**
Examination: **13 SRPs**
– *If discussion is not linked to a developed economy: 7 SRPs*
– *A third example may be credited from the SRPs*

ANSWER **A**

The development of transport/communications in Ireland and Paris has undergone significant transformation in recent decades.

IRELAND When Ireland joined the EU in 1973, the country was a rural, underdeveloped economy with few urban centres and a weak transport network. As a member of the EU, the economy has benefited from significant capital transfers from the Common Regional Policy in the form of Structural Funds, which have helped fund the transformation of Ireland's transport network. In the Southern and Eastern region, the creation of hubs (Mallow, Tralee and Kilkenny) and gateways (Cork, Limerick and Waterford) and the linking of these by upgraded and new road corridors has increased transport efficiency in the region. Investment has also been provided for the expansion of Dublin and Cork ports and new airport terminals at both Dublin and Cork. Road and rail improvements have also been made in the BMW region. These include the upgrading of the Galway–Dublin railway line and improvements in the Galway city road network, which now has an extensive new access corridor based on the western ring road. Upgrading has also occurred on the Galway, Mayo, Sligo, Donegal road infrastructure and the Galway, Ennis, Limerick, and Galway, Loughrea, Athlone corridor. Telecommunications networks in Ireland have also been expanded, particularly the availability of broadband in both urban and rural areas.

PARIS Paris is centrally located in the lowland fertile plain of the Paris Basin, which is well drained by the Seine, Marne and Oise and has become a focal point of routeways and trade. This has allowed the city to become the centre of France's national and international transport systems, including road, rail, river and airports (Orly to the south, the centrally located Charles de Gaulle and

Beauvais, 75km to the north, used by low-cost airlines). The rail network includes the high-speed TGV, carrying trains that can travel at 300km per hour, which links Paris to key regional areas and cities. Paris is also linked to other European high-speed rail networks in the Netherlands, Germany, Spain and Switzerland. Paris has a highly efficient Métro system which connects with the national rail network and the regional rail system (RER). Private car commuters can avail of a large underground parking network. Overall, the transport system in Paris reflects its dynamic core characteristics and forms a critical component of tertiary activities.

ANSWER **B**

The development of financial services in Ireland and in Cayman Island has undergone significant transformation in recent decades.

IRELAND Ireland's entry to the service economy came relatively late – because of our late industrialisation – but by 1981 more than half of total employment was in services. Services have a tendency to locate in urban centres directly related to demand, so the geographic distribution of the service economy is heavily concentrated in the south and east of the country. Ireland has experienced significant growth in international financial services (IFS) in the recent past. The concentration of financial services in Dublin is related to:

• The region's excellent communications systems, which has allowed the city to become a key centre for national and international financial services.
• The availability of a skilled and well-educated workforce, particularly in banking and related financial activities.
• A proactive government policy which has provided the physical and social infrastructure to promote the development of national and international financial institutions. The government has also provided generous grants and tax incentives to develop the sector.

In particular, the development of the International Financial Services Centre (IFSC) in Dublin was very successful in job creation and improving the inner city. Other cities to benefit from the growth in financial services include Cork, Galway and Limerick.

CAYMAN ISLAND Cayman Island, located 480 miles south-east of Miami, has developed into a key location for financial activities. The island has a no tax policy regime and by law there is no tax on income, profit or wealth. This system has attracted significant interest from global investors seeking a tax free base for their operations. The island is a registered base for 32,000 companies, 550 banks, 900 mutual funds and 400 insurance companies. Cayman Island has a population of 36,000 and the financial sector is a key employer, utilising a highly skilled and educated workforce.

Other major centres of financial services include New York, Tokyo and Zurich.

The International Financial Services Centre (IFSC) in Dublin

DEVELOPED ECONOMIES 2010 QUESTION 8 PART B

*Explain the growth of any **one** developed economy you have studied under one or more of the following headings:*
- *Financial services*
- *Tourism*
- *Industrial decline.* (30 marks)

 MARKING SCHEME ✓

Developed economy named: **2 marks**
Examination: **14 SRPs**
- *Maximum of 7 SRPs for discussion without reference to growth*
- *Maximum of 7 SRPs for discussion without reference to at least one heading*

Ireland is a developed economy that has experienced significant growth in the key areas of financial services and tourism.

Ireland's entry to the service economy came relatively late due to our late industrialisation, but by 1981 more than half of total employment was in services. Services have a tendency to locate in urban centres directly related to demand, so the geographic distribution of the service economy is heavily concentrated in the south and east.

IFSC

The development of the International Financial Services Centre (IFSC) in Dublin was very successful in terms of job creation and improving the image and composition of the inner city. The development of this key part of the tertiary sector was directly related to the availability of a well-educated and flexible workforce. Dublin is an important centre of educational opportunity, with TCD, UCD and DCU and institutes of technology in Tallaght, Dún Laoghaire and Blanchardstown. By 2006, up to 450 financial service companies were located at the IFSC, creating an estimated 17,000 direct and indirect employment opportunities.

TOURISM

Tourism in Ireland is a key growth industry, and in 2005 there were 6.8 million visitors to Ireland, resulting in foreign earnings of €4.8 billion. Total tourist revenue for the country was €5.4 billion, and one in five jobs in the country were tourism related. The major tourist region is the south and east, with 75 per cent of total tourist revenue (Dublin receiving 25 per cent). This is directly related to Dublin's gateway function and the region's cultural and historical attractions.

The growth of the global tourist industry is directly related to:

- higher incomes
- increased annual paid leave
- growth of package holidays
- better transport and accommodation
- higher levels of education leading to greater awareness of destination areas.

TOURISM IN THE BMW REGION

Tourism is important to the economy of the BMW region. Attractions include its physical landscape, historic artefacts and culture, pace of life, rural economy and lack of congestion. Yet growth of the industry here is not as substantial as in the south and east. Problems for tourism development in the BMW region include: lack of direct access; under-utilisation of Ireland West Airport Knock; and declining trans-Atlantic passenger traffic through Shannon. Additionally, the seasonality of the industry and the high cost of food, beverages and accommodation represent real challenges for the tourism industry.

The growth of financial services and tourism are immensely important to the Irish economy, but these sectors need to remain competitive in an increasingly globalised world economy.

The European Parliament in Strasbourg

EUROPEAN UNION: POLICIES AND IMPACTS
2006 QUESTION 7 PART B

*Examine how European policies have influenced the development of any **one** sector of the Irish economy.* (30 marks)

The sector of the Irish economy I have studied which has been positively affected by European Union policies is the tertiary sector. The two key activities in this sector which have been influenced by EU policies are transport and tourism.

TRANSPORT   Transport development in Ireland has been positively affected by the Common Regional Policy (CRP) and its funding mechanism, the European Regional Development Fund, which is part of the EU's Structural Funds. Ireland has received significant capital transfers in the form of Structural Funds: 1975–88, €3.2 billion; 1989–99, €11 billion; 2000–2006, €3.3 billion; 2007–13, €3 billion. These funds have been used in part to upgrade our transport network, particularly roads, rail, ports and airports. These improvements have been a significant part of the National Spatial Strategy, which was introduced in 2002. The creation of hubs (including Mallow, Tralee and Kilkenny) and gateways (including Cork, Limerick, and Waterford) in the Southern and Eastern region, and the linking of these by upgraded and new road corridors, has increased the transport efficiency of the region.

Road and rail improvements have also taken place in the BMW region, including improvements in: the Galway–Dublin railway line; the Galway city road network, with an extensive new access corridor based on the western ring road; the Galway, Mayo, Sligo and Donegal road infrastructure; and the Galway, Ennis, Limerick, and Galway, Loughrea, Athlone corridor.

TOURISM   The tourism industry has also been helped by the CRP and Structural Funds. The investment made in roads, rail, ports and airports has made Ireland more accessible, cut transport costs and reduced our geographic isolation. In addition, significant investment has been provided to increase the range of tourist products in Ireland (for example golf, angling, hill-walking and farm tourism). Regional tourist organisations such as Shannon Development and Western Regional Tourist Organisation have received EU funding to help in product development and marketing. Funding has also been provided to host tourist conferences and tourism marketing fairs. The LEADER programme has also been instrumental in promoting the development of tourism in Ireland, and significant funds were given to Ireland for tourism development under a number of operational programmes.

EUROPEAN UNION: POLICIES AND IMPACTS
2007 QUESTION 9 PART C

*Examine the impact of any **two** European Union policies on the Irish economy.* (30 marks)

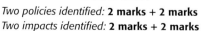

Two policies identified: **2 marks + 2 marks**
Two impacts identified: **2 marks + 2 marks**
Examination: **11 SRPs**
– Discussion without link to Irish economy: 5 SRPs maximum
– Discussion of one policy only: 5 SRPs maximum

– A third impact may be credited from SRPs
– Amalgamate all relevant discussion points

One sector of the Irish economy that has been greatly affected by European Union policies is the primary sector, especially agriculture and fishing.

AGRICULTURE

Agriculture in the Southern and Eastern region has been positively affected by the Common Agricultural Policy (CAP), which was established in 1962. CAP's key objectives were to increase farmers' incomes, increase food production and stabilise food supplies in the EU.

FOOD PRODUCTION

Food production output increased under CAP's guaranteed price scheme, as many farms developed more modern and scientific production practices.

Exports of agricultural activity grew enormously in value, from €0.4 billion in 1970 to over €6 billion by 2005. Average farm incomes increased from €5,000 per annum in 1984 to €17,000 in 2008. The most profitable sectors were dairying and tillage, and these large-scale farmers were predominately located in the south and east.

However, the reforms of CAP during the post-1992 period led to a reduction of output in some sectors, most notably the dairy sector following the introduction of milk quotas in 1984. As a result, many smaller farmers, particularly in the BMW region, turned to beef and sheep farming. Cereal production output also fell with the introduction of the set-aside system. The overall increase in farm output since our membership of the EU in 1973 was greater in the Southern and Eastern region than in the BMW. This reflects a more suitable physical landscape and younger, more progressive farmers who were able to take advantage of the guaranteed price.

Even so, the number of farmers declined from 26 per cent of the labour force in 1971 to less than 5 per cent in 2006, as average farm size increased from 18 hectares in 1970 to 33 hectares in 2007 and production became more specialised, with greater emphasis on large-scale production.

ENVIRONMENT

With the introduction of CAP in 1962, emphasis was placed on increasing productivity by utilising more scientific methods of production, including consolidating farm size, greater specialisation and increased use of fertilisers. This proved to be very successful in terms of productivity levels. However, over-intensification of agricultural activity had negative implications for the landscape and, in response to this, during the 1990s CAP began to reduce its emphasis on production. The Rural Environment Protection Scheme (REPS) was introduced to encourage farmers to work in a more environmentally sustainable manner. Emphasis is now placed on more environmentally aware methods of production which preserve and protect the natural landscape. In return for promoting more environmentally sustainable practices, farmers receive monetary support from CAP. REPS has been a vital source of income, particularly for farmers in the BMW.

FISHING   The commercial fishing industry in the BMW was affected by the Common Fisheries Policy (CFP), introduced in 1983. The main objective of this policy was to implement conservation measures to reduce the negative impact of over-fishing. The fishing industry in the BMW has been negatively affected by the introduction of the total allowable catch system (TAC), a reduction in fishing days for certain species and the entry of Spanish boats into the Irish Fishing Box. Ireland owns 16 per cent of EU waters yet has only 11 per cent of TAC, and only 20 per cent of the value of fish landed in the Irish Box is by Irish-registered boats. There has been a significant decline in the number of fishermen, from a peak of 9,000 in 1980 to 5,000 by 2005. In the same period, the number of vessels halved, from 3,000 to 1,500.

In addition, the Irish fishing industry has been forced to restructure its landing and processing operations. Many small ports are no longer economically viable for processing, and activities have become concentrated in the key ports of Killybegs and Castletownbere. These two ports now account for 33 per cent of the total value of the Irish fishing catch. The decline of small ports has had a negative effect on several local coastal communities such as Rossaveal, Dingle, Schull and Dunmore East.

More recent reforms of the CFP (2003) have placed further TAC restrictions on traditional fish species, including cod, herring and mackerel, which is restricting the growth potential of this valuable natural resource, unless the Irish fishing industry diversifies its activities to non-TAC species. However, this degree of diversification will require significant investment, and this may prove difficult to secure in the current economic circumstances. A possible area of expansion is aquaculture, but again capital investment will be required to ensure that the fish farming industry is sustainable and economically viable.

EUROPEAN UNION: POLICIES AND IMPACTS
2008 QUESTION 9 PART B

*Examine **one example** of how the policies of the European Union have influenced Ireland's economic development.* (30 marks)

MARKING SCHEME ✓

Influence named: **2 marks**

SOCIAL FUNDING

TARGET AREAS

The European Union policy I have studied which has had significant implications for the Irish economy is social funding.

Social funding is provided through the Common Regional Policy (CRP) by the European Social Fund. Capital is allocated to reduce social exclusion and promote social inclusion in order to allow all citizens to benefit from economic development.

Social funding has been targeted at particular areas, including the following.

1. Training and retraining for people in long-term unemployment and those affected by youth unemployment. One of the critical challenges facing the Irish economy at the current time is the increasing rates of youth unemployment: figures suggest that a third of the workforce under the age of 25 is currently unemployed. This represents a huge drain on the economy in terms of social welfare payments, but it is also a huge waste of potential economic talent, especially if these people are forced to emigrate in search of employment opportunities.

2. Affordable housing for the poorer sections of society. One of the very negative aspects of the Celtic Tiger era was the huge rise in house prices, leaving many sections of society unable to purchase family homes. The provision of affordable housing is important to both the economy and society of Ireland.

3. Centres and facilities to help the integration of minority groups, including Travellers and refugees. The integration of all people into the Irish economy and society will result in significant economic benefits, increasing the skills and availability of the labour force and reducing dependency on the social welfare system. Social benefits will also result as inclusion reduces tensions within society and problems associated with anti-social behaviour.

4. Funds to support gender equality and to encourage greater female participation in the workforce. Increased female participation in the workforce has obvious benefits to the economy in terms of increasing skill levels and flexibility and reducing dependence on state support.

5. The support of community projects to improve the quality of life for

people in disadvantaged urban and rural areas. Community projects include support for people over 65, and programmes include the rural transport initiative, provision of day care centres and support for active retirement groups. An ageing population can place significant strain on health care provision; however, if people are encouraged to remain active and engaged within society, they will require less medical intervention and can continue to enjoy a productive and active retirement.

The availability of social funding has resulted in significant economic benefits to Ireland since our membership of the EU in 1973.

EUROPEAN UNION: POLICIES AND IMPACTS
2009 QUESTION 9 PART C

*Examine the importance of any **one** of the following to the development of the Irish economy:*
- *Common Agricultural Policy*
- *Common Fisheries Policy*
- *Regional Development Funds*
- *Social funding.* (30 marks)

See earlier answers on EU policies.

EUROPEAN UNION: POLICIES AND IMPACTS
2010 QUESTION 9 PART B

*Examine how any **one** major policy of the European Union has influenced Ireland's economic development.* (30 marks)

See earlier answers on EU policies.

ENERGY 2006 SAMPLE PAPER QUESTION 9 PART B

Examine:
1. *The potential economic implications of the continuing dominance of oil as an energy source.*
2. *The environmental implications of the 122.8 per cent growth in transport consumption.* (30 marks)

RELIANCE ON OIL

The economic impacts of our reliance on the use of oil as a key energy resource are, and will continue to be, highly significant. Oil is a fossil fuel and a non-renewable resource. Continual use will result in depletion over time, and the inevitable shortages of supply will lead to higher prices for consumers. Energy resources are the lifeline of any economic system, and rising oil prices will lead to greater production costs in all sectors of the economy, which will then be passed on to consumers. For example, an increase in oil prices affects every aspect of the economic system from primary to secondary and tertiary activities; and domestic users of oil will be affected as many rely on oil for domestic heating and transport.

OIL CRISES The oil crises in 1973, 1989 and more recently were contributing factors in the economic recessions experienced by the global economy. Continuing reliance on oil represents a significant economic risk to all consumer countries, while producers continue to reap rich rewards. Oil resources are concentrated in particular areas of the world: currently the Middle East controls up to 70 per cent of total global oil production. Tensions between Iran, Iraq and the Western world have increased over time, and our reliance on these countries for oil production represents a significant economic, political and strategic risk.

ENVIRONMENTAL IMPACT Transport is a critical component of any economic system; however, the expansion of the global transport system and its dependence on oil has significant environmental implications. Transport is a key contributory factor in the increasing levels of CO_2, which is a highly efficient greenhouse gas. Increasing levels of greenhouse gases appear to be resulting in global warming and significant climate change. Global warming is likely to result in the increased melting of the polar ice caps; this will lead to a rise in sea levels. Low-lying coastal areas will thus be exposed to increased flooding and erosion. Countries such as the Netherlands and Bangladesh are most at risk, but all coastal communities will be negatively affected. Global warming will also result in climatic change, and this may cause increased rainfall in some areas and serious droughts in others. Furthermore, emissions from transport will result in a reduction in air quality, particularly in urban areas; this may cause an increase in respiratory problems, particularly for the young and old.

ENERGY **2006 QUESTION 9 PART C**

*Examine the economic **and** environmental impact of our world's continued reliance on fossil fuels.* (30 marks)

MARKING SCHEME

Two impacts named: **2 marks each**
Discussion: **11 SRPs**
Overall coherence: **4 marks graded**
– *Economic and environmental impacts may overlap*
– *If only one impact treated, overall coherence: 0 marks*

ECONOMIC IMPACT The economic impact of our reliance on coal, oil and gas is extremely significant and will continue to be so in the future. Since fossil fuels are non-renewable resources, if we continue to use them stocks will become depleted, which in turn will lead to high costs of extraction, leading to higher prices to consumers. All economic systems – primary, secondary and tertiary activities – are reliant on energy, so rising fuel prices will also lead to greater production costs: costs that will then be passed on to consumers. The oil crises in 1973, 1989 and more recently contributed to economic global recessions. Continued reliance on fossil fuels is a significant economic risk to all consumer countries, while producers continue to reap the rewards.

ENVIRONMENTAL IMPACT
The risks and damage to the environment associated with the continual use of fossil fuels are significant. Fossil fuel consumption increases the problem of acid rain, which results in damage to forests, vegetation and soil. An estimated one in four trees in Europe is affected by acid rain. This represents both an economic and environmental loss. Acid rain also affects rivers, lakes and streams, raising their acidity levels, which can result in the creation of dead lakes that are unable to support any aquatic life. An estimated 20,000 lakes in Sweden are affected. Acid rain also causes the chemical weathering of buildings, particularly those built of sedimentary rocks, including limestone and sandstone. Many buildings in Dublin have been affected, as have historic buildings and structures in Athens, for example. Burning fossil fuels also causes smog in cities, making life uncomfortable or even dangerous for people with respiratory conditions. An estimated 4,000 deaths occurred during the great London smog of 1952. During the lead up to the Olympics in China in 2008, there was real concern that the very high levels of smog in Beijing would cause serious problems for the athletes. Burning fossil fuels can also lead to an increase in global warming related to CO_2 emissions.

The continued reliance on fossil fuels raises significant economic and environmental concerns.

ENERGY 2008 QUESTION 9 PART C

*Examine the economic **and** environmental significance of current major trends in global energy consumption.* (30 marks)

See earlier answers including 2006 Sample Paper Question 9 Part B (page 155) and 2006 Question 9 Part C (page 156).

THE ENVIRONMENT 2009 QUESTION 8 PART C

Describe and explain the impact of the burning of fossil fuels on the environment. (30 marks)

MARKING SCHEME   ✔

Environmental impact named: **2 marks**
Examples of two fossil fuels named: **2 marks + 2 marks**
Discussion: **12 SRPs**
– *Discussion must refer to the environmental impact*
– *Credit a maximum of 3 SRPs for economic references*

The burning of fossil fuels, which include coal, oil, gas and peat, has a serious impact on the natural environment. Fossils fuels contain high levels of carbon and sulphur oxides, which are released during combustion. These gases have significant implications for the natural environment, increasing the levels of greenhouse gases, reducing air quality and intensifying the acidity of precipitation.

GLOBAL WARMING   Scientific evidence suggests that the combustion of fossil fuels to generate electricity for industrial and domestic consumption, and as fuel for transport, is a key factor in increasing greenhouse gases, which have in turn been linked to global warming. While the issue of global warming and its causes are hotly debated, the consensus view suggests that there is a link between the growing volume of greenhouse gases, fossil fuel combustion and global warming or climate change.

ENVIRONMENTAL IMPACT   Changing climatic conditions have huge implications for the natural environmental. Some areas are experiencing higher levels of rainfall as a result, and this is causing flooding. Such flooding affects many global populations, both in terms of agricultural output and damage to settlements and infrastructure. Other areas are experiencing less rainfall, which can result in drought, causing famine, death and/or significant population migration in the worst affected areas. In addition, global warming has been linked to the melting of polar ice caps, which again has huge implications for the natural environment and global populations.

ACID RAIN   Acid rain is another environmental issue which has been linked to the combustion of fossil fuels, particularly in urban and industrial economies. Greater levels of acidity in precipitation have negative impacts on the natural environment, particularly as regards soil and water supplies, which absorb them. The increased level of acidity in soils affects the natural vegetation, and has serious implications for local ecosystems and native fauna and flora. In Sweden, acid rain is having a detrimental effect on the productivity of the country's forestry industry and is also affecting many freshwater lakes, which now have such levels of acidity that they are not capable of supporting aquatic life.

AIR QUALITY   Fossil fuel combustion has also been linked to declining air quality, particularly in urban-industrial economies. Poor air quality in cities has negative effects on human populations, especially those who suffer from respiratory conditions. Smog and bad air quality also have negative implications for the natural environments of urban areas, a fact that has been confirmed by many studies.

SUSTAINABLE DEVELOPMENT
2008 QUESTION 8 PART C

Examine, with reference to an example/examples you have studied, the importance of ensuring that development is environmentally sustainable. (30 marks)

MARKING SCHEME ✓

Aspect identified: **2 marks**
Named example: **2 marks**
Examination: **13 SRPs**
– *General examination without reference to sustainability: maximum of 6 SRPs*
– *Broad interpretation of 'development'*

Sustainable development policies try to ensure that economic activities do not result in short- or long-term negative environmental effects. The concept of sustainable development was adopted by the Bruntland Commission in 1987. Many global resources are renewable, if adequate management practices are put in place to ensure that exploitation rates do not exceed natural regeneration. The activity I am going to discuss with reference to environmental sustainability is the tuna fishing industry in the Coral Triangle.

TUNA FISHING   The Coral Triangle is located in the Indian Ocean and is a rich tuna spawning and fishing ground. It is also a migratory route for southern bluefin, bigeye, yellowfin, skipjack and albacore tunas from the Indian and Pacific oceans.

Tuna is a vital fishery resource for both developed and developing countries. Between 1950 and 2006, about 27.5 million tonnes of tuna were caught by fishing fleets operating in the Coral Triangle area. These fish are traded, shipped and eaten in many countries around the world.

In addition, an abundance of small tuna species such as frigate, bullet and bonito provide a vital food source for millions of people in the Coral Triangle, while they also serve as prey for other species of fish. The marine food chain is highly interconnected, and failure to manage this vital resource properly will result in irreversible damage.

INVESTMENT   Due to increasing global demand for fish as a food source, the fishing industry has invested significant capital and technology in the harvesting industry. Key investments have been made in sonar, radar, factory ships and mechanised methods of landing and processing. The expansion of the fishing fleets in the region is placing pressure on heavily fished stocks, such as yellowfin tuna in the Indian Ocean. If the current level of fishing continues or increases, these stocks will collapse.

OVER FISHING   International laws and standards support sustainable fisheries management, and are applicable to tuna regional fisheries management organisations (RFMOs) and their member states. However, tuna RFMOs have been unable to prevent over-exploitation of tuna, rebuild depleted stocks or protect the wider ecosystem. A significant proportion of global tuna fishing is unsustainable, and unless emphasis is placed on reducing fish catches and conserving current stocks, the industry will experience irreversible damage. This will not only affect global food supplies and fishermen's incomes, but will also result in a transformation of the ecosystem of the world's oceans.

SUSTAINABLE DEVELOPMENT
2010 QUESTION 9 PART C

Discuss the environmental and economic advantages of using renewable energy sources. (30 marks)

 MARKING SCHEME   ✓

Environmental advantage identified: **2 marks**
Economic advantage identified: **2 marks**

Renewable energy resources: **13 SRPs**
Examination: **11 SRPs** (6/5 SRPs per advantage)
– Credit other named advantage for a maximum of 2 SRPs

The key renewable energy resources currently available for consumption are solar, wind, hydro-electric, wood and biomass. There is also significant investment in developing and harnessing wave energy. The utilisation of renewable energy has many positive environmental and economic implications.

ENVIRONMENTAL BENEFITS

In terms of the environment, the use of renewable energy resources will:

- reduce carbon emissions (except for wood burning)
- reduce air pollution (acid rain and smog)
- reduce greenhouse gas emissions
- allow countries to use fewer fossil fuels
- preserve vital fossil fuel resources
- help countries reach their Kyoto Treaty obligations.

ECONOMIC BENEFITS

The economic benefits of using renewable energy include:

- a more diversified energy base
- reduced dependence on finite resources
- greater competition within the energy market, resulting in lower prices for consumers
- reduced dependence on oil, in particular, resulting in lower prices and greater economic and political stability as the power of OPEC will be reduced
- a long-term solution to global energy needs
- sustainable development policies which will have positive economic and environmental impacts for the global community.

CONFLICTS OF INTEREST (ECONOMIC VERSUS ENVIRONMENTAL) 2006 QUESTION 8 PART B

 *With reference to **one** example you have studied, examine how conflicts may develop between local and global interests where economic and environmental issues are concerned.* (30 marks)

 MARKING SCHEME ✓

Reference to example: **2 marks**
Two conflicts identified: **2 marks each**
Discussion: **10 SRPs**
Overall coherence: **4 marks graded**
– *At least two of the four operative words to be referred to in discussion, otherwise overall coherence: 0 marks*

COMMERCIAL WHALING

The exploitation of the sea's resources dates back thousands of years and, for many coastal communities, this has provided a vital source of food and income over the centuries.

Commercial whaling was developed in the early twentieth century. Whale fishing has a strong historical tradition in countries such as Iceland, Norway and Japan, and it has been a source of food and valuable oils. During the 1930s, annual global whale catches were estimated at nearly 50,000. This level of exploitation resulted in a significant decrease in whale numbers, and some countries, including Australia, began to express concern about the unsustainable nature of the industry. In 1986, the International Whaling Commission imposed a worldwide moratorium on killing whales for commercial purposes with the intention of allowing global whale stocks time to recover. In the period since 1986, whale stock numbers have increased, and Iceland, Japan and Norway have proposed that the ban on commercial whaling should now be removed. However, anti-whaling countries want the ban to remain, taking the view that commercial whaling will result in over hunting and the possible extinction of many species of whales, including humpbacks, minkes and finbacks.

Despite the ban on commercial whaling, Japan has continued to hunt whales, claiming that they are doing so as part of a programme of scientific research – allowing scientists to collect valuable data on age, birthing rate and diet. (The whale meat is then packaged and sold.) However, opponents claim that this type of research can be undertaken by tagging and monitoring whales' movement and habits rather than by killing them. The Sea Shepherd Conservation Group and Greenpeace have raised awareness of the conflict of interest between pro- and anti-whaling groups. Conservationists and environmentalists are insistent that the commercial ban remain, while Japan, Iceland and Norway want the ban removed.

AQUACULTURE   Aquaculture is another area of conflict between local and global interests. Aquaculture refers to fish farming, including breeding and rearing freshwater and marine fish. It also includes the cultivation and harvesting of oysters, mussels and other shellfish, normally for human consumption, in both inland and coastal locations. This activity has experienced significant growth in the recent past, due to over fishing of wild species. The activity offers an alternative source of employment opportunity for coastal/fishing communities. However, the scale of development has resulted in growing concerns among local communities regarding potential negative environmental impacts, including:

- impact on water quality, especially resulting from the use of chemicals and the build-up of food and waste material in the aquacultural environment
- the incidence of disease among farmed stock and the possible impact of diseases on wild species of fish; for example, the spread of sea lice in salmon and sea trout
- farmed stock escaping into the natural environment and the potentially

deleterious impact of this on wild species of fish
- visual pollution from cages, nets and buoys
- restricted access to scenic, unpolluted areas.

CONFLICTS OF INTEREST (ECONOMIC VERSUS ENVIRONMENTAL) 2007 QUESTION 7 PART C

Examine, with reference to examples you have studied, how conflict often occurs between the need to exploit natural resources and the need to protect the environment. (30 marks)

MARKING SCHEME

Conflict identified: **2 marks**
Reference to two examples: **2 marks + 2 marks**
Examination: **12 SRPs**
– *Discussion of one side of the argument only: 6 SRPs maximum*
– *A second conflict may be credited from the SRPs*
– *Example can refer to region/conflict*

The two natural resources I have studied are tropical rainforests in the Amazon and soil in the Sahel. Conflict has occurred between economic interests and environmentalists regarding the exploitation of these resources.

AMAZON RAINFORESTS

Deforestation in the Amazon has been escalating since the 1960s. Timber is an important natural resource with significant economic potential as a raw material. Commercial logging interests in the Amazon area remove large tracts of rainforest annually – in 2005 over 26,000km^2 of forestry was cut down. Environmentalists maintain that this rate of deforestation is unsustainable and that it will have a serious environmental impact. The tropical rainforests have a vital role to play in reducing the amount of greenhouse gases in the atmosphere – they are sometimes described as the 'lungs of the earth' – and removing the trees at an unsustainable rate will have huge implications for global climatic conditions.

The Brazilian government has supported deforestation in order to clear land for agriculture, but the soil structure in the area is not suitable for intensive agriculture, and as a result soil erosion and desertification are occurring at an increasing rate.

DESERTIFICATION IN THE SAHEL

In the Sahel region, soil is a crucial natural resource and has been used by nomadic farmers for generations. However, agricultural practices in the region have changed, as countries in the region encourage the production of cash crops in order to reduce debt. The imposition of intensive long-term agricultural activity results in damage to the fragile soil structure. Soils very quickly lose inherent fertility, and this causes a reduction in vegetation cover. Over time, soil becomes exposed to harsh climatic conditions, and human-induced desertification occurs. In the Sahel, poor soil management combined with very low levels of rainfall are causing the desert to expand at a rate of between 5.5km and 9km per year. In addition, population pressure is increasing, as is the number of grazing animals, and this is placing additional pressure on a very fragile environment. Many areas of the Sahel are now overpopulated, increasing the conflict between man and environment.

CONFLICTS OF INTEREST (ECONOMIC VERSUS ENVIRONMENTAL) **2009 QUESTION 9 PART B**

*Conflict may develop between economic interests and environmental interests. Examine this conflict with reference to **one** example you have studied.* (30 marks)

See answers to 2006 Question 8 Part B (page 163) and 2007 Question 7 Part C (page 165).

CONFLICTS OF INTEREST (ECONOMIC VERSUS ENVIRONMENTAL) **2010 QUESTION 8 PART C**

Examine how conflict can arise between local interests and global interests when a resource is exploited for economic reasons. In your answer refer to an example of such conflict that you have studied. (30 marks)

See answers to 2006 Question 8 Part B (page 163) and 2007 Question 7 Part C (page 165).

ECONOMIC DEVELOPMENT VARIES OVER TIME
2006 SAMPLE PAPER **QUESTION 7 PART C**

*Explain how levels of economic development vary **over time**.*
(30 marks)

A region I have studied which shows that economic development varies over time is the Sambre-Meuse region in Belgium. This coalfield region is located in a valley stretching 120km from the French border to the city of Liège.

GROWTH   During the industrial revolution, industrial development was concentrated in specific geographic locations which had access to energy, raw materials, labour and markets. The geography and resources of the Sambre-Meuse facilitated its economic development in the early nineteenth century, and key industries, including coal mining and iron and steel production, developed in the region. These industries were labour intensive, so employment opportunities expanded and the region became a centre for in-migration. Its industrial base continued to grow in the twentieth century, and the south of Belgium, which is known as Wallonia, became the economic core of the country.

CHANGING ECONOMIC FORTUNES   In the years after World War II, the factors influencing industrial location underwent a transformation, and a great dispersal of industrial activity took place as more energy sources (oil in particular) and raw materials became available. However, as coal resources became depleted and the cost of extracting coal increased, traditional industrial locations like the Sambre-Meuse began to experience economic difficulties. Furthermore, coastal portal locations started to develop strong industrial bases, and as new technologies and more efficient methods of production were introduced in these areas, industries in the Sambre-Meuse began to decline. Over time, iron, steel and related industries in the region began to rationalise and restructure, resulting in significant job losses in what had been very labour intensive sectors.

The gradual decline of this industrial base had a very negative impact socially and economically. Unemployment rates soared and alternative sources of work were not to be found locally. As a consequence, many of the younger population migrated to the new industrial zone of the north, which contained the key cities of Antwerp and Ghent.

In the mid-1980s, the last coalfield in the Sambre-Meuse closed. The area is now classified as a declining industrial region which is over-dependent on traditional industries and suffering high levels of unemployment and out-migration. It receives significant capital assistance under the EU's Common Regional Policy to help regenerate its economic base.

Looking at the change in the Sambre-Meuse region's fortunes from the nineteenth to the twentieth century, gives us a clear illustration of how economic development can vary over time.

THIS CASE STUDY CAN ALSO BE APPLIED TO 2010 QUESTION 8 PART B (PAGE 147)

TRADE PATTERNS
2006 SAMPLE PAPER **QUESTION 8 PART B**

Explain how the producers of commodities such as coffee receive so little of the final price. (30 marks)

*COFFEE
PRODUCTION*

The production of cash crops and the price received for them are influenced by market demand and supply and by competition among producers and buyers.

Coffee production over the last 20 years has expanded at a huge rate, but coffee consumption has remained relatively static during the same period. As a result, there is a huge over supply of coffee, and this has a negative impact on the price paid to producers. Coffee exports have grown by 15 per cent since 1990 due to increased outputs by established producers and by the arrival of new producers in the market. Ten years ago, Vietnam was not a major coffee producer, yet today it is second only to Brazil. During the same period, Brazil and Columbia have expanded production.

COFFEE PRICES   Over production is reducing the price paid to producers. In response to the reduced price of coffee, some producers have been forced to expand production and increase output to remain economically viable.

Oxfam has suggested that a radical change in coffee production practices is required in order to stabilise the market. Production levels have to come down or the price to producers will continue to decline. As a against that, the coffee federation of Brazil suggests that the solution is to increase consumption of coffee in the key global markets of China and India.

COMPETITION   Another reason why the price paid to producers remains low is the huge level of competition between them. This allows the manufacturers to exploit the producer market and keep prices as low as possible. Wholesale prices for coffee have fallen from $2.40 to just 50 cents per pound. This is the lowest level paid for over 30 years. Yet consumers have not benefited from this as coffee prices in supermarkets remain high.

PATTERNS & PROCESSES IN THE HUMAN ENVIRONMENT

POPULATION **2008 QUESTION 10 PART C**

*Describe and explain, using examples which you have studied, the difference between the terms **population density** and **population distribution**. (30 marks)*

MARKING SCHEME

Terms defined: **2 marks + 2 marks**
Two named examples: **2 marks + 2 marks**
Explanation: **11 SRPs**
– If explanation refers to one term only: maximum of 5 SRPs

POPULATION DENSITY

Population density is measured by calculating the number of people living in a specific area. The result is usually expressed as a number per square kilometre. The highest population densities are generally associated with urban areas, and it is estimated that by 2030 up to 60 per cent of the world's population will live in urban areas. In Ireland the highest population densities are in the key urban centres of Dublin, Belfast, Cork, Waterford and Limerick. Low population densities are associated with rural areas and upland locations which are not suitable for human settlement or productive economic activities. The population density for Ireland is approximately 54 per square kilometre.

However, this figure does not take into consideration areas with very high or very low density.

POPULATION
DISTRIBUTION
Population distribution refers to the location and number of people living in a particular region, country or continent. Many areas of the earth's surface are not suitable for human settlement, primarily because of climatic and physical constraints. The highest concentration of cities with a population greater than one million people is between the Tropic of Cancer and 40°N. Key areas of urbanisation include South East Asia and the western and eastern American seaboard. In India, the highest distribution of population is in the Indus-Ganges plain and in key urban areas, primarily old colonial ports and the inland cities of Bengaluru (formerly Bangalore), Delhi and New Delhi.

By combining statistics relating to both population distribution and population densities, demographers can gain a greater understanding of the dynamic of global and regional populations.

MIGRATION **2007 QUESTION 12 PART C**

*Migration, both internal and international, continues to play an important role in shaping the population of states and regions. Examine **one** impact of population movement on donor regions and **one** impact on receiver regions.* (30 marks)

MARKING SCHEME ✓

Impact on donor regions: **2 marks**
Impact on receiver regions: **2 marks**
Explanation: **13 SRPs**
– *Give credit for up to three examples from the SRPs*
– *If answer is based on donor or receiver region only: 7 SRPs maximum*

*POPULATION
DENSITY*

Donor Region Impact: Border, Midlands and West (BMW)

The BMW region is a peripheral region which lacks the economic opportunities of other areas. This has resulted in considerable out-migration in the past, which has had a significant negative impact on the population structure and the social and economic dynamics of the region. Migrants from the region have traditionally been the younger, educated section of the population, which has resulted in an ageing population lacking the dynamism and education to meet the demands of the modern global economy. Many counties in the BMW have experienced serious brain drains, inhibiting their economic potential.

The loss of the younger section of the population also has negative cultural implications, as seen in the decline of some GAA clubs and the resulting need for the amalgamation of rural clubs in order to field teams in underage and senior competitions.

Connacht's population has declined from 1.4 million in 1841 to approximately 500,000 today, while Mayo experienced a 32 per cent decline in population between 1926 and 2002.

Receiver Region Impact: Greater Dublin

With the advent of the Celtic Tiger economy and the significant increase in employment opportunities, the Greater Dublin area has experienced considerable in-migration in recent decades. Some of these migrants were from regions within Ireland; however, there was also a notable level of migration from eastern European countries. During a time of economic growth, economic migration is critical in order to ensure adequate numbers of workers for an expanding economy. Migrant labour was hugely important, particularly in the service sector and the construction industry. Economic migrants ensure the flexibility of a labour force, and they bring substantial economic benefits to the receiver regions in terms of taxation and consumer spending. In addition, they enhance the cultural diversity of the receiver regions in such areas as language, dress, food, festivals, etc. During the period 2002 to 2006, Dublin's population increased by 5.7 per cent.

However, in a time of economic recession, migrants can find it difficult to secure adequate employment, and their social and financial conditions can decline significantly as a result. Additionally, increased migration into a region can put pressure on its physical and social infrastructure – housing, transport, schools, hospitals and recreational facilities.

MIGRATION 2008 QUESTION 11 PART C

*Examine **one** positive and **one** negative potential consequence of human migration.* (30 marks)

Connacht is a peripheral economic region that lacks the economic opportunities of other areas. The out-migration that was caused by Connacht's underdevelopment led to a 64 per cent decline in the population of the province between 1841 and 2006. This has had a serious impact on the region's population structure and social and economic dynamics.

NEGATIVE IMPACT ON A SOURCE REGION

Traditionally, it is younger, educated people who migrate, and this drain on the population of the region has resulted in an ageing population largely lacking the education and drive to participate fully in the modern global economy. Many counties in Connacht have experienced serious brain drains, which has inhibited their economic potential. Sligo's population fell by 18.5 per cent and Leitrim's by 58.8 per cent during the period 1926 to 2002. The loss of younger people in a community also has negative cultural effects. For example, many GAA clubs have declined, and rural clubs have had to amalgamate in order to field teams in underage and senior competitions.

POSITIVE IMPACT ON A RECEIVER REGION

The Celtic Tiger economy led to an expansion of employment opportunities, which in turn led to high in-migration to the Greater Dublin area. Some migrants came from other parts of Ireland, but there was also a marked level of migration from eastern Europe. Economic migration is important at times of economic growth because an expanding economy needs more workers. Migrant labour was vital, particularly for the service sector and the construction industry, to ensure a flexible and plentiful workforce. Economic migrants bring great economic benefits – taxation and consumer spending – to receiver regions, and they also contribute to cultural diversity in such areas as language, dress, food, festivals, etc. However, during recessionary times, it is harder for migrants to find work, leading to a reduction in their social and financial well-being.

MIGRATION **2009 QUESTION 12 PART B**

*With reference to examples you have studied, examine **two** impacts of rural to urban migration.* (30 marks)

MARKING SCHEME

Two impacts named: **2 + 2 marks**
One migration named: **2 marks**
Examination: **12 SRPs (6 SRPs per impact)**
– *Credit one further named migration as SRP from examination*

INDIA

One impact of rural to urban migration in India is the growth of shanty towns. In many parts of rural India, population growth has increased rapidly due to falling death rates and rising birth rates (natural increase). Many young people are unable to find work in rural areas and migrate to cities such as Kolkata, Delhi and Bengaluru. However, poor levels of education, inadequate skills and limited employment opportunities mean that many of the migrants are unable to secure employment and are forced to live in slums or shanty towns. In Kolkata, over four million people live in these *bustees*. Conditions in shanty towns are very poor, and problems include lack of access to clean water, poorly constructed homes, high death rates, particularly among children, the spread of disease, poor sanitation and widespread poverty.

BMW REGION

A second example of rural to urban migration is the BMW region. One impact this has had on the region is rural depopulation. In 1926, 68 per cent of the Irish population was rural; however, by 2030 only approximately 30 per cent of the population will reside in rural areas. Many of these migrants are young people, and they leave behind an ageing population with negative levels of natural increase. The rural depopulation of areas has significant negative implications for the economy and society of the BMW region. The lack of a young, educated, dynamic workforce hinders economic development and can increase the economic and geographic isolation of areas. Decreasing population numbers also have a negative impact on the provision of services, including transport, infrastructure, education and health care. Depopulated areas may also experience cultural erosion, such as the decline of the native Irish-speaking population in Gaeltacht areas and the drop in the numbers of players and members in local GAA clubs.

MIGRATION AND IRELAND
2010 QUESTION 10 PART B

*Examine **two** major changes in the patterns of Irish migration within the last one hundred years.* (30 marks)

OUT-MIGRATION

Two key patterns of Irish migration can be identified since the end of World War II.

Emigration rates of Irish people to foreign labour markets were very high, particularly during the 1950s. This emigration was directly related to a significant lack of employment opportunities in the Irish economy. The 1950s were characterised by very low levels of economic growth, and many people, particularly in rural areas, could not find work. The Irish government was unable to promote or sustain economic activity, and many people were forced to emigrate in search of work. The main push factors were lack of employment opportunity, low living standards and lack of access to services and education. The destination economies included Britain, the USA and Australia, and the main pull factors were jobs, higher standards of living and the prospect of a better life. During the 1950s, an estimated 409,000 people emigrated from Ireland; the highest rate was in 1958, when 58,000 people emigrated. According to census figures, the Irish population fell to a historic low of 2.8 million in 1961. This level of emigration from the country had many negative effects: a brain drain; the loss of cultural identity, particularly in rural areas; an ageing population; and the depopulation of many rural areas.

IN-MIGRATION   The second key change in Irish migration occurred during the Celtic Tiger period of the mid-1990s to 2007/8. During these years, the Irish economy experienced exceptional growth rates and employment opportunities grew, particularly in the manufacturing and tertiary industries. This resulted in a significant return migration of many people who had emigrated to foreign labour markets during the economic recession of the late 1980s. During the period, net migration (the difference between in- and out-migration) increased significantly. Not only did Ireland experience high levels of return migration, but the country now became a key destination for foreign nationals as employment opportunities rose in key areas, including the construction industry and services (especially low-order services). Key source locations for foreign nationals coming to Ireland were Poland (17 per cent of in-migrants in 2005) and Lithuania (9 per cent of in-migrants in 2005).

The booming economy of the mid-1990s to 2007/8 resulted in a significant population increase within the economy, and this resulted in many positive effects, including a vibrant consumer market, greater demand for housing and services, increased tax returns and greater cultural diversity.

MIGRATION AND IRELAND
2010 QUESTION 12 PART B

'Ethnic and religious issues can arise as a result of migration.'
Examine this statement with reference to example(s) you
have studied. (30 marks)

MARKING SCHEME ✔

Ethnic issue identified: **2 marks**
Religious issue identified: **2 marks**

Example: **2 marks**
Examination: **12 SRPs**
- *Credit one extra example from examination*
- *Issues can be negative or positive*
- *Maximum of 6 SRPs for discussion of one issue only*

NORTHERN IRELAND

'Ethnic' or 'ethnicity' refers to a minority group of people who live within a large host population. These minority groups have a unique self-identity, generally expressed in terms of place of birth, language and religion.

In Northern Ireland, Catholics were seen as an ethnic group within the majority Protestant community, and during the 'Troubles' many Catholic families migrated into the Republic seeking respite from civil unrest. The creation of ethnic tensions in Northern Ireland can be traced back to the colonisation and plantation of Ulster by the British Crown during the seventeenth and eighteenth centuries. During this period, many English and Scottish planters migrated to Ulster and began to take control of the economic and political institutions and resources of the region. These planters belonged to the Protestant faith, and over time cultural conflict developed between the planters and the domestic population.

IRISH DIASPORA

Ethnic Irish groups can be found in many countries of the world, including the UK, USA, Australia and Canada. The Irish diaspora has become part of the global economy, and expresses its culture through language, religion and sporting activities. However, tension can exist among ethnic groups as people compete for available economic opportunities.

FORMER COLONIAL POWERS

Ethnic and religious tension can also be seen in former colonial powers, including Britain, France and the Netherlands. These former colonial countries have been key centres of in-migration of populations from the newly independent colonial areas. In Britain there are many ethnic groups in urban areas, and their roots can be traced from former colonial regions, including India and Africa. In France, many African migrants have sought to establish enclaves in several cities, but there have been tensions between migrants and resident populations. This was clearly seen during the social unrest and riots in Paris in 2005. The migration of Muslims from Arabic regions has influenced the cultural composition of many countries and cities; in the more recent past, the growth of Islamic fundamentalism has increased religious tension between Islamic groups and Western society.

IMMIGRATION POLICIES

2006 SAMPLE PAPER **QUESTION 12 PART C**

Comment on the need for the development of a common immigration policy by the countries of the European Union. (30 marks)

ECONOMIC MIGRANTS

The EU as a core economic region has a long tradition of economic migrants, especially from north Africa and Turkey. More recently, significant numbers of migrants have come from eastern Europe following the break-up of the Soviet Union. Despite this history of immigration, the EU has failed to establish a common immigration policy. This failure may encourage the economic exploitation of migrants and may also be leading to a growth in xenophobia – the fear or hatred of foreigners.

POLICIES NEEDED

The EU needs approximately 20 million economic migrants to sustain supply in the labour market. However, in the interest of protection for migrants, the EU must develop a fair and equitable common immigration policy. This policy should take a number of issues into account, including the establishment of a common border guard in order to allow all EU states to adopt a uniform approach to migrant applications. The issue of asylum seekers also needs to be addressed in a timely manner, in order to reduce the stress and anxiety of genuine asylum applicants. Furthermore, all migrants should have to sign up to an EU database which can store information relating to origin, gender, family ties, economic resources, etc. This system would reduce the number of illegal entries and discourage illegal trafficking.

Efforts also need to be made to assist common entry countries such as Spain, Italy and eastern European countries to update and overhaul their immigration controls and policies. These entry point countries should not be expected to carry the total economic costs of establishing a common immigration policy.

Finally, it is of critical importance that efforts are made to reduce illegal immigration and the potential exploitation of migrants. All migrants need to be protected by the EU and their rights upheld, while all those involved in any form of exploitation should be prosecuted by strict EU laws.

URBAN AREAS **2010 QUESTION 11 PART C**

 'Problems can develop as urban centres expand and grow.'
Discuss this statement with reference to one developing
world city that you have studied. (30 marks)

 MARKING SCHEME ✓

Developing world city identified: **2 marks**
Two problems identified: **2 marks + 2 marks**
Examination: **12 SRPs**
– *Maximum of two SRPs if answer is not tied to a named developing world city*
– *Credit a third named problem from within examination if discussed*

URBANISATION

The urban region I have studied in a developing economy is Kolkata.

India is a developing economy, and its current rate of urbanisation is about 28 per cent. According to experts, the rate of urbanisation in developing countries is expanding rapidly, and it is estimated that by 2030 almost 60 per cent of people in developing countries will live in cities.

This level of growth will lead to serious problems, especially in terms of pressure on both physical infrastructure – roads, transport, housing, water supply, waste disposal – and social infrastructure – health services, education, employment opportunities and recreational facilities.

POPULATION GROWTH AND POVERTY

Many of India's large cities, including Delhi and Kolkata, are unable to cope with increasing population numbers. In Kolkata, poverty is a critical problem, and it has been exacerbated by growing urbanisation. Kolkata's population is estimated at 12.7 million, with a natural increase of 2 per cent. Many residents do not have access to adequate food, shelter, clothing or clean water. Thirty per cent of the population live in slums known as *bustees* and survive by collecting waste food and material in landfill sites, and by begging on the streets. The vicious cycle of poverty in the city is undermining development efforts to improve the social conditions of the population.

Access to medical and health facilities is limited. Sanitation and access to clean water is poor, and diseases such as cholera and typhoid are common. Child infant mortality rates are high. An estimated 500,000 people who live on the streets of the city have no access to government services and are largely ignored by government. Many international agencies work in the city trying to improve living conditions for thousands of people, but despite their best attempts Kolkata remains one of the most underdeveloped urban areas in the developing world.

Because India is still a developing economy, the government does not have adequate economic resources to address the significant economic challenges posed by increasing levels of urbanisation.

URBAN PROBLEMS **2006 QUESTION 10 PART B**

*The growth of urban centres may lead to the development of problems. Examine any **two** of these problems, with reference to examples you have studied.* (30 marks)

The urban centres I have studied are Dublin and Paris.

One critical problem related to the growth of Dublin in recent times is traffic congestion. The expansion of the Dublin population (city and county) in recent decades has been enormous. In 1946, 636,200 people lived in Dublin city and

DUBLIN county: this grew to 852,200 in 1971 and 1,186,159 in 2006. This expansion has put huge pressure on a transport infrastructure which was outdated, poorly developed and unable to meet the demands of the modern global economy. Increasing levels of private car ownership, particularly during the Celtic Tiger era of the 1990s and the 2000s, resulted in huge traffic delays, and it was estimated that travel speeds during peak traffic travel times were only 14km per hour. An estimated 60 per cent of work-related travel was by car, while only 17.6 per cent of people used public buses and a mere 4.2 per cent travelled by train or DART (2006 figures).

In recent years, there has been considerable investment in building a modern transport system for the capital. Key developments include the DART, the Luas, the port tunnel, upgrading of the M50, and the establishment of bus lanes and Quality Bus Corridors. However, Dublin still suffers from significant traffic congestion, and the daily commuting journey times are still very high.

PARIS   Paris is a primate city with a population of over ten million. It is a historic city, but suffers from some critical problems related to population expansion. One area of concern for planners is urban decay.

Many areas in the city are suffering from industrial decline and urban decay. These locations have become ghettos for immigrants, particularly those from Africa and South East Asia. In these areas, housing standards are low, and many low-income groups cannot afford rising rent values. One particular area of concern was the La Défense district, close to the city centre. However, due to good urban planning with an emphasis on urban renewal, this area has been transformed from a decaying district to a vibrant area with an expanding population, redeveloped housing and the creation of over 100,000 jobs in the service sector. Throughout the inner city, over 200,000 units of social housing have been built in order to reduce urban decay and to provide a community focus for inner city zones.

URBAN PROBLEMS **2006 QUESTION 11 PART B**

*The rapid growth of cities in the developing world has led to social and economic problems. Examine any **two** such problems, referring to examples you have studied.* (30 marks)

MARKING SCHEME ✓

Two problems identified: **2 marks each**
Two named examples: **2 marks each**
Discussion: **9 SRPs**

Two cities in the developing world that I have studied which experience both economic and social problems are Kolkata and Delhi in India.

Kolkata has a population of 12.7 million people with a natural increase of 2 per cent. An estimated 500,000 people are homeless, with over four million people living in slums known as *bustees*. Housing in the *bustees* is of a very poor standard: many houses are constructed using scrap material, including cardboard, plastic and galvanised iron. In some areas in Kolkata, concrete pipes are used for shelter. Houses often consist of just one room, and overcrowding is a serious problem. There is basic provision of water and light, but living conditions are poor and represent a serious health hazard, particularly for the young and the elderly. Water contamination is common, particularly during monsoon rains, and diseases such as malaria, typhoid and cholera thrive in these conditions. Similar conditions also occur in slums in Sao Paulo, Mexico City and Mumbai.

SOCIAL PROBLEM: LACK OF ADEQUATE HOUSING

Kolkata was once a key trading, financial and industrial centre; however, since the late 1950s, it has experienced significant economic decline, leading to high levels of unemployment. People living in the *bustees* have no access to work, no right to social welfare, no adequate health care provision and are trapped in a vicious cycle of poverty. The lack of employment opportunities is a huge hindrance to development for millions of residents. Many survive by begging or by working in the informal service sector economy: services here include transport (rickshaws), street trading, shoe shining and selling waste products. People are living at subsistence level, and many children suffer from malnutrition because their parents are unable to provide them with an adequate diet. Children spend their days searching through rubbish heaps and dumps, trying to find usable waste materials and even food.

ECONOMIC PROBLEM: UNEMPLOYMENT

The Indian government has tried to promote employment opportunities in the city, but key problems of a poorly developed transport system, poverty and lack of adequate education are hindering the process.

URBAN PROBLEMS **2007 QUESTION 11 PART C**

Cities are places of opportunity, but also have problems. Examine this statement with reference to a city or cities of your choice. (30 marks)

ELECTIVE 2: **PATTERNS & PROCESSES IN THE HUMAN ENVIRONMENT**

*ECONOMIC
OPPORTUNITIES*

The city I have studied is Paris.

Paris is a capital and primate city and a centre of administration, banking, commerce, finance, retail and tourism. Seventy per cent of all France's service-based employment is centred on the Paris region. Paris is the seat of government and administration; it is a well-developed educational centre and noted as a financial services centre, with employment opportunities in banking, commerce and business consultancy. It is also the hub of the French transport and telecommunications network. The area is a nodal centre of transport and communications and has become a key point of immigration. The resulting population growth has led to the development of five new satellite towns. This city is also a fashion, cultural and tourist centre, providing a variety of service-based employment opportunities.

Because of its level of urbanisation, Paris employs a significant labour force and has a large internal market of ten million people. The industrial base is very diversified, with craft industries, including jewellery, porcelain, perfumes and fashion goods, located in the older part of the city. Emphasis is placed on high-value, high-quality output. Heavy industries, including car manufacturing (Renault and Citroën), engineering, machine tool manufacturing and railway components, are located in the northern and eastern suburbs. In the portal area, raw materials are imported and have allowed for the development of oil-refining and important petro-chemical industries. More modern and footloose industries, including electronics, pharmaceuticals, food processing and consumer appliances, are located in the outer suburbs and satellite towns.

PROBLEMS

Paris suffers from some critical problems related to population expansion. One area of particular concern for planners is urban decay. Many areas in the city suffer from industrial decline and urban decay and have become ghettos for immigrants, particularly those from Africa and South East Asia. Housing is poor, and many people on low incomes cannot afford to pay rising rents. One particular area of concern was the La Défense district, close to the city centre, but this area has been transformed from a decaying district to a vibrant area with an expanding population, redeveloped housing and the creation of over

100,000 jobs in the service sector. Throughout the inner city, over 200,000 units of social housing have been built in order to reduce urban decay and to provide a community focus for inner city zones.

A second problem experienced by Paris is the decline of its traditional industrial base. Paris has a long history of industrialisation, and traditional industries included iron and steel, textiles and shipbuilding. However, the factors influencing industrial location have changed over time, and many of these industries are no longer able to survive in the highly competitive modern global economy. Paris is now experiencing restructuring and rationalisation of many of its older industries, and this is resulting in job losses. Workers from these industries require retraining, reskilling and help to find alternative employment opportunities.

URBAN PROBLEMS 2008 QUESTION 12 PART C

*Examine **two** of the main problems created by the continued pace of urban growth in a region you have studied.* (30 marks)

MARKING SCHEME

Two problems identified: **2 marks** + **2 marks**
Named urban centre/region: **2 marks**
Examination: **9 SRPs**
Overall coherence: **12 SRPs (6 SRPs per problem)**
– *Examination not tied to a named urban centre: maximum of 6 SRPs*
– *Urban centres/regions can be worldwide*
– *Accept a broad interpretation of urban centre*
– *Both problems must be tied to the same region*

TRAFFIC CONGESTION IN DUBLIN

Traffic congestion is a massive problem in Dublin. The population of the city and county has grown enormously in recent decades: from 636,200 people in 1946 to 852,200 in 1971 and 1,186,159 in 2006. As a result, huge pressure has been placed on an outdated, poorly developed transport infrastructure which was unable to meet the demands of the modern global economy. Increasing levels of private car ownership, particularly during the Celtic Tiger period of the 1990s and 2000s, resulted in huge traffic delays, and it was estimated that travel speeds during peak traffic travel times were only 14km per hour. In 2006, it was estimated that 60 per cent of work-related travel was by car, while only 17.6 per cent of people used public buses and a mere 4.2 per cent travelled by train or DART.

In response to these problems, there has been significant investment in building a modern transport system for the capital. Important developments include the DART, the Luas, the port tunnel, upgrading of the M50, and the establishment of bus lanes and Quality Bus Corridors. However, Dublin still suffers from significant traffic congestion, and commuting journey times are still very high.

URBAN SPRAWL IN DUBLIN

Dublin's population expansion has also led to urban sprawl as the city spreads outwards into the surrounding countryside. The Wright Plan of 1967 recommended the establishment of three new towns: Tallaght, Lucan-Clondalkin and Blanchardstown. However, these new towns have now become part of the greater Dublin area.

Urban sprawl places considerable pressure on the physical environment and also on the provision of services. In particular, the rate of expansion has put serious strain on the transport infrastructure, which is proving incapable of meeting the demands of the growing population. In addition, providing basic services such as water, waste collection, sewage treatment and roads is putting increasing pressure on the economic resources of the various local authorities.

URBAN PROBLEMS 2010 QUESTION 11 PART B

(i) Explain the term 'traffic congestion'.
*(ii) Explain **two** methods used to overcome traffic congestion.*
Use examples you have studied in your answer. (30 marks)

MARKING SCHEME ✓

Explanation: **2 marks graded**
Two methods named: **2 marks + 2 marks**
Named examples: **2 marks + 2 marks**
Examination: **10 SRPs (5 per method)**
– Allow for transfer of information from part one to part two if it refers to methods used to overcome traffic congestion

Traffic congestion refers to a significant build-up of traffic in an area, and results in limited movement. It is generally associated with rush hour periods (7–9 a.m. and 5–7 p.m.); traffic in urban areas; the build-up of traffic between towns and villages; and congestion in small towns which are on main travel routes (e.g. Gort, Co. Galway, which is on the Limerick–Ennis–Galway route).

Method 1: Bypasses/Ring Roads

Traffic congestion in Ennis in Co. Clare, which is on the main routeway between Limerick and Galway, was a major problem for the town and its residents. In an attempt to reduce congestion and to improve the commercial potential of the town, the National Roads Authority (NRA) developed a bypass system. The aim was to create a ring road around Ennis, allowing commuter and goods traffic to bypass the town; and a motorway linking Limerick and Shannon traffic to the Crusheen/Gort road. Construction began in early 2000, and the bypass opened in 2006. Access time between Limerick and Galway has been reduced by up to 25 minutes; and traffic congestion in Ennis town has been greatly eased, which is benefiting the commercial potential of the town.

In Loughrea, Co. Galway, located on the Galway–Dublin axis, traffic congestion was also a major problem: not only did it have a negative effect on the town, it was increasing the travel time for people driving from the west of Ireland towards Dublin. This problem has been ameliorated by the construction of the Loughrea bypass, which was opened in 2010.

Method 2: Public Transport

Many Irish cities experience high levels of traffic congestion, especially during the rush hour, and this congestion is directly related to high dependence on private modes of transport. In an effort to reduce the need for private transport and to encourage the use of public transport, many local authorities have attempted to upgrade and increase the efficiency of public transport. In Cork city, bus corridors/lanes have been introduced to reduce travel times, and bus frequency has been increased (e.g. bus 8 from Bishopstown to Mayfield). In addition, a park and ride system has been introduced to encourage people to park their cars in the public authority car parks on the outskirts of the city and to use public transport for the remainder of their journey (for example, the Blackash park and ride at the Kinsale roundabout).

In Dublin, the DART and Luas systems have been developed to reduce the need for private transport. Other examples include the Paris Métro, the London Underground and the New York subway. Dublin city has also introduced a public bicycle system which allows people to access bikes at a very low cost and use these to travel around the city.

Dublin city

URBAN PLANNING **2009 QUESTION 11 PART B**

*With reference to **one** example that you have studied, examine the effectiveness of urban planning strategies in dealing with urban problems.* (30 marks)

MARKING SCHEME ✓

Two named strategies: **2 marks + 2 marks**
Two named urban problems: **2 marks + 2 marks**
Examination: **11 SRPs**
– Allow a named urban area as 1 SRP from the examination
– Maximum of 5 SRPs if not related to 'effectiveness'

The city I have studied is Dublin.

In 1967, the Wright Plan was formulated to provide a planning strategy to manage the future growth of Dublin. It proposed the establishment of three new towns in the greater Dublin area which would relieve urban sprawl from the *WRIGHT PLAN* city. Three new towns were established: Tallaght, Lucan-Clondalkin and Blanchardstown. It was anticipated that these towns would be linked to Dublin by a well-developed road network system and that there would be a green belt to ensure adequate agricultural and recreational areas.

However, in the decades since the Wright Plan was drawn up, urban sprawl has become a critical problem for Dublin city. The three new towns are now part of the urban population, and green belts have disappeared under increasing demand for housing. The transport infrastructure has been unable to keep pace with increasing demand. Levels of private car ownership have grown dramatically, and 60 per cent of the population use private transport for travelling to and from work.

NATIONAL
SPATIAL
STRATEGY
The National Spatial Strategy, introduced in 2002, aims to reduce the growth of Dublin and to create a more even distribution of urban areas, employment opportunities and the provision of services and facilities outside the Dublin region. Plans include the development of:

- Gateways: designated urban areas with good infrastructure which will reduce the dominance of Dublin. Examples: Galway, Limerick, Cork, Waterford, Athlone, Tullamore, Mullingar, Sligo and Letterkenny.
- Hubs: smaller urban centres to increase dispersal of growth in regional economies. Examples: Ennis, Mallow, Tralee, Killarney, Wexford, Kilkenny, Tuam, Castlebar.
- Strategic road corridors: good infrastructural links between hubs, gateways and Dublin.

The most effective component of the strategy has been the development of infrastructural links between the hubs, gateways and Dublin. Significant investment has been devoted to increasing transport efficiency, particularly in terms of the road networks. Travel times between Cork and Dublin have been reduced by 40 minutes. The Limerick–Galway network now bypasses Ennis, while road journey times from Galway to Dublin have also been reduced.

Cork city

LAND USE CHANGE IN URBAN AREAS
2006 QUESTION 11 PART C

Different activities compete for space in urban areas. As a result, different land use zones develop. Referring to examples you have studied, examine how these land use zones change as urban centres grow. (30 marks)

 MARKING SCHEME ✓

Two land use zones identified: **2 marks each**
Discussion: **11 SRPs**
Overall coherence: **4 marks graded**
– Credit two specific examples from SRPs
– Examples may refer to two urban centres or to two named
  areas/sectors within the one urban centre

Cork city has experienced significant land use changes over time. These changes have occurred due to the outward expansion of the city in key directions.

    The central business district (CBD) of the city is sited along the axis of
CBD   Patrick's Street, Oliver Plunkett Street and South Mall. However, within this zone

READING ORDNANCE SURVEY MAPS

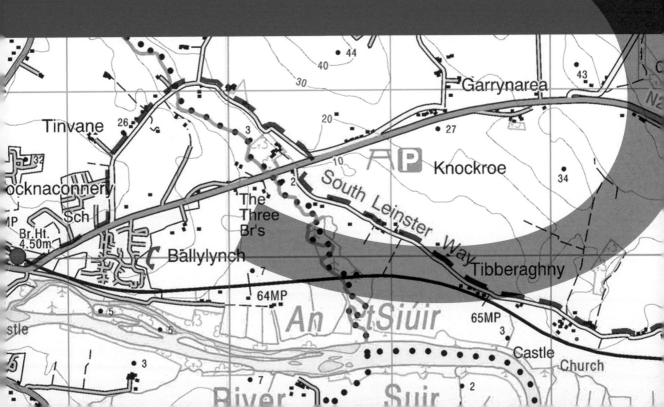

READING ORDNANCE SURVEY MAPS

The key to success in answering map questions is to answer exactly what is asked and to support every part of your answer with evidence from the map. Use the concept *Statement – Evidence, Statement – Evidence.* Remember, questions on Ordnance Survey maps are about map reading.

 ## SYMBOLS

Be completely familiar with the map legend and conventional symbols used. Focus on key details, for example: modes of transport; tourist-related information, including tourist offices, parking and viewing sites, marinas and marked walkways; antiquities; relief; water features; and forestry areas. Also be familiar with the use of colour coding for roads; relief; antiquities; provision of services, including post offices, fire stations, and public telephones; and built-up areas.

Recent Exam Questions on Conventional Symbols

- 2011 (Short Questions): Question 2
- 2010 (Short Questions): Question 2
- 2009 (Short Questions): Question 2
- 2008 (Short Questions): Question 2
- 2007 (Short Questions): Question 2

 ## SCALE

The scale of the maps used in the Leaving Certificate examination is 1:50,000. This figure is known as a representative fraction (RF) and it means that 1cm on the map represents 50,000cm (500m) on the ground: so 2cm on the map represents 1km on the ground.

   Note: A street map generally has a scale of 1:2,500 while a world atlas scale is generally 1:100,000,000.

Recent Exam Questions on Scale

- 2006 Sample Paper (Short Questions): Question 10

MEASURING DISTANCE AND AREA

Straight Line

Mark the two points on the map and measure the distance in centimetres.
Remember: 2cm = 1km.

Crooked Line

Mark the starting point on the straight edge of a piece of paper.
Follow the route by moving the paper against the map, marking
each divergence from a straight line on the edge of the sheet of paper.
Measure the distance from the first mark to the last in centimetres.
Remember: 2cm = 1km.

Regular Area

Measure the length in centimetres and divide by two.
Then measure the breadth in centimetres and divide by two.
Multiply the two figures to get the total area in square kilometres.

Irregular Area

Each full square equals 1km^2, so count the number of full squares.
Then count the number of partial squares (halves and quarters, etc.).
Add the full and partial numbers together to calculate the total area.

Recent Exam Questions on Distance

- 2009 (Short Questions): Question 2
- 2008 (Short Questions): Questions 2, 9
- 2007 (Short Questions): Question 2
- 2006 (Short Questions): Question 7
- 2006 Sample Paper (Short Questions): Question 8

GRID REFERENCES AND COMPASS DIRECTIONS

Grid References

The sub-zone letter comes first, followed by the easting and then the northing. Use a six-figure reference for a particular point on a map and a four-figure reference for an area on a map.

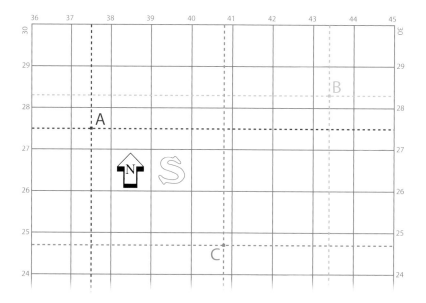

Examples of grid references
A = S 375 275
B = S 434 283
C = S 408 247

Compass Directions

Divide the compass into eight reference points: north, north-east, east, south-east, south, south-west, west and north-west. You can use compass directions to locate a feature or to establish the trend of a road network or the trend of relief. Remember that the trend of something contains two opposite compass points; for example, the trend of a mountain range might be north-east/south-west.

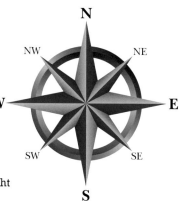

Recent Exam Questions on Grid References and Compass Directions

- 2010 (Short Questions): Question 5
- 2007 (Short Questions): Question 2

SKETCH MAPS AND ORDNANCE SURVEY MAPS

These are an important part of the exam curriculum and have featured in several papers since 2006. There are a number of basic rules which should be followed when drawing Ordnance Survey sketch maps.

1. Draw to half scale. The required size on recently used maps is 9cm by 12cm.
2. Using graph paper (if indicated in the question) or ruled paper, draw the outline in pencil.
3. If a major lake or coastline is on the extract you should include it: this will help you to draw to scale.
4. Otherwise only include features you are asked for, e.g. relief, roads, coastline, etc.
5. Use colour for clarity (e.g. shading for uplands and lowlands), but don't waste time.
6. Insert all required information in a key.
7. Mark and label (or show and name) information on the sketch map.
8. Add a title to the sketch map.
9. Insert a north sign.
10. Insert a scale. If the sketch map is drawn to half scale, the new scale will be 1:100,000.

Note: Sketch maps must not be traced.

Recent Exam Questions on Ordnance Survey Sketching

- 2011: Question 1 Part A
- 2010: Questions 1 Part A, 9 Part A
  SEE PAGES 212 – 214 FOR SAMPLE ANSWERS
- 2009: Question 1 Part A
- 2008: Question 1 Part A
- 2007: Question 1 Part A

ORDNANCE SURVEY MAP
2010 QUESTION 1 PART A

Examine the Ordnance Survey map that accompanies this paper.
(MAP REPRODUCED ON PAGE 216)
In your answer book, draw a sketch-map **to half scale** *of the area shown. On it, mark and name* **each** *of the following:*
*   *One landform created by the processes of river deposition*
*   *A V-shaped valley*
*   *An area with a trellised drainage pattern*
*   *The complete course of the Glen River.* (20 marks)

MARKING SCHEME ✓

Proportion: **4 marks graded (4-2-0)**
Four features: **4 marks each (shown 2 marks graded, named 2 marks)**
– *Proportion involves showing the correct scale*
– *Required size is 9cm x 12cm (allow a difference of up to ½cm)*
– *If sketch is traced or a section of the map is drawn, lose 4 marks for proportion and 2 marks for showing per item*

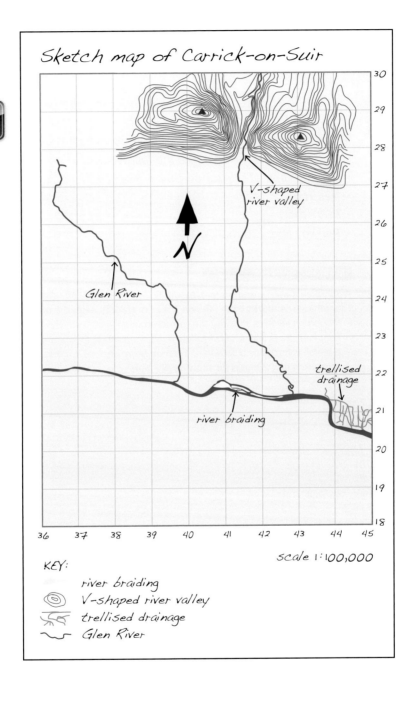

Sketch map of Carrick-on-Suir

V-shaped river valley

N

Glen River

trellised drainage

river braiding

scale 1:100,000

KEY:

river braiding
V-shaped river valley
trellised drainage
Glen River

ORDNANCE SURVEY MAP
2010 QUESTION 9 PART A

Examine the Ordnance Survey map that accompanies this paper.
(MAP REPRODUCED ON PAGE 216)
*In your answer book, draw a sketch-map **to half scale** of the area shown. On it, show and name the following:*
* *Built-up area of Carrick-on-Suir*
* *N24 road*
* *R697 road*
* *Railway line. (20 marks)*

MARKING SCHEME ✓

Proportion: **4 marks graded (4-2-0)**
Four features: **4 marks each (shown 2 marks graded, named 2 marks)**
– *Proportion involves showing the correct scale*
– *Required size is 9cm x 12cm (allow a difference of up to ½cm)*
– *If sketch is traced or a section of the map is drawn, lose 4 marks for proportion and 2 marks for showing per item*

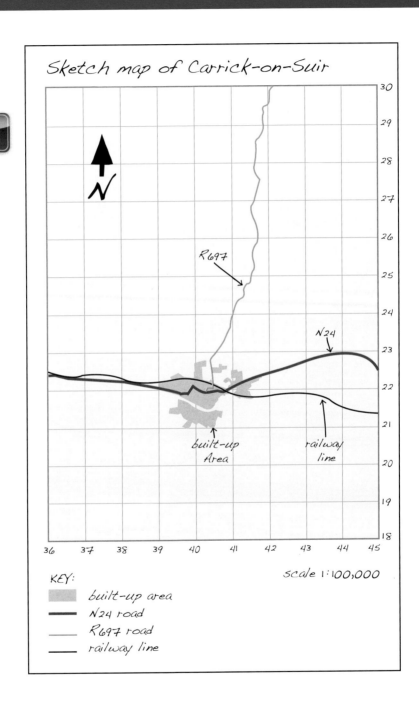

Sketch map of Carrick-on-Suir

a

R697

N24

built-up
Area

railway
line

KEY:
built-up area
N24 road
R697 road
railway line

scale 1:100,000

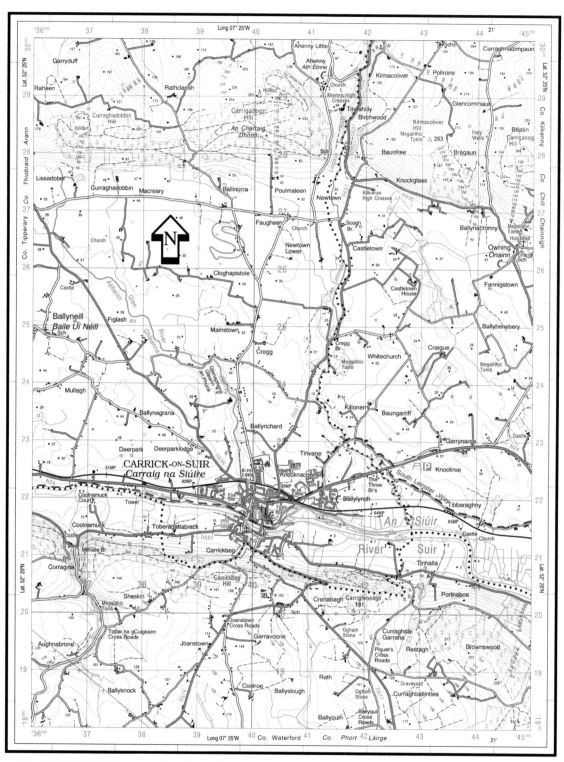

RELIEF

The relief of an area refers to height above sea level. Areas of lowland are generally below 200m, while upland areas are above 200m. There are a number of different methods used to show the relief of areas on Ordnance Survey maps:

1. Shading: lowland areas have green shading patterns; uplands have brown shading.
2. Contour lines: lines drawn on a map which indicate areas of equal height and are normally shown at 10m and 50m intervals.
3. Spot heights: black dots with a number which indicates height in metres.
4. Triangulation pillars: shown as a triangle and a number which indicates height in metres.

SLOPES

A slope is described by its gradient.

- The formula for calculating the gradient is vertical interval (VI) divided into the horizontal equivalent (HE).
- The VI is the difference in height between the two points, measured in metres. The HE is the distance between the two points.
- When calculating the HE, first measure the distance between the two points in centimetres, convert this into kilometres (2cm = 1km), then convert the kilometres into metres (1km = 1,000m).
- Then divide the VI into the HE and you will get 1 over _____ metres.

Note: The smaller the denominator, the steeper the slope; i.e. 1/8 is steeper than 1/10. The gradient of a road can also be calculated using the same formula.

Types of Slope

- Convex: a slope with a gentle upper section and a steep lower section. It is represented on a map by tightly packed contours at the lower level and widely spaced contours at the upper level.
- Concave: a slope with a steep upper section and a gentle lower section. It is represented by widely spaced contours at the lower level and tightly packed contours at the upper level.
- Even: a slope represented by equally spaced contours.
- Stepped: a slope which has tightly packed and widely spaced contours at equal intervals.

Recent Exam Questions on Slopes

- 2007 (Short Questions): Question 10
- 2006 Sample Paper (Short Questions): Question 9

CROSS SECTION

A vertical cross section shows the relief of an area between two points. Other aspects of interest, e.g. roads, towns, lakes, rivers, etc. can be annotated on the cross section.

Recent Exam Questions on Cross Sections

- 2007 (Short Questions): Question 12
- 2006 (Short Questions): Question 9

PHYSICAL FEATURES

Physical features include uplands, mountains, lowlands, rivers, lakes, streams and features created by surface physical processes including rivers, glaciers and marine features.

Rivers

Key Terms

- Source: the point of origin of a river in an upland area. Use a six-figure grid reference to pinpoint the source of a river.
- Tributary: streams which join a main river.
- Mouth: where a river enters the sea.
- River basin or catchment area: area of land drained by a river and all its tributaries.
- Watershed: area of high ground which divides one river basin from another.
- Ria: a V-shaped valley which has been drowned due to a rise in sea levels.

Rivers have three main stages: youthful, mature and old age. You should be able to identify the different stages and associated physical features as shown on Ordnance Survey maps.

Youthful Stage

Associated with upland areas, i.e. areas above 200m. Identifiable physical features in the youthful stage include:

1. Narrow V-shaped valley: this will have steep-sided slopes, illustrated by tightly packed contour lines.
2. Waterfall: generally notated on maps in blue writing.
3. Interlocking spurs: can be seen if a river takes a winding path in upland areas, thereby avoiding areas of hard rock. (**Note:** Do not confuse these with meanders, which only occur in lowland areas.)

In the youthful stage a river may be joined by a number of tributaries (small streams). These can result in distinctive drainage patterns which can be identified on Ordnance Survey maps. (See drainage patterns diagram, page 220.)

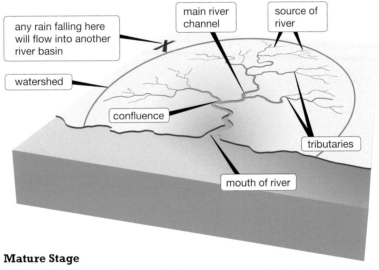

Mature Stage

Identifiable physical features in the mature stage include:

- Wider V-shaped valley.
- Meanders: the river takes a widening path in a low-lying area.
- Flood plain: look for low-lying relief, the avoidance of roads and the absence of houses on the river bank.

Old Age Stage

Identifiable physical features in the old age stage include:

- Well-developed meanders.
- Extensive flood plain.
- Oxbow lake: former part of the river now cut off from the main river channel.
- Delta: look for evidence of the build-up of deposition (shading colours) and distributary channels.

Drainage Patterns

- Radial: associated with upland areas as streams radiate outwards and down a natural slope.
- Trellised/rectangular: streams and tributaries entering the main river at right angles.
- Dendritic: tree-like pattern of drainage as tributaries branch into the main river.
- Deranged: a chaotic pattern of drainage usually associated with poorly drained lowland areas which have been affected by glacial deposition, or in limestone areas which are very porous.
- Parallel: tributaries flowing parallel to the main river.

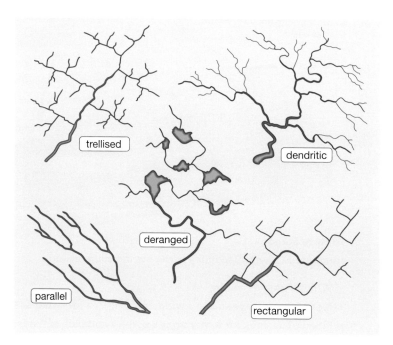

Marine Environment and Physical Features

Identifiable physical features of erosion include:

- Cliff: shown by tightly packed contours lines at the coastline.
- Sea stack: area of land disconnected from the headland.
- Wave-cut platform: shown by colour shading at the base of a cliff.
- Bay: indentation in the coastline.

Features of marine erosion

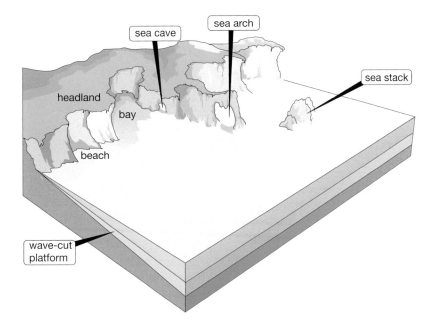

Identifiable physical features of deposition include:

- Beach: occurs between the high and low tide mark and is composed of a variety of material deposited by constructive waves. Shown by yellow shading.
- Sand spit: area of deposition attached at one end to the coastline. Shown by yellow shading.
- Bay mouth bar: area of deposition which is attached to a coastline at both ends. May enclose a water area, which becomes known as a lagoon.
- Tombolo: area of deposition which links an island to the mainland.
- Sand dunes: windblown deposition found at the back of beaches. Look for contour lines showing small hill-like features.

Glacial Environments and Physical Features

Identifiable physical features of glacial erosion include:

- Corrie/cirque/coom/tarn lake: an armchair-shaped hollow in an upland area, shown by tightly packed contours on three sides, opening into a U-shaped valley. May contain water.

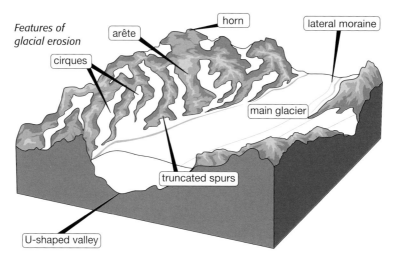

Features of glacial erosion

- **U-shaped valley or glacial trough:** steep-sided valley with a flat valley floor. Valley sides shown by tightly packed contours; wide contours on the valley floor.
- **Hanging valley:** small U-shaped valley joining a larger one at a right angle. May include a small river.
- **Arête:** knife-edge ridge between two corries. Tightly packed contours.
- **Pyramidal peak:** mountain peak in a glacial environment.
- **Ribbon lakes or paternoster lakes:** small lakes on the valley floor connected by small streams.
- **Truncated spurs:** cut-off interlocking spurs, shown as an area of high land at right angles to a U-shaped valley.

Identifiable physical features of glacial deposition include:

- **Drumlins:** known as a 'basket of eggs' topography; shown as clusters of oval-shaped hills in a low-lying area. Placenames may indicate the presence of drumlins ('Drum' in townland names).
- **Eskers:** long winding ridges of sand and gravel, shown as ridges with contour lines. Placenames of townlands may indicate the presence of eskers (e.g. Esker in Co. Galway and Esker Hills in Co. Offaly).

Recent Exam Questions on Physical Features

- 2011 (Short Questions): Question 7
- 2010 (Short Questions): Questions 2 and 5
- 2009 (Short Questions): Question 10
- 2007 (Short Questions): Question 11

SETTLEMENT PATTERNS

The distribution and density of settlements are influenced by the physical landscape and the functions of settlement.

Human settlement tends to favour low-lying areas (below 200m), which are undulating, have access to a water supply, are not prone to flooding and are well serviced by a road network. Settlement tends to avoid upland areas (above 200m) as these locations experience harsher climatic conditions, may be unsuitable for many economic activities, especially agriculture, and will have poor access to road networks.

The main patterns of settlement which can be identified on Ordnance Survey maps include:

Clustered/Nucleated Pattern

Associated with low-lying areas which are well drained and have access to a freshwater supply. The functions of this type of settlement will be directly related to size: the greater the size of any settlement, the greater the complexity of its functions.

Functions may include:

- Historic: look for evidence of antiquities (see Historic Settlement, page 224).
- Market: serving the needs of the internal population and the population of the surrounding hinterland. The larger the site, the greater its market function.
- Service centre: serving the needs of the internal population and the population of the surrounding hinterland. Look for evidence of post offices, Garda stations, tourist information offices, public telephones, fire stations, etc.
- Educational function: look for evidence of schools and colleges.
- Health care: look for evidence of hospitals (Hosp) on maps.

Dispersed

Associated with low-lying areas which are well drained, have fertile soils and have access to freshwater supplies. This type of settlement is mainly composed of single-family homes which are owner occupied and are associated with agricultural activity, though more recently there has also been a major increase in one-off housing.

Linear

Develop along roadways which radiate from clustered nucleated areas, or can be found on third-class roads. Linear settlement allows residents access to public utilities, including water supply, electricity, telecommunications and waste collection. Land values in linear settlements are generally lower than those in clustered nucleated areas.

Absence

An absence of settlement usually occurs in areas above 200m or in low-lying areas which are prone to flooding.

Note: Settlement *density* refers to the *amount* of settlement in an area. Settlement *distribution* refers to the *location* of settlement throughout an area. Distribution of settlement can be dense or sparse and is generally influenced by the physical landscape.

Recent Exam Questions on Settlement Patterns

- 2009: Question 10 Part B
- 2006 Sample Paper: Question 10 Part B

HISTORIC SETTLEMENT

The 1:50,000 Ordnance Survey maps are a rich source of information about historic settlements in Ireland. Different eras of settlement can be identified on these maps because they include a wide range of antiquities (check the map legend). Historical settlements in Ireland that can be identified on Ordnance Survey maps include, in chronological order:

- Mesolithic or Middle Stone Age. Settlers arrived approximately 9,000 years ago and were associated with hunting and gathering. Evidence of these settlers includes middens, which were sites of waste disposal.
- Neolithic or New Stone Age settlers appeared approximately 5,000 years ago and were the first farmers in Ireland. Neolithic settlements are located in low-lying fertile areas with access to freshwater supplies, including lakes or rivers. These settlers began to domesticate livestock and grow crops. Neolithic antiquities include megalithic tombs and cairns. Megaliths were large stone structures and were either religious sites or burial grounds; they are usually associated with higher ground. Cairns were also burial sites; they were constructed out of mounds of stones. Dolmens are also associated with the period: they were built with large rock slabs and are associated with early burial grounds.

- Bronze and Iron Age settlers began to influence the Irish landscape around 4,000 years ago, when they started to clear forested areas for agricultural use. They built defensive settlements in lowland areas and on elevated slopes. Defensive sites associated with these settlers include ringforts and raths, which were constructed of earthen mounds and a trench and may have also contained underground passages known as souterrains. Crannogs (artificial islands) were also constructed in small lakes, and these were linked to land by underwater stone paths. Other antiquities associated with these settlers include *fulachta fia* (open cooking sites); standing stones, which marked religious sites; ogham stones, large slabs of rock on which early writings and symbols were carved, associated with religious sites; and barrows, burial sites composed of earth mounds. Placenames on maps that suggest Bronze and Iron Age settlements include Rath, Lios and Dun.
- Early Christian settlements date from the fifth to the twelfth century. Examples include monasteries, priories and friaries (marked in red on OS maps). Other evidence of Christian settlement includes round towers, holy wells, stone crosses and cillins (oratories). Placenames that provide evidence of Christian settlement include Cill or Kil.
- Viking settlements: many of the surface remains of Viking settlements have disappeared from the landscape. Viking settlers were associated with the portal settlements of Dublin, Wicklow, Arklow, Wexford, Waterford, Cork and Limerick. The original street patterns of these towns were narrow and winding, with some evidence of radial developments.
- Norman settlements, dating from the twelfth century, were initially defensive, later evolving into market centres. Evidence of this type of settlement includes the presence of earthen enclosures which were composed of a motte and bailey. Over time, these structures were replaced by stone castles. Many of these defensive sites evolved into market centres and nodal points of transport and communications. Streets were generally constructed in a gridiron pattern. Large Norman settlements developed at strategic sites on low-lying rivers, which were easy to defend and also supplied the settlers with access to freshwater supplies.
- Plantation settlement: the plantation of many parts of Ireland occurred during the sixteenth and seventeenth centuries, when English and Scottish settlers were granted lands in Ireland by the English Crown. New towns were built on fertile low-lying sites. Examples include Bandon, Adare and Birr. Planters built large estate homes known as demesnes, and these are shown on Ordnance Survey maps. Placenames indicating the presence of plantation settlements include Manorhamilton and Newtown.

Recent Exam Questions on Historic Settlements

- 2010: Question 10 Part C
- 2007: Question 11 Part B
- 2006: Question 12 Part C

URBAN DEVELOPMENT

The development of urban areas is related to:

- A suitable physical landscape, generally low-lying, well drained, with access to a freshwater supply and sheltered from harsh climatic conditions.
- The functions of a settlement (which can change over time).
- The development of transport and communications, which will influence the nodality of a settlement. In dealing with nodality you must consider all modes of transport, including roads, rail, rivers, canal, ports and airports. Remember: the greater the nodality of a site, the greater the size of population. Complexity of functions is directly related to population density and distribution.

Recent Exam Questions on Urban Development/Functions

- 2010: Question 12 Part C
- 2008: Question 7 Part B
- 2007: Question 8 Part B
- 2006: Question 10 Part C

SITE LOCATION

The location of a particular type of land use is directly related to the requirements of that land use. For example, an industrial estate will be developed at a particular location according to:

- suitable physical landscape and size of the site
- proximity to a labour force
- proximity to transport networks
- access to internal and external markets for inputs and outputs.

The development of a new school will be influenced by:

- suitable physical landscape and size of the site

- access to road networks – safety of passage may be an issue
- the population of the surrounding hinterland.

The development of a tourist and leisure centre will be influenced by:

- suitable physical landscape and size of the site
- access and proximity to different modes of transport
- scenic potential of an area
- potential issues of noise and traffic pollution
- target market of visitors and proximity of site to tourist activities.

The development of a wind farm will be influenced by:

- suitable physical landscape and size of the site
- climatic conditions, particularly wind patterns
- potential issues of noise and scenic pollution
- identification of possible objections by the resident population.

 ## FORESTRY DISTRIBUTION

For questions on the distribution of forestry in Ordnance Survey maps, you should consider the following.

- Where you can, use either a four-figure grid reference or compass locations: e.g. 'a large area of forestry can be seen on the south-west slopes of mountain X'.
- Absence of forestry: why is it not located in a particular area? Consider relief, soil fertility, climatic conditions, land values and alternative land use, including agriculture. For example, many upland areas above 600m experience harsh climatic conditions and have shallow infertile soils, which limits tree growth. In contrast, some lowland areas may have significant agricultural potential and thus will not be forested.
- Why is forestry located in particular areas? Consider relief, soil fertility, climatic conditions and the functions of forestry, which include economic, environmental and tourist/recreational functions.
- What type of forestry is it? Remember, all types are clearly shown in the key or legend of the map.

Different types of forestry in Ireland include coniferous, deciduous or native woodland and mixed woodland.

Coniferous

Most conifer species are not native to Ireland, but they are very suitable to Irish climatic conditions, and growth rates to maturity are faster than those experienced in higher latitudes. They are suited to upland areas ranging from 200m to 600m, can grow in shallow soils and are not negatively affected by harsher climatic conditions. The key tree species include spruce and pine. Up to 80 per cent of all coniferous plantations are state owned and managed by the state-owned company Coillte. Coniferous plantations may also occur in low-lying areas which are prone to flooding and unsuitable for agricultural activity. Coniferous forestry can provide significant positive economic, environmental and tourist/recreational benefits to individual regions and the Irish economy.

Deciduous or Native Woodland

Native Irish deciduous trees include oak, ash and birch. They are suited to low-lying areas which have natural levels of inherent soil fertility. However, due to extensive deforestation in the past, related to agriculture and the development of settlements, many of Ireland's native woodlands have been removed from the landscape. Their distribution is mainly limited to forest parks, such as Glenveagh in Co. Donegal, Killarney in Co. Kerry and Lough Key forest park in Co. Roscommon, and small clusters around former landlords' houses or demesnes or on steep-sided slopes along low-lying river valleys.

Mixed Woodlands

These are normally associated with landlord estates. These trees offered privacy and also a location for native fauna which could be hunted by the landed gentry. Some of these forested areas still remain on the landscape today. Their purpose is more environmental and recreational than economic. Coillte is now promoting the plantation of mixed woodlands in order to enhance the scenic potential of areas and to increase native biodiversity of fauna and flora.

TRANSPORT AND COMMUNICATIONS

A modern transport network is the lifeline of a modern economic system. The main modes of transport in Ireland that are illustrated on Ordnance Survey maps include roads, rail, rivers, canals, ports and airports.

Roads

The development of the road network in Ireland was originally based on linking Dublin to other key market centres. However, over time Ireland has developed a very modern road transport network which is vital to the economic and social expansion of the country. The EU has played a huge role in aiding the development of an advanced road network in Ireland. Since we joined the EU in 1973, Ireland has received significant capital transfers from the Common Regional Policy to upgrade our road and transport networks. Under a number of National Development Plans (NDPs) and the National Spatial Strategy and Transport 21, the road network of Ireland has been transformed into a more efficient and effective system.

Note: Make sure you are familiar with the different types of roads shown in the map legend.

Rail

The development of the rail network in Ireland is directly related to British colonial influence, and much of the rail network was constructed during the nineteenth century. The importance of rail as a mode for transporting industrial goods has declined over time, but it remains important for passenger travel. Under the Transport 21 programme, many rail networks have been upgraded, including the Cork–Dublin and the Dublin–Belfast lines; and other areas, including the Western Rail Corridor, are also being upgraded.

Rivers

Rivers are the oldest form of transport in Ireland; however, rivers are today seldom used for the transport of raw materials or finished goods. Other modes of transport are more efficient.

Canals

The development of the canal system in Ireland is directly related to British colonial influence, and many canals were constructed during the mid-eighteenth century. Canals were in the past an important mode of transport for raw materials and industrial goods. Today, the canal system in Ireland plays an important role in promoting and enhancing the tourism and recreational potential of many inland areas. Important canals include the Royal and Grand canals, which connect Dublin to the river Shannon, and the Shannon–Erne Waterway, which connects the Shannon to Lough Erne in Northern Ireland.

Ports

The development of ports in Ireland can be traced to the Viking period and, more significantly, to British colonialism. Portal areas were concentrated on the eastern and southern coastline, and key ports for import and export developed at major sites, including Dublin, Waterford and Cork. The development of ports on the western coastline was associated with the fishing industry, and today the only notable western port for import and export is Foynes on the Shannon estuary.

Airports

The development of air transport in Ireland began after independence. Over time, international airports have been developed in Dublin, Cork, Shannon and Knock. Regional airports are also located in Galway, Farranfore and Donegal. The development of an air transport network has been critically important for the growth and expansion of the Irish tourist industry in recent decades.

TOURISM POTENTIAL

The tourism potential of areas/regions can be clearly seen by a careful examination of three key attributes.

- Activities. When looking at the availability of tourist attractions or activities, consider the physical landscape, human-constructed tourist/leisure features and areas of cultural and historical significance. Physical landscape attractions may include rivers, lakes, glacial and marine environments. Human-constructed features of tourist interest include tourist information offices, parking areas and viewing points, marked and unmarked walkways, marinas, golfcourses, racecourses, retail areas, etc. Areas of cultural and historical significance will be indicated by the presence of antiquities (see Historic Settlement).
- Access. The tourism potential of regions is greatly enhanced by accessibility: you need to consider all modes of transport, including road, rail, river, canal, port and airport. Be familiar with the map legend, which clearly shows the different modes of transport on the map.
- Accommodation. Some types of tourist accommodation are clearly shown on the 1:50,000 maps, so be familiar with all the types that are shown on the key or legend. In addition, it is possible to infer the availability of hotels, B&Bs and self-catering accommodation in areas/regions with high tourist potential.

Note: The use of the term 'potential' in an exam question can refer to the present day or the future.

INDUSTRIAL LOCATION
2006 QUESTION 8 PART A

STUDY THE 1:50,000 ORDNANCE SURVEY EXTRACT [KILLARNEY] WHICH ACCOMPANIES THIS PAPER.
*Identify by **grid reference** a suitable site for a major industry of your choice. Using map evidence to support your answer, explain **two** reasons why you chose this site.* (20 marks)

MARKING SCHEME ✔

Site identified: **2 marks (6-figure grid reference)**
Two reasons identified: **2 marks each**
Discussion: **5 SRPs**
Overall coherence: **4 marks graded**
– *If one reason only, overall coherence: 0 marks*
– *Wrong grid reference or no grid reference, overall coherence: 0 marks*

A suitable site for a major industry in this extract would be V 956 917.

Reason 1: Suitable Physical Landscape
This site is located in a low-lying area at an average height of 30m (see contour line at V 955 915). The area is well drained by the river Deenagh, which runs to the south of the site. This river could provide a source of water for industrial purposes. Due to the presence of a number of major roads to the south (e.g. the N72) and the N22 to the north-east, it is possible to suggest that the underlying rock geology is solid and stable, thus making the area suitable for the construction of a site for a major industry. The site is also large enough to allow for the construction of a car park for workers and loading facilities for industrial goods. It is also large enough for expansion in the future if required.

Reason 2: Proximity to a Local Labour Force
The site is in close proximity to the large urban centre of Killarney (V 96 90), which could supply a local labour force. The size of Killarney suggests that it has a large number of schools and colleges which would provide an educated workforce for industrial activity. Additionally, the connectivity of the site to major roadways, including the N72 and N22, would allow workers to travel from the surrounding hinterland in search of employment opportunities. As the site is on the outskirts of the town, it would not present an environmental risk, nor would it have a negative impact on the economic and social functions of Killarney – in fact it would enhance these functions over time.

ORDNANCE SURVEY MAP 2007 QUESTION 8 PART B

STUDY THE 1:50,000 ORDNANCE SURVEY MAP [DROGHEDA] *THAT ACCOMPANIES THIS PAPER.*
'Drogheda is an important centre of economic activity.'
Examine the above statement, using map evidence to
support your answer. (30 marks)

MARKING SCHEME ✓

Three activities at 10 marks... **or** *Two activities at 16/14 marks...*

Activity identified: **2 marks**   *Activity identified:* **2 marks**
Map reference: **2 marks**   *Map reference:* **2 marks**
Examination: **3 SRPs**   *Examination:* **6 (5) SRPs**

- *Examination must be based on relevant explanation rather than on further map references*
- *If answer is based on aerial photograph, allow marks for identifying activity only*

Drogheda (O 08 75) is a key centre of economic activity, and this can be clearly seen in terms of its nodal, educational and secondary and service functions.

NODALITY

Drogheda is well served by a variety of modes of transport, which has a positive influence on all economic activities. Transport is a cost of production, and a well-developed transport network reduces transport costs, increases access to markets and facilitates economic development. Drogheda is served by a well-developed road network. The M1 motorway runs to the western edge of the town and is connected to the N51 and to a number of important regional roads, including the R152 to the south-west and the R168 to the north-west. The town itself has a high density of regional roads, including the R166, R167, R108 and R150.

In addition, Drogheda is serviced by a railway line with a station located at O 099 748. This station would enhance the economic viability of the town particularly in terms of passenger travel.

The town is connected to the river Boyne, with a docking area located at O 108 759. This could allow for the import and export of goods by ship and may facilitate container traffic.

The nodality of the town appears to have a positive impact on its economic functions.

EDUCATION CENTRE

From the extract it is clear that Drogheda is a centre of educational activity. A large number of schools and colleges are shown, including those located at O 093 745, O 075 747, O 071 749 and O 105 758. The centres of education could supply the town with a well-educated workforce, which would enhance the economic potential of the area and provide it with a competitive advantage in the modern global economy, which demands a well-educated, flexible, adaptive workforce capable of meeting the demands of both multinational and native industries and services. The built-up nature of the town also suggests an expanding population, and this is reflected in the high density of schools and colleges in the town.

INDUSTRIAL AND SERVICE CENTRE
There are a number of industrial estates shown in the built-up area of Drogheda: examples include estates located at O 078 741 and O 075 745. These estates are well connected to the road network and may also benefit from rail and river connections. There are a number of service activities: educational (O 075 756); hospital (O 088 759); post office (O 087 753); tourist information office (O 084 749); fire station (O 093 753); bus station (O 086 747). The size of the settlement also suggests that it could have an important central business district (CBD) function which serves the economic needs of the internal population and those of the surrounding hinterland.

ORDNANCE SURVEY EXTRACT
2008 QUESTION 7 PART B

STUDY THE 1:50,000 ORDNANCE SURVEY MAP [GALWAY] THAT ACCOMPANIES THIS PAPER.
*Using map evidence to support your answer, explain **three** reasons why Galway has developed as a growing economic centre.* (30 marks)

 MARKING SCHEME ✓

Three reasons at 10 marks each...
Reason identified: **2 marks**
Map reference: **2 marks**
Examination: **3 SRPs**
– Examination must be based on relevant explanation rather than on further map references
– Accept any relevant aspect regarding growth

Galway has developed as a growing economic centre due to its physical location, nodality and tourist potential.

LOCATION
Galway is located in a low-lying area, at an average height of 40m (contour line at M 330 262). This site is well drained by the river Corrib and by Lough Atalia. These water systems may provide the city with water for domestic and industrial use. The density of settlement is evidence that the site is composed

of solid underlying rock geology. The site is also a coastal location, and this may have had a positive impact on its market and trading potential in the past, and today may encourage the development of industries and tourism.

NODALITY Galway is a nodal site and is well serviced by a variety of modes of transport. The road network is highly developed, and there are numerous regional roads, including the R338 to the east, the R336 to the west and the R339 to the north-east. These regional roads are linked to the N6 and N17 and the N84 and N59. The city also contains a railway station at M 302 253. Portal transport may also be possible, indicated by the pier at M 302 246. Air transport is available, shown by the airport located at M 37 28; this is about five miles from the city. The nodality of the site would be of significant benefit to its economic and social development, as transport is the lifeline of any urban centre.

TOURISM The tourism potential of Galway has been enhanced by its well-developed transport network, which increases its accessibility for visitors. The modes of transport favoured by tourists are airport, rail and road, and Galway is well served by these. Galway is a historic site, and this can be seen clearly from the number of its antiquities, ranging from pre-Christian to Norman. Key areas of interest for historical and cultural tourists might include the holy well located at M 307 255, the castle at M 285 277, and the star-shaped fort at M 312 247. Accommodation sites are also shown, including the camping and caravan site at M 323 246 and a number of youth hostels, e.g. at M 300 253. A tourist information office is located at M 302 253, and this provides information about activities and accommodation in the city and surrounding hinterland. The site, with its river, lakes and coastline, is an attractive scenic location for visitors who are interested in walking and boating and/or angling, and a beach is located at M 27 23.

ORDNANCE SURVEY MAP 2009 QUESTION 7 PART B

EXAMINE THE ORDNANCE SURVEY EXTRACT [WICKLOW] *THAT ACCOMPANIES THIS PAPER.*
Using map evidence to support your answer, state and explain **three** *reasons why the industrial estate is located at* **T 285 955**. (30 marks)

MARKING SCHEME ✔

Three reasons at 10 marks each...
Reason identified: **2 marks**
Map reference: **2 marks**
Examination: **3 SRPs**
– *Examination must be based on relevant explanation rather*

than on further map references
- *Accept a maximum of two reasons on transport*
- *Accept any location on the map providing the reason is related to the site*

PHYSICAL LANDSCAPE

The industrial estate located at T 285 955 may have developed at this site due to a suitable physical landscape. The site is low-lying at an average height of 30m (see contour line located at T 285 956). Additionally, the area surrounding the site is relatively undulating, shown by the widely spaced contour lines; this would have aided construction. The small unnamed river which flows to the north of the site would ensure the area is well drained and may provide the site with a water supply for domestic and industrial use. Finally, the industrial estate is large, and thus the underlying rock geology must be solid and stable.

NODAL SITE FOR TRANSPORT

The site is located at the centre of a number of intersecting roads, including the N11 to the west, the R761 to the north and the R750 to the east. These roads would allow for the arrival of raw materials and the departure of finished goods. Centrality to these roads must have influenced the location of this estate. In addition, a railway line and station is located in Wicklow town at T 308 948; this could be used to transport goods in and out of the industrial estate. Transport is a critical consideration in the location of industrial estates as it allows the movement of goods and labour. A well-developed transport system reduces the costs of production and increases access to markets.

PROXIMITY TO LABOUR

A third reason for the location of the industrial estate may be access to a labour force. Wicklow town is a large nucleated settlement and contains a number of educational centres, including those located at T 307 947 and T 318 936. This suggests that the town has an educated and expanding workforce. The site is also close to the settlements of Rathnew and Ashford, which may also supply a local labour force. The labour force of the town and hinterland would be able to commute to and from work easily, using the well-developed road and rail network.

URBAN DEVELOPMENT **2006 QUESTION 10 PART C**

STUDY THE ORDNANCE SURVEY MAP EXTRACT [KILLARNEY] *THAT ACCOMPANIES THIS PAPER.*
*Using map evidence to support your answer, explain **three** reasons why Killarney developed at this location.* (30 marks)

READING ORDNANCE SURVEY MAPS

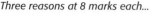

Killarney has developed at this location for three reasons: its physical landscape is suitable; it is a nodal point; and it is a tourism centre.

SUITABLE PHYSICAL LANDSCAPE

Killarney is located in a low-lying area at an approximate height of 50 to 60m (see spot height V 964 917). This area is well drained by the river Flesk, which is located to the south of the main settlement. The site is also in close proximity to a large lake – Lough Leane – which borders the settlement to the west and south. These two water areas would in the past have supplied the settlement with fresh water for washing, cooking, drinking and the disposal of waste. Today, these water supplies could potentially meet the domestic and industrial requirements of the large Killarney settlement. The site is also sheltered by the large upland area located in the south-west of the extract, V 89 86.

NODAL POINT

Killarney is a nodal point of transport and communications and is a meeting point of many important roads, including the N72, the N22 and the N71. It also has a well-developed network of regional and third-class roads which converge on the settlement, for example at V 96 90. The site is also serviced by a railway line and a railway station located at V 970 907. In the past, the river Flesk may have been an early mode of transport for the site and its residents. The nodality of the site would have encouraged economic activities ranging from a market function to commercial and retailing activities. The site is very accessible in terms of transport networks, and this would benefit the local population of Killarney and the population in the surrounding hinterland, which could use Killarney as a service and economic centre.

TOURISM CENTRE

The extract shows clearly that Killarney and its surrounding hinterland have significant tourism potential. The built-up area of Killarney is very accessible for tourists, and a variety of modes of transport are available, including road and rail. The presence of a tourist information office located at V 965 905, which is open all year, is a clear indication of its tourism potential. Killarney's attractions for visiting tourists include accommodation (for example, the youth hostel located at V 966 908), and its CBD may offer significant retailing and entertainment options. The surrounding hinterland, including the large inland lake and the mountains to the south-west of the settlement, may be very attractive as a sightseeing location, and parking facilities are located at strategic points, including V 953 888 and V 880 890. There are also a large number of historic antiquities shown on the extract, including a castle at V 972 883, Muckross friary at V 975 870 and a round tower at V 935 927. These areas of historical interest could attract cultural and historical tourists to the area. Recreational sites are also available, including a golfcourse at V 953 896 and a racecourse at V 961 895. These attractions all encourage the development of the town of Killarney.

HISTORIC SETTLEMENT 2007 QUESTION 11 PART B

The area shown on the Ordnance Survey map that accompanies this paper [DROGHEDA] *shows evidence of a wide range of **historic settlement**. Examine this statement using map evidence, with reference to any **three** different aspects of historic settlement.* (30 marks)

 MARKING SCHEME ✓

Three historic settlements at 10 marks each…
Settlement identified: **2 marks**
Map reference: **2 marks**
Examination: **3 SRPs**
– *Examination must be based on relevant explanation rather than on further map references*
– *At least one aspect should refer to an antiquity (red)*
– *If answer is based on aerial photograph, allow marks for identifying historic settlement only.*

The extract exhibits a wide range of historic settlements, including pre-Christian, Christian and Norman.

PRE-CHRISTIAN

Pre-Christian settlement in Ireland included those of Stone Age and Bronze Age settlers, dating from 4000 BC. These settlers were originally food gatherers who survived by hunting and fishing. As time passed, they began to farm the land. Many of their settlements were located near water sources or coastal sites. There is limited physical evidence of their occupation on the landscape; however, some religious sites can be identified, including standing stones, which can be seen at O 145 782, and burial grounds (O 115 753 and O 068 783).

CHRISTIAN

Christian settlement is associated with the period AD 500 to AD 1300. Christian settlements were often located in lowland areas. This was to facilitate transport and the construction of homes and religious sites. Many Christian settlers farmed the land and settled in areas which were well drained and had fertile soils. Over time, some Christian settlements evolved into educational and market centres. Examples of Christian settlements in this extract include holy wells located at O 104 703 and O 055 786 and the abbey at O 087 752.

NORMAN   Many Norman features date from the twelfth and thirteenth centuries and are associated with the Norman occupation of Ireland. The Normans originally settled in coastal areas but moved inland as their position became more secure. Initially, the settlements were defensive in nature and were located on the defensive sites of rivers or elevated sites. Examples of Norman settlements in this extract include the castle located at O 145 706 and a motte at O 088 746.

SETTLEMENT PATTERNS **2009 QUESTION 10 PART B**

EXAMINE THE ORDNANCE SURVEY MAP EXTRACT [WICKLOW] *THAT ACCOMPANIES THIS PAPER.*
Using map evidence to support your answer, identify and explain
***three** patterns of **rural** settlement.* (30 marks)

MARKING SCHEME ✓

Three patterns at 10 marks each…
Pattern identified: **2 marks**
Map reference: **2 marks**
Examination: **3 SRPs**
– *Examination must be based on relevant explanation rather than on further map references*
– *If answer is based on aerial photograph, allow marks for naming pattern only*

Three patterns of rural settlement that can be identified in the Wicklow extract are: linear (T 31 90); dispersed (T 27 90); absent (T 31 91).

The linear settlement is located on a third-class road, and a number of individual homes can be identified, including one at T 313 905. The area is at *LINEAR*   an average height of 70m (see spot height at T 308 906). The site is well drained due to the presence of a small stream at T 312 906. This stream may provide a water supply for this rural population. The site is served by a third-class road which joins the R751 at T 303 921 when it travels through Wicklow town. Linear settlement takes advantage of cheaper land values and also the availability of service utilities, including water supply, waste disposal and electricity and telecommunications.

DISPERSED   Dispersed settlement is located at an average height of 50m (see spot height at T 267 907); the surrounding land is relatively flat, which can be inferred from the absence of contour lines. These dispersed houses may be associated with agricultural activity and may be family owned. The houses are in close proximity to a third-class road at T 27 90 which connects to the N11 at T 279 908 and the R751 at T 281 908. These roads allow the residents to travel to the town of Wicklow for services and economic needs. The site of this dispersed settlement is drained by two small unnamed rivers.

ABSENT   There is an absence of settlement in the upland area to the east of the N11 at T 28 92. This area is above 100m, rising to a height of 187m at T 285 922. To the west of this point, the contour lines are tightly packed, indicating steep slopes. The absence of roads in the surrounding upland is obvious. This would hinder the development of settlement in the area, as would the height and the presence of steep slopes. This elevated site would also be exposed to harsher climatic conditions, which would inhibit settlement development.

HISTORIC SETTLEMENT 2010 QUESTION 10 PART C

EXAMINE THE 1:50,000 ORDNANCE SURVEY MAP OF CARRICK-ON-SUIR [PAGE 216] THAT ACCOMPANIES THIS PAPER.
*Using evidence from the map, describe and explain **three** different examples of historic settlement. (30 marks)*

MARKING SCHEME

Three historic settlements at 10 marks each…
Settlement identified: **2 marks**
Map reference: **2 marks**
Examination: **3 SRPs**
- *Examination must be based on relevant explanation rather than on further map references*
- *If answer is based on aerial photograph allow marks for identifying historic settlement only*

The extract exhibits a wide range of historic settlement, including pre-Christian, Christian and Norman.

Pre-Christian settlement in Ireland included those of Stone Age and Bronze Age settlers, dating from 4000 BC. These settlers were originally food gatherers
PRE-CHRISTIAN who survived by hunting and fishing. As time passed, they began to farm the land. Many of these settlements were located near water sources or coastal sites. There is limited physical evidence of their occupation on the landscape;

however, some religious sites can be identified, including megalithic tombs which can be seen at S 375 200 and S 445 243 and ogham stones at S 422 187 and S 419 197.

CHRISTIAN   Examples of Christian settlements in this extract include holy wells located at S 442 284 and S 449 265 and high crosses at S 423 275 and S 414 292.

Christian settlement is associated with the period AD 500 to AD 1300. Many of the Christian settlements were located in lowland areas. This was to facilitate transport and the construction of homes and religious sites. Many Christian settlers farmed the land, and they settled in areas which were well-drained and had fertile soils. Over time, some Christian settlements evolved into educational and market centres.

NORMAN   Examples of Norman settlements in this extract include the castles located at S 367 215 and S 449 232. Many of these features date from the twelfth and thirteenth centuries and are associated with the Norman occupation of Ireland. Originally, the Normans settled in coastal areas but moved inland as their position became more secure. Initially, the settlements were defensive in nature and were located on the defensive sites of rivers or elevated sites.

CENTRAL PLACE 2010 QUESTION 12 PART C

EXAMINE THE 1:50,000 ORDNANCE SURVEY MAP [PAGE 216] AND AERIAL PHOTOGRAPH [PAGE 253] OF CARRICK-ON-SUIR ACCOMPANYING THIS PAPER.

*Using evidence from the Ordnance Survey map **and** aerial photograph, show that Carrick-on-Suir performs the functions of a central place or market centre for the surrounding hinterland.* (30 marks)

MARKING SCHEME ✓

Ordnance Survey evidence: **2 marks**
Aerial photograph evidence: **2 marks**
Examination: **13 SRPs**
– *Maximum of 6 SRPs if reference to map or photograph only*
– *Maximum of 2 SRPs if the answer is theory-based and without relevant reference to Carrick-on-Suir*

There is clear evidence to support the view that Carrick-on-Suir is a centre of socio-economic activity for its surrounding hinterland.

The services provided by Carrick-on-Suir include a post office located at S 395 215, a tourist information office at S 401 217, a fire station at S 396 220 and

SERVICES   public telephones at S 403 217. These services would benefit the internal population of the town and also the residents of the surrounding hinterland, where settlement is very dispersed and rural in nature (for example, the linear settlement located at S 39 19). In addition, Carrick-on-Suir also provides an administrative function for the town and its hinterland, evidence of which is the Garda station. Educational needs are also catered for: there is a school located at S 402 220. The town is also a nodal point of transport as many roads, including the N24, R697, R696 and R680, all converge in the town. Additionally, a railway station is located at S 407 220. These modes of transport would allow the population of the surrounding hinterland access to the town and all its service and market functions.

MARKET CENTRE The importance of Carrick-on-Suir as a market centre for the population of the surrounding area is also supported by evidence from the aerial photograph. There is a large car park in the middle ground of the photograph, which would facilitate parking for non-residents of the town, allowing people from the surrounding hinterland to park and have access to the town's services and market functions. A significant main street runs parallel to the right bank of the river, and it is possible that this area of the town may be a key area of retail and commercial activity. A church can be clearly identified in the centre background, and this would cater for the religious needs of the resident population and people living in the surrounding hinterland. Near the church there is a large recreation area, including playing pitches, which could be used by both the internal and external population. Another large recreation area can be seen in the left background of the photograph.

COMMERCIAL/
LEISURE Some commercial or leisure facilities appear to be located on the right bank of the river between the two bridges – these may also cater for the needs of the internal and external population of the town. Overall, it is apparent from both the map and the photograph that Carrick-on-Suir serves a central place function for the surrounding hinterland.

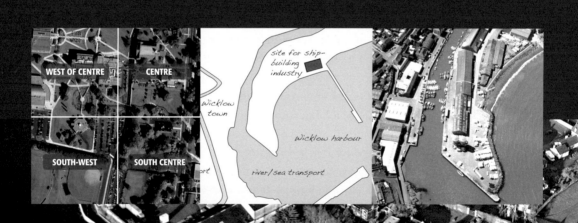

WEST OF CENTRE

CENTRE

SOUTH-WEST

SOUTH CENTRE

Wicklow
town

...ort

site for ship-
building
industry

Wicklow harbour

river/sea transport

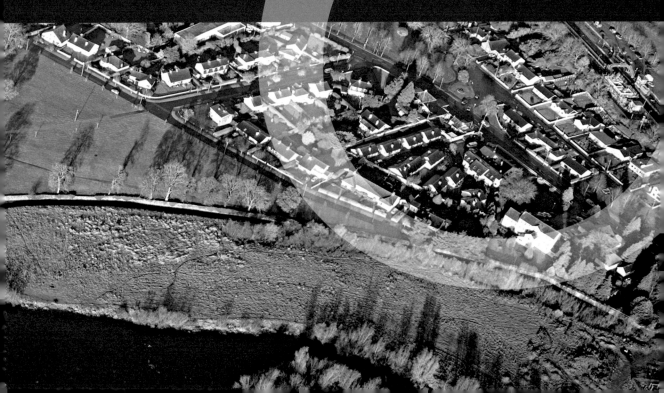

VIEWING AERIAL
PHOTOGRAPHS

VIEWING AERIAL PHOTOGRAPHS

Aerial photographs are pictures of areas taken from aircraft flying at low altitude. These photographs are of interest to a wide range of users, including:

- military – to update maps
- engineers – for site location, road construction and elevations
- archaeologists – to find locations of mounds and changing elevations
- scientists, including botanists and geologists
- geographers, including cartographers and urban and rural planners
- the general public.

TYPES OF AERIAL PHOTOGRAPH

Vertical Photographs

Vertical photographs are taken from directly overhead, and there is no distortion of scale of features. These photographs may contain a north sign, and this can be used to indicate directions. When locating features on a vertical photograph, divide the photograph into nine grid squares and label each square according to compass directions:

Oblique Aerial Photographs

These can be high oblique or low oblique. Oblique aerial photographs are taken at an angle to the ground, so there is a distortion of scale from the back to the front of the photograph. High oblique photographs may include a horizon; low oblique photographs will not. Oblique photographs do not contain a north sign, so we have to use a different method to locate features. Divide the photograph into nine grid squares and label each square using the concept of background, centre ground and foreground, and left and right.

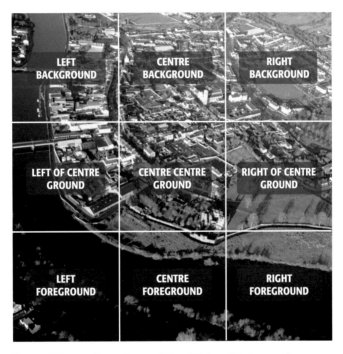

Recent Exam Questions – Identifying Photographs

- 2009 (Short Questions): Question 3
- 2008 (Short Questions): Question 5
- 2006 (Short Questions): Question 11

Locating Features on Aerial Photographs

- 2011 (Short Questions): Question 3
- 2010 (Short Questions): Question 8
- 2009 (Short Questions): Question 4
- 2008 (Short Questions): Question 6
- 2007 (Short Questions): Question 7
- 2006 (Short Questions): Question 11

SKETCH MAPS OF AERIAL PHOTOGRAPHS

This is an important part of the curriculum: questions on this topic have featured in every examination since 2006. There are a number of basic rules to follow when drawing sketch maps from aerial photographs:

1. Draw a rectangle to the size indicated in the question. You can divide this into nine grid squares.
2. If a major lake or coastline is in the photograph, you should include it as it will help you draw to scale.
3. Otherwise only include the features you are asked for, e.g. relief, roads, coastline, land use, etc. You only need to show one example of the information asked for. Enclose types of land use by using a box.
4. When sketching roads or rivers, you need to draw double lines as this indicates the scale of features.
5. Use colour for clarity, but don't waste time.
6. Insert all required information in a key.
7. Mark and label information on the sketch map.
8. Add a title to your sketch map.
9. Remember, in oblique photographs there is a distortion of scale from the background to the foreground.

Note: Sketch maps must not be traced.

AERIAL PHOTOGRAPHS & ORDNANCE SURVEY MAPS

It is possible to identify the area of a photograph on an Ordnance Survey map. This allows you to collate information from both. In order to match up the photograph with the map:

- Draw a straight line through the centre of the photograph from background to foreground. This line corresponds with the line of sight of the camera.
- Identify the main features that are on or close to the line.
- Locate these features on the map and draw a straight line through the map. This line indicates the direction of the camera when the photograph was taken.

Recent Exam Questions

- 2011 (Short Questions): Question 3

- 2010 (Short Questions): Question 4
- 2009 (Short Questions): Question 3

LAND USE IDENTIFICATION

FEATURE	LAND USE
Church	Religious
School	Education
Road, railway, airport, canal	Transport
Houses	Residential
Park, marina, walkway, playing pitches	Recreational
Industrial estate	Industry
Fields	Agriculture

Recent Exam Questions – Sketching and Land Use Identification

- 2011: Questions 8 Part A, 10 Part A
- 2010: Question 7 (Short Questions); Question 11 Part A
- 2009: Questions 9 Part A, 12 Part A
- 2008: Question 6 (Short Questions); Questions 8 Part A, 11 Part A
- 2007: Questions 9 Part A, 12 Part A
- 2006: Question 11 Part A

Physical Landform Identification

- 2009 (Short Questions): Question 8

AERIAL PHOTOGRAPHS 2009 QUESTION 9 PART A

Examine the aerial photograph of Wicklow that accompanies this paper [PAGE 249]. *Draw a sketch map to half the length and half the breadth. On it show and name examples of the following which would make the area an attractive location for industry.*
- *Two different modes of transport*
- *Suitable site for a shipbuilding industry*
- *A new residential development.* *(20 marks)*

MARKING SCHEME ✓

Outline: **4 marks graded**
Each of attractions : **4 marks each (shown 2 marks graded, named 2 marks)**
– *Required size is 10.2cm x 9.5cm (allow a difference of up to ½cm)*

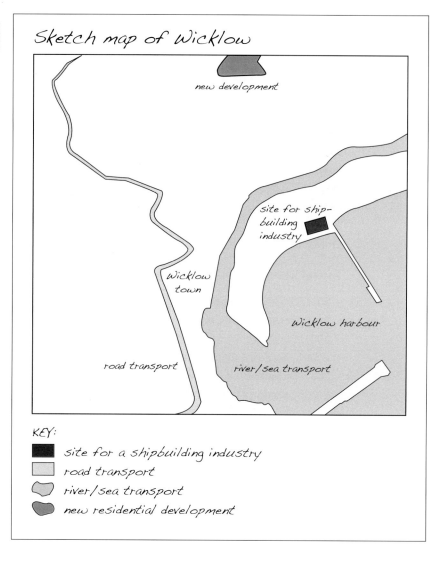

Sketch map of Wicklow

new development

site for ship-building industry

Wicklow town

Wicklow harbour

road transport

river/sea transport

KEY:

- site for a shipbuilding industry
- road transport
- river/sea transport
- new residential development

Wicklow

- car parks (it is sometimes possible to distinguish between areas for cars and buses)
- two-way systems and dual carriageways.

7 Discuss the relative merits of the map and aerial photograph in showing information about area X.

Ensure that you make reference to both in your answer.

MULTINATIONAL COMPANIES
2010 QUESTION 7 PART B

EXAMINE THE AERIAL PHOTOGRAPH [PRINTED OPPOSITE] *AND THE ORDNANCE SURVEY MAP* [PAGE 216] *ACCOMPANYING THIS PAPER.*
Using evidence from the Ordnance Survey map **and** the aerial photograph, explain **three** reasons why Carrick-on-Suir would be a suitable location for a multinational company. (30 marks)

MARKING SCHEME ✓

Three patterns at 10 marks each…
Reason identified: **2 marks**
Map/photograph evidence: **2 marks**
Examination: **3 SRPs**
– A minimum of one reference to the Ordnance Survey map and one reference to the aerial photograph is required as evidence
– Accept a maximum of two reasons on modes of transport

NODAL POINT

From viewing both the aerial photograph and the Ordnance Survey map, it is clear that Carrick-on-Suir is a nodal point in terms of the transport network. The road network is well developed, and the town is well serviced by the N24 which travels in an east–west direction; the town is also connected to a regional road network, which includes the R697 and R696 to the north and the R680 and R676 to the south, and to a railway network – a station is located at S 407 220. These modes of transport would facilitate the movement of goods and labour and would be an attractive competitive advantage for a multinational company. The town also has a key river which dominates the left and foreground of the aerial photograph, and a docking area can be identified in the left background, which could be used to transport goods. The river may also supply a source of water for the MNC if required. The nodality of the area would reduce the costs of transport and enhance the potential of the region to attract an MNC.

Carrick-on-Suir

SUITABLE SITE　　Evidence from both the aerial photograph and the map suggests that Carrick-on-Suir offers a suitable physical landscape for the establishment of an MNC. The area is low lying at an average height of between 5m and 10m (see spot heights located at S 422 213 and S 381 215). The area is also well drained by the river Suir, and this river might also supply a mode of transport and a source of water for industrial consumption. In addition, the aerial photograph shows a number of sites that could be used for the construction of an MNC, including a suitable location in the right background and one in the left foreground on the banks of the river.

LABOUR SUPPLY　　Both the aerial photograph and the map suggest that Carrick-on-Suir and its surrounding hinterland may offer a suitable labour force. The town itself is reasonably large (S 40 21), and the aerial photograph shows many residential areas, including those located in the left, centre and right centre ground. In addition, a new residential area can be identified in the right background. The town also has a school, located at S 404 222, which could provide an educated workforce. The nodal nature of the town may also allow workers to travel from the surrounding hinterland.

URBAN FUNCTIONS **2007 QUESTION 10 PART B**

*Examine the aerial photograph of Drogheda that accompanies this paper. Examine any **three** functions of the town, using evidence from the photograph to support your answer.* (30 marks)

MARKING SCHEME ✓

Three patterns at 10 marks each…
Function identified: **2 marks**
Photo reference: **2 marks**
Examination: **3 SRPs**
- *Examination must be based on relevant explanation rather than on further map references*
- *Answer based on OS map*
- *If answer is based on OS map, allow marks for identifying function only*

The three main functions of Drogheda are bridging point, service centre and residential site.

The town of Drogheda is located on the lowest possible crossing point of the river Boyne, which can be clearly seen in the left foreground, centre ground and right background of the photo. This river would have been an important source of transport in the past and may also be important today. The location of storage tanks in the right background on the right-hand side of the river suggests that the river might be used as a mode of transport for the import and export of goods. The river has a large number of bridges, linking settlement on the right and left banks. The bridge in the left foreground appears to be a very modern structure. Its size and two-way system allow it to be used by both cars and large transport vehicles. The proximity of the town to the river bank, especially on the left-hand side of the photograph, suggests that the land is well drained by the river and may not be prone to flooding.

BRIDGING POINT

SERVICE CENTRE The area of Drogheda shown on the photograph shows evidence of a well-developed service function. Many churches can be identified, including one large structure located in the centre ground and another in the left background. These churches would serve the religious needs of the internal population and the population of the surrounding hinterland. The town also has a number of car parks, including one located on the bank of the river in the centre foreground. The provision of car parking spaces would encourage the economic and service functions of the town. The large multi-storey building located in the left foreground may be an educational centre, which would provide for the educational needs of an expanding population both within the built-up area and in the surrounding hinterland. It is possible to suggest that the CBD of the settlement located in the centre ground would support the provision of a wide range of services ranging from high order to low order.

RESIDENTIAL SITE There is evidence in the photograph that Drogheda serves as a key centre for residential land use. The density of buildings in close proximity to the river bank, especially on the left-hand side, suggests significant residential activity. It is also apparent from the density of new residential estates, particularly in the left and centre background of the photograph, that the town has an expanding residential function. The residential development of the town appears to be well planned with an availability of open spaces for recreational activities, including the large areas in the left centre ground and left background. The development of new bridges in the right background and left foreground suggests that this is an expanding settlement with an important residential function. Many of the new residential estates in the background of the photograph comprise high-density building in planned formations.

URBAN FUNCTIONS 2008 QUESTION 10 PART B

*Examine the aerial photograph of part of Galway that accompanies this paper. Examine any **three** functions of the city, using evidence from the photograph to support your answer. (30 marks)*

MARKING SCHEME

Three patterns at 10 marks each…
Function identified: **2 marks**
Photo reference: **2 marks**
Examination: **3 SRPs**
*– Examination must be based on relevant explanation
  rather than on further photographic references*
– Answer based on OS map
*– If answer is based on OS map, allow marks for
  identifying function only*

The key functions of Galway city are: a religious site, a service centre and a tourism centre.

RELIGIOUS SITE
From viewing the aerial photograph, it is clear that a large cathedral/church is located in the centre background. This site also has significant parking space and is well connected to a variety of road networks. This church would serve the religious needs of the internal population and the external population who could access the site through a well-developed road network which has enhanced the nodality of the church.

SERVICE CENTRE
The photograph provides evidence of a significant variety of services. Located in the centre/right background is a large multi-storey structure with significant parking spaces to the front and side of the building. This could be a hospital, catering for the health care needs of the resident and external population of the surrounding hinterland. In close proximity to this structure is a large well-preserved quadrangle building located in the right background, which could be associated with education or government administration. Other service functions can also be identified, including a significant number of open spaces which might be associated with recreational activities: examples include the green area in the centre centre ground on the bank of the river and a large green area in the right foreground.

TOURISM CENTRE
The photograph contains evidence of a potential tourism centre, both in terms of physical landscape and cultural/historical attributes. The river in the centre ground and, in particular, the marina in the right centre ground could be

significant tourist attractions. This area has a large number of boats and ample parking available for visitors. The weir located in the centre ground could be an attractive location for sightseeing and angling. The cathedral/church in the centre background could attract historical/cultural tourists. The accessibility of the built-up area in terms of a well-developed road network would have a positive impact on the tourism potential of the city, as would the availability of ample parking, including the car park located in the centre and left foreground.

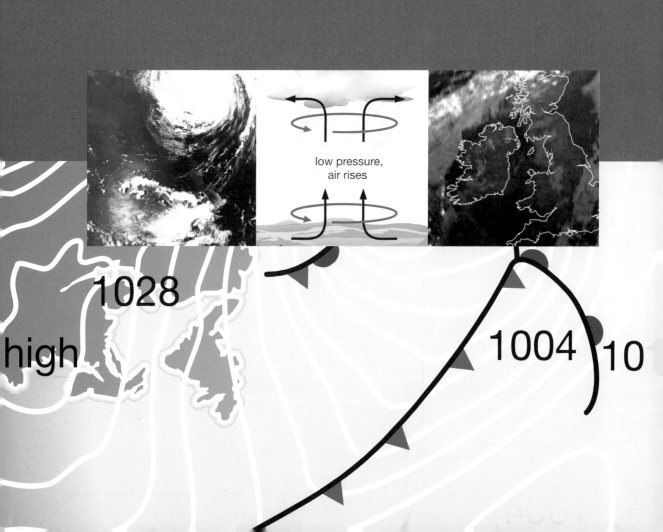

low pressure,
air rises

1028

high

1004

10

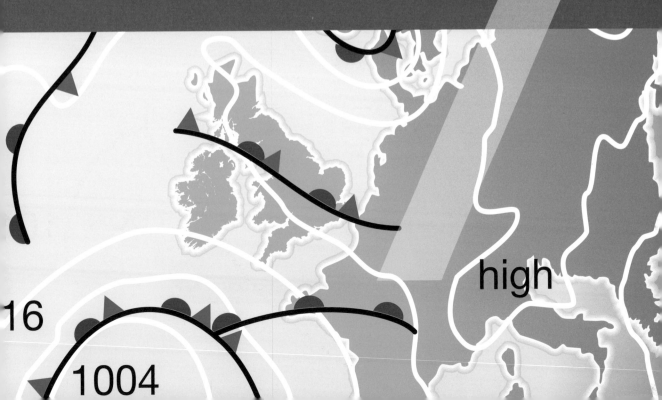

WEATHER MAPS
& CHARTS

high

16

1004

WEATHER MAPS AND CHARTS

Synoptic Charts

A synoptic chart is the scientific term for a weather map. These charts are used to report on the current weather and to predict future weather patterns. Synoptic charts provide information on:

- air pressure, including distribution and movement
- rainfall
- wind
- temperature.

Air Pressure

The most important feature of a synoptic chart is air pressure. This is shown by lines called isobars. Isobars connect points that share the same atmospheric (air) pressure. Tightly packed isobars indicate strong winds, while widely spaced isobars indicate light or calm conditions. Air pressure is measured by a barometer and is calculated using hectopascals (hPa).

The average air pressure at sea level is 1013 hPa. Any measurement above this number is called a high pressure system and is considered to be an area of descending air. An anticyclone, also known as a 'high', can be identified on a weather chart as a large area of widely spaced isobars, where pressure is higher than surrounding areas. In the northern hemisphere, winds blow in a

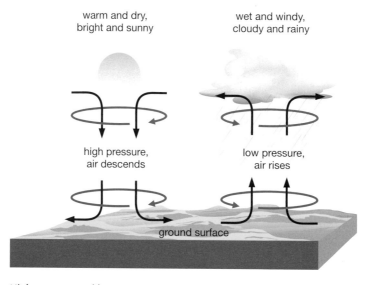

High pressure and low pressure systems

clockwise direction around a high pressure system. The highest pressure occurs at the centre and is known as the 'high pressure centre'. Anticyclones are associated with warm and sunny weather in summer and cold and foggy/clear weather in winter. High pressure systems are also associated with light winds.

Any measurement below 1013 hPa is called a low pressure system and is an area of rising air. A depression, also known as a 'low', can be identified on a weather chart by an area of closely packed isobars. In the northern hemisphere, winds blow around depressions in an anticlockwise direction. The lowest pressure occurs at the middle of a depression: this is known as the 'low pressure centre'. In Ireland, Atlantic depressions are associated with strong winds and heavy rain.

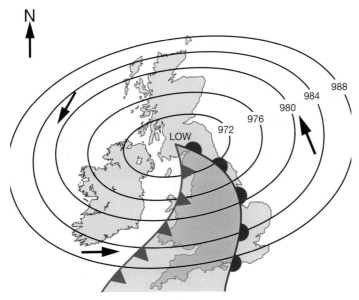

Low pressure system on a synoptic chart

Fronts

When two masses of air with different characteristics (warmer or colder) collide with one another, it is called a front.

Cold fronts are shown on weather charts as bold lines with triangles. These are blue when displayed on coloured charts. The points of the triangle indicate the direction in which the front is moving. A cold front indicates a change in air mass, where warmer air is being replaced by colder air. They often bring short spells of heavy rainfall in the form of showers and squally winds, and are accompanied by a decrease in temperature, a change in wind direction and a change to brighter showery conditions.

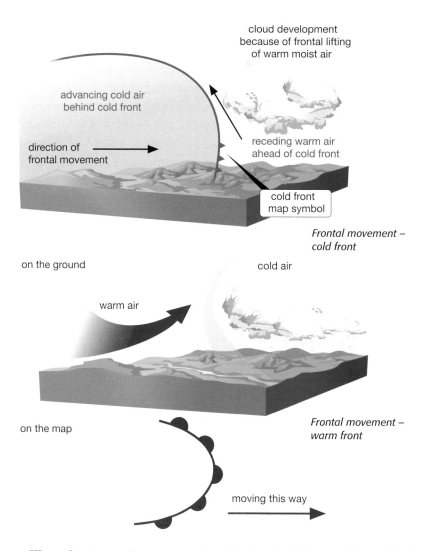

cloud development
because of frontal lifting
of warm moist air

advancing cold air
behind cold front

direction of
frontal movement

receding warm air
ahead of cold front

cold front
map symbol

*Frontal movement –
cold front*

on the ground

cold air

warm air

on the map

*Frontal movement –
warm front*

moving this way

Warm fronts are shown on weather charts as bold lines with semi-circles. These are coloured red when displayed on coloured charts. The direction of the semi-circles indicates the direction in which the front is moving. A warm front indicates a change from a colder to a warmer air mass. They often bring spells of prolonged and sometimes heavy rainfall, with strong winds.

Occluded fronts are shown on weather charts as bold lines with sets of triangles and semi-circles. These are coloured purple on coloured charts. The direction in which the symbols face indicates the direction in which the front is travelling. Occlusions are formed when a cold front overtakes a warm front, so they have similar characteristics to a cold front, but are less intense.

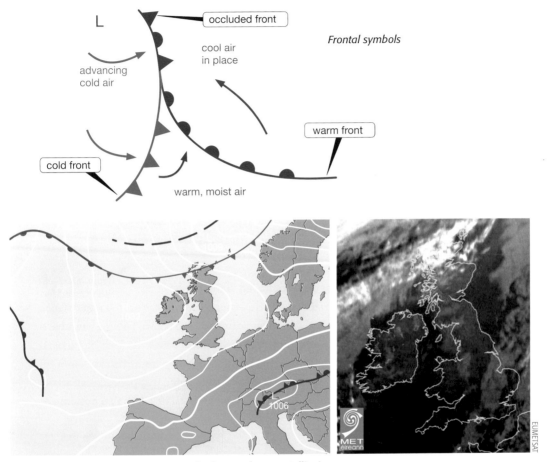

Frontal symbols

L

occluded front

cool air
in place

advancing
cold air

warm front

cold front

warm, moist air

High pressure system on a synoptic chart and on a satellite image

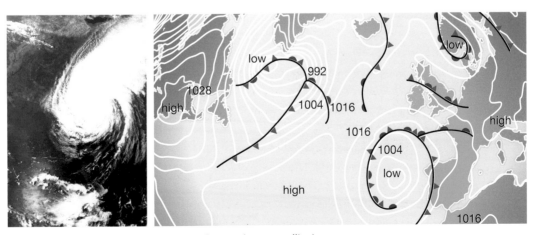

Low pressure system on a synoptic chart and on a satellite image

Precipitation

Precipitation includes snow, hail, dew and rainfall. The most common form of precipitation is rainfall. Rainfall is a regular feature on synoptic charts and is usually shown using shading. Low pressure systems and cold and warm fronts are usually associated with precipitation, while high pressure systems are associated with dry conditions.

Wind Direction and Speed

Wind generally refers to the horizontal movement of air. The earth produces local winds, which include land breezes and sea breezes, as well as permanent global winds, such as trade winds and the polar easterlies. Wind direction is indicated by using a weather vane, which is a device that turns on an axis to point in the direction of the wind.

Wind direction is indicated by a weather vane

Wind speed is measured using an anemometer, which uses rotating cups/blades to determine speed.

On a synoptic chart, wind speed and direction are shown using a wind barb (a dot with a straight line attached). The direction in which the stem of the barb points shows the direction that the wind is coming from. To represent an increase in speed, lines are added to the barb to make it appear like an arrow. The greater the wind speed, the more lines the barb has. It is also possible to

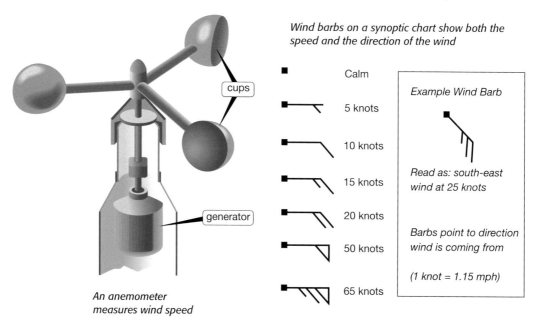

Wind barbs on a synoptic chart show both the speed and the direction of the wind

Calm

5 knots

10 knots

15 knots

20 knots

50 knots

65 knots

Example Wind Barb

Read as: south-east wind at 25 knots

Barbs point to direction wind is coming from

(1 knot = 1.15 mph)

An anemometer measures wind speed

refer to how close together the isobars are to determine how windy it is.

Weather charts generally use wind arrows to depict the speed and direction of wind. The head of the arrow points in the direction towards which the wind is blowing. But remember, winds are described by the direction from which they are blowing: a south wind is a wind blowing from the south.

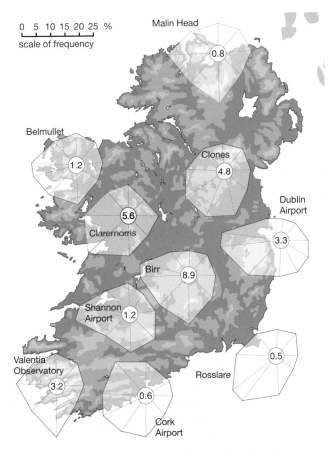

Wind direction and wind speed according to selected stations

Recent Exam Questions

- 2011 (Short Questions): Question 6
- 2010 (Short Questions): Question 6
- 2009 (Short Questions): Question 12
- 2008 (Short Questions): Question 7
- 2007 (Short Questions): Question 8
- 2006 (Short Questions): Question 4

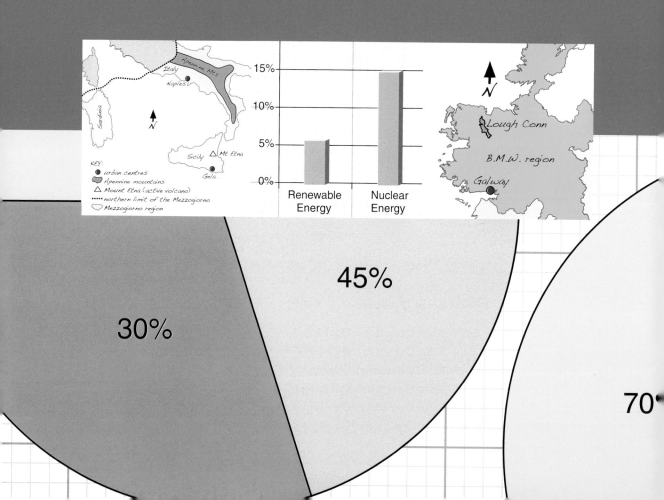

KEY:
● urban centres
 Apennine mountains
△ Mount Etna (active volcano)
•••• northern limit of the Mezzogiorno
 Mezzogiorno region

Apennine Mts
Italy
Naples
Sardinia
N
Sicily   △ Mt Etna
Gela

15%
10%
5%
0%
Renewable Energy
Nuclear Energy

N
Lough Conn
B.M.W. region
Galway

30%

45%

70%

SKETCHING REGIONS & DRAWING GRAPHS

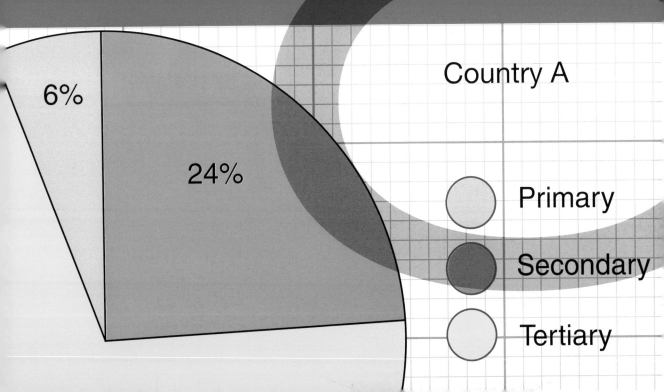

6%

24%

Country A

Primary

Secondary

Tertiary

SKETCHING REGIONS

Regions can be Irish, non-Irish European or continental/sub-continental.
All sketch maps should include:

- a title
- a key/legend
- a north symbol
- a border.

Remember:

- Only put in what you are asked for.
- Use colour for clarity.
- Overall presentation and perception of scale is important.

Recent Exam Questions

- 2011: Questions 4 Part A
- 2010: Questions 4 Part A, 6 Part A
- 2009: Questions 5 Part A, 6 Part A
- 2008: Questions 4 Part A, 6 Part A
- 2007: Questions 4 Part A, 6 Part A
- 2006: Sample Paper, Question 6 Part A

SKETCHING REGIONS (IRELAND)
2010 QUESTION 4 PART A

 *In your answer book, draw an outline map of **Ireland**. On it, show and name the following:*
- ***Two** Irish regions you have studied*
- ***One** urban centre in **each** region*
- ***One** feature of the physical landscape in **each** region. (20 marks)*

MARKING SCHEME ✓

Map outline: **2 marks graded**
Showing and naming region: **2 marks (2 marks graded + 1 mark)**
Showing and naming urban centres: **2 marks (2 marks graded + 1 mark)**
Showing and naming physical features: **2 marks (2 marks graded + 1 mark)**

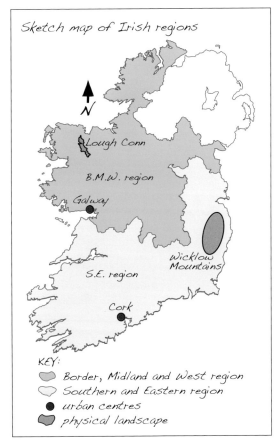

SKETCHING REGIONS (EUROPE)
2010 QUESTION 6 PART A

*In your answer book, draw an outline map of a **European region** (not in Ireland) that you have studied. On it, show and name the following:*
- *Any **two** physical features in the region*
- *Any **two** urban centres in the region.* (20 marks)

Map outline: **2 marks graded**
Showing and naming physical feature: **2 marks (2 marks graded + 2 marks)**
Showing and naming urban centres: **2 x (2 marks graded + 2 marks)**

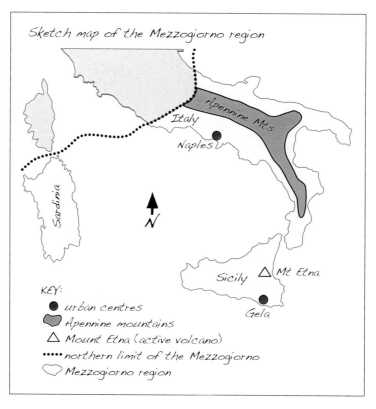

SKETCHING REGIONS (CONTINENTAL/ SUB-CONTINENTAL)
2008 QUESTION 6 PART A

*In your answer book, draw an outline map of a **European region (not Ireland)** OR a **continental/sub-continental region** that you have studied. On it, show and name the following:*
- *Any **two** physical features in the region*
- *Any **two** urban centres in the region. (20 marks)*

MARKING SCHEME ✓

Showing and naming map outline of region: **2 marks graded + 2 marks**
Showing and naming physical feature: **2 x (2 marks graded + 2 marks)**
Showing and naming urban centres: **2 x (2 marks graded + 2 marks)**
– *Do not accept a country in Europe as a region*
– *Accept a country as a region in a continental/sub-continental region*

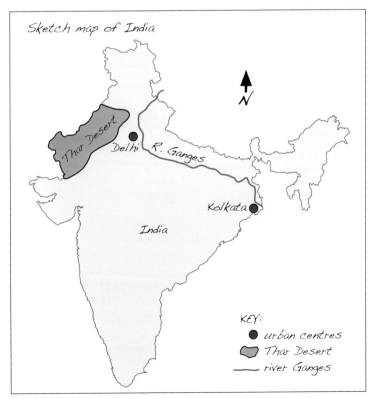

DRAWING GRAPHS

When you are drawing graphs, follow these rules:

- Use graph paper if you are asked to do so.
- Pick a suitable graph type to represent the data.
- Use a title.
- Label all axes indicating what information is being graphed on each axis.
- Use regularly spaced intervals.
- Clarity of presentation and clear plotting of points is important.
- Use of colour or shading is optional but will improve overall presentation.

Recent Exam Questions

- 2011: Question 7 Part A
- 2010: Questions 8 Part A, 10 Part A
- 2009: Questions 7 Part A, 11 Part A
- 2008: Questions 5 Part A, 7 Part A, 9 Part A, 12 Part A
- 2007: Question 7 Part A
- 2006: Questions 4 Part A, 9 Part A

DRAWING GRAPHS
2008 QUESTION 5 PART A

Energy Sources	% of Total Consumption
Renewable Energy	6%
Nuclear Energy	15%
Solid Fuels	18%
Gas	24%
Oil	37%

Examine the data in the table, showing the percentage of total energy by source consumed in the 25 EU member states in 2004. Using **graph paper***, draw a suitable graph to illustrate this data.* (20 marks)

MARKING SCHEME ✓

Bar Chart/Pie Chart...

Title: **2 marks**
Use of graph paper: **2 marks**
Scaled axis: **2 marks**
5 items illustrated: **2 marks each graded**
Overall presentation: **4 marks each graded**

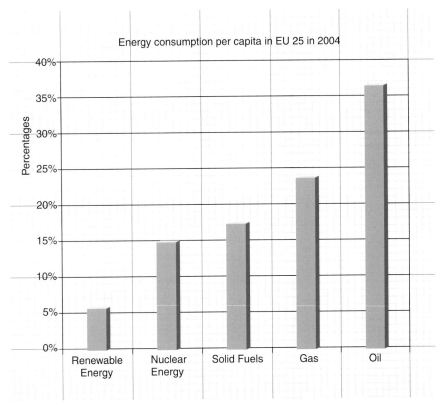

Energy consumption per capita in EU 25 in 2004

Percentages

40%
35%
30%
25%
20%
15%
10%
5%
0%

Renewable Energy | Nuclear Energy | Solid Fuels | Gas | Oil

DRAWING GRAPHS

2008 QUESTION 9 PART A

	Country A	Country B
Primary	6%	45%
Secondary	24%	30%
Tertiary	70%	25%

Examine the data in this table. Using **graph paper** *draw a suitable graph to illustrate the data.* (20 marks)

MARKING SCHEME

Bar Chart/Pie Chart...

Title: **2 marks**
Use of graph paper: **2 marks**
Scaled axis: **2 marks**
6 items illustrated: **2 marks each graded**
Overall presentation: **2 marks graded**

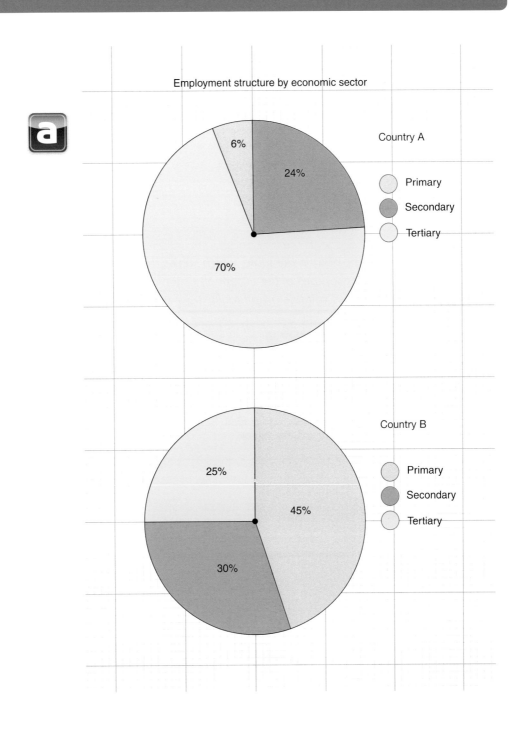

Employment structure by economic sector

Country A

6%

24%

70%

Primary

Secondary

Tertiary

Country B

25%

45%

30%

Primary

Secondary

Tertiary

DRAWING GRAPHS
2008 QUESTION 7 PART A

EU Unemployment Rates – July 2007

Ireland	4.7%
Germany	6.4%
United Kingdom	5.3%
Poland	9.7%
France	8.5%

*Examine the data in the table, which shows the rate of unemployment in selected countries of the European Union in July 2007. Using **graph paper**, draw a suitable graph to illustrate the data.* (20 marks)

MARKING SCHEME

Bar Chart/Histogram...

Title: **2 marks**
Use of graph paper: **2 marks**
Scaled axis: **2 marks**
5 items illustrated: **2 marks each graded**
Overall presentation: **4 marks graded**

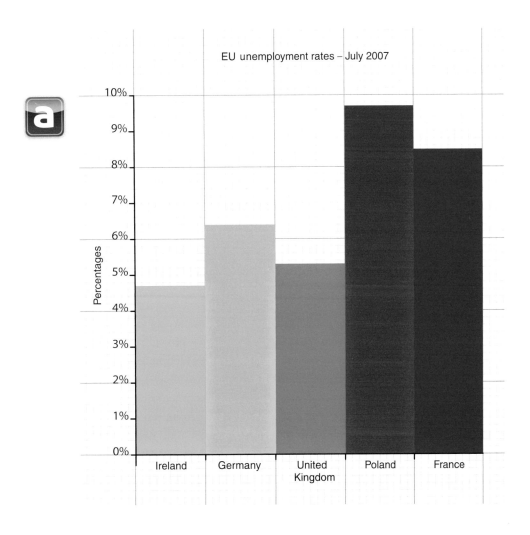

EU unemployment rates – July 2007

INTERPRETING GRAPHS
2006 SAMPLE PAPER QUESTION 7 PART B

Ireland Unemployment Rate as % of Total Workforce: 1993–2003

1993	1995	1997	1999	2001	2003
15.6	12.3	9.9	5.6	3.9	4.6

Examine the major reasons for the trend shown by these data.
(30 marks)

1993–2001

The data shows that during the period 1993 to 2001 there was a reduction in the level of unemployment in Ireland. This reduction was directly related to the Celtic Tiger economy, which was associated with an expansion of employment opportunities, particularly in secondary and tertiary economic activities. In the secondary sector, significant investment by multinational companies, particularly from the USA, resulted in the creation of additional employment opportunities in key sectors, including electronics, computers, medical and pharmaceutical industries. Key companies which expanded operations at this stage in Ireland included Dell Computers in Limerick, Intel in Kildare and Pfizer in Cork. There was also employment growth during this period in tertiary activities, including tourism, transport and financially traded services, particularly in Dublin and surrounding urban areas in the south and east. The establishment of the International Financial Services Centre (IFSC) in Dublin resulted in significant employment growth in the capital city.

2001–2003

A slight increase in unemployment levels occurred during the period 2001–2003. This may be related to the influx of foreign nationals into the country, particularly from countries in eastern Europe. During this period, Ireland's economic growth rates had created significant employment opportunities, and the country became a key centre for people migrating from eastern Europe in search of work. Many of these people found jobs in the low-paid service and construction sectors; this may have resulted in a slight displacement of native workers from these sectors and thus in an increase in unemployment levels. Additionally, during this period, the Irish labour force was continuing to expand, and employment opportunities in high-wage sectors may not have been able to keep pace with demand.

INTERPRETING GRAPHS

2006 SAMPLE PAPER QUESTION 12 PART B

Population Structure – Ireland – Census 2002

Age [years]	Number	Percentage
65–85+	436,001	11
15–64	2,653,774	68
0–14	827,428	21
Totals	3,917,203	100

*Examine **two** of the major implications for Ireland of such a population structure.* (30 marks)

LARGE LABOUR FORCE

According to the data, the 2002 census showed that 68 per cent of the Irish population was in the 15–64 age group. This suggests that a significant proportion of Ireland's population was in the working age category. The availability of a large labour force is a critical competitive advantage to an economy in today's modern, highly competitive global economic system. Many MNCs which have located manufacturing and service activities in Ireland in the recent past have highlighted the importance of a large, well-educated labour force. During periods of economic growth, the availability of a large labour force may encourage increased economic expansion and competition in the labour market. However, during a period of economic recession the labour force may experience high levels of unemployment and may be forced to emigrate to foreign labour markets to find work. Moreover, it is the younger, flexible, educated labour force which will emigrate, resulting in a brain drain and representing a significant loss to the Irish economy and society.

RETIRED POPULATION

According to the data, in 2002, 11 per cent of the Irish population was over the age of 65. This type of population structure has implications for social welfare, private pensions and health care provision.

The official retirement age for workers in Ireland is 66 years, although there are some exceptions in certain sectors of the economy. On reaching retirement, people are entitled to a pension. There are two main types of state pension: contributory, for people who have built up PRSI stamps; and non-contributory, for people who were not in paid employment. As the percentage of the population ages, the payment of state pensions becomes an issue of debate: during periods of economic downturn, paying state pensions can put pressure on the national budget. For those who have them, private pensions are paid on their retirement and represent a secure income; however, fewer than 50 per cent of the Irish workforce has private pensions, and thus as they enter the 66+ age group, these people may be totally dependent on state support. Another critical aspect of an ageing population structure is the implications that this has in terms of health care provision. Older people have greater health care needs than younger people, and pressure may increase on the public health care system, on community care facilities and on private and public nursing homes.

INTERPRETING GRAPHS

2008 QUESTION 11 PART B

Increase in artificial land cover 1990–2000 (Source: EPA/EEA)

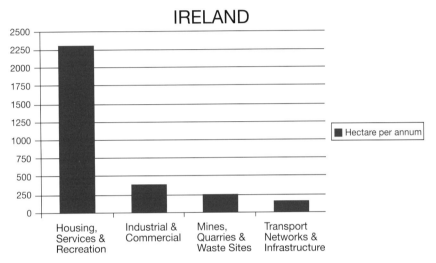

IRELAND

*Study this graph which shows the annual increase in artificial land cover in Ireland 1990–2000. Describe and explain, using examples you have studied, **two** of the ways in which the landscape of Ireland is being changed by human activities.* (30 marks)

MARKING SCHEME ✓

Two named examples: **2 marks + 2 marks**
Description/explanation: **2 marks**
– Only one way discussed – maximum of 5 SRPs
– Credit reference to chart for a maximum of 2 SRPs

According to the graph, the main change in artificial land use cover in Ireland is construction associated with housing, services and recreation, which has increased by 2,250 hectares per annum. The least change is associated with transport networks and infrastructure, which has increased by 100–250 hectares per annum. However, the graph does not contain any reference to one major change in the landscape which has occurred in the recent past: the construction of wind farms.

WIND FARMS   Energy is a critical component of any modern global economy, and Ireland has attempted to reduce its dependence on imported energy by developing wind farms. These farms are best suited to exposed upland areas, which have low population densities and which are affected by prevailing winds. Since the mid-1990s, many rural areas have been chosen as suitable sites for the construction of wind farms (for example Derrybrien in Co. Galway). This rural location now contains up to 40 huge wind turbines which supply electricity to the ESB national grid. In constructing these farms, the rural upland raised bog landscape was transformed as roads were built, land cleared of forestry and heather and raised bogs drained. The turbines are in an elevated position and can be clearly seen for miles around. In the initial construction, a number of bog bursts occurred as construction activities destabilised some raised bogs in the area. As a consequence, significant movement of peat occurred, which damaged the local road infrastructure and also negatively affected water quality in local rivers and streams.

TRANSPORT NETWORKS
The development of a new transport network, with particular emphasis on roads, has transformed the Irish landscape in recent decades. This transformation has been enabled by the availability of significant capital from EU Structural Funds and, in particular, from the European Regional Development Fund. Major bypasses have been built, including the M1 ring road in Dublin, the link road in Cork and the western road network in Galway. Ennis has now been bypassed as a result of the upgrading of the Limerick–Galway road. Other transport improvements include the Jack Lynch Tunnel in Cork, the Port Tunnel in Dublin and the Shannon Tunnel in Limerick; and new motorways linking Galway to Dublin, Waterford to Dublin and Cork to Dublin. Investment in transport networks has not been limited to roads – the rail system has also benefited, with work on the DART and Luas in Dublin, the Cork–Cobh–Midleton railway line and the Ennis–Galway line. This transformation of the landscape has resulted in the development of more modern, efficient transport, which is increasing the economic potential of the economy.

However, not all of these developments have been welcomed by the general public, and in some areas developments were opposed by local communities on environmental (destruction of natural flood plains and/or native woodlands) and historic grounds (Hill of Tara).

OPTION 1
GLOBAL
INTERDEPENDENCE

OPTION 1: GLOBAL INTERDEPENDENCE

Questions 13, 14 and 15 in the options section cover Global Interdependence.
The following instruction is given at the beginning of the section:
'It is better to discuss three or four aspects of the theme in some detail, rather than give a superficial treatment of a large number of points.'
Thus the following marking scheme is utilised throughout the Global
Interdependence option:

MARKING SCHEME ✓

Number of aspects: **3 (27 + 27 + 26) (4 at 20 marks each)**
Identifying aspect: **4 marks**
Examination: **8 SRPs (6 x SRPs)**
Overall coherence: **7/6 marks graded (4 marks graded)**

Learning Outcomes

– *Evaluate the different views on development and underdevelopment.*
– *Exhibit a detailed understanding of the global economy with reference to one multinational company.*
– *Evaluate the impact of globalisation on producer and consumer regions.*
– *Examine the environmental, political, human and economic impacts of globalisation.*
– *Understand and evaluate the concept of sustainable development with reference to examples you have studied.*

E.R. SCHIFFAHRT/NORDCAPITAL

GLOBAL ECONOMY AND TRADE
2007 QUESTION 14

Examine the part national debt and global trade patterns play in the continuing cycle of poverty in many countries. (80 marks)

National Debt

Many developing economies have adopted a policy of borrowing to aid the economic and social development of their countries. Capital is borrowed from governments or international banks in the developed world and invested in projects such as education, agricultural reform, health care provision, water supply networks and transport. In some cases, the loans are provided over a long period of time with low interest rates, and borrowing countries are able to pay back the capital and interest. However, in other cases, the loans are offered at high commercial interest rates, and many countries experience significant difficulty in paying back the capital and accumulated interest. When this occurs, the national debt of borrowing countries can become a huge problem. For example, Zambia has a significant national debt problem, and it spends four times more capital in servicing its national debt than it does on investing in education and health care. According to international research, for each $1 received from the developed world, the developing world is paying back $9, and this is directly related to the financing of national debt. This situation is increasing the cycle of poverty and underdevelopment in many developing countries.

Rising international interest rates during the 1980s placed huge pressure on the ability of developing economies to manage their national debt. In 1982, Mexico became unable to continue repayments on its loans. This resulted in panic among lenders and bankers, and in an effort to ensure that loans would be repaid, the International Monetary Fund (IMF) was consulted and the debt payments rescheduled according to IMF guidelines. Borrowing countries were required to restructure their economies to facilitate loan repayments.

This led to a significant increase in the growth of cash crops and a reorganisation of agricultural practices. In many cases, there was a change in land ownership systems and a consolidation of farms into larger units. This caused peasant displacement and the reorganisation of local social settlement systems. The transfer of agricultural activity from local food production to cash crops had negative implications for food supply and income levels of local people. Food shortages became common, and the cycle of poverty became more pronounced in many communities.

Many countries were also forced to reduce expenditure on unprofitable public programmes, including education and health care. This resulted in significant setbacks to the potential of local communities to be self-reliant and self-sufficient.

The national debt of many developing countries is hampering development, and the vicious cycle of poverty is actually becoming worse rather than better.

Global Trade Patterns

In the colonial period, global trading patterns established a distinctive geography of consumer and producer countries. Colonialism resulted in the economic exploitation of colonies by powerful colonial masters. Colonies were often forced to produce primary products for export and manufacture in the developed economy; as a result, many underdeveloped countries became producers of cash crops, including coffee, tea and sugar.

Today, price for outputs is controlled by the consuming countries, and these unfair trading patterns prevent the advancement of many developing countries. Large multinational companies, including Nestlé (coffee) and Chiquita (bananas), control the price paid for primary products, and they reap the rewards from the processing, manufacturing, distribution and marketing of the finished products. In addition, many developing economies have become reliant on growing monocultural products; for example, Sri Lanka on tea. If the value of these products declines, the producing countries face an economic crisis resulting from significant reduction in income. This places additional strain on government capital resources, and public expenditure in key areas such as education, health care, housing and water supplies may be reduced, resulting in a negative effect on local populations. In 1975, the Zambian government went bankrupt as the price of copper, whose export accounted for 83 per cent of government revenue, collapsed on the world market.

Coffee production over the last 20 years has expanded at a huge rate; however, coffee consumption has remained relatively static during the same period. As a result, there is a huge oversupply of coffee, and this is having a negative impact on the price paid to producers. Coffee exports have grown by 15 per cent since 1990 as a result of increased outputs by established producers and the arrival of new producers in the market. The huge level of competition between producers also ensures that the price paid to them remains low. This allows the manufacturers to exploit the producer market and keep prices paid to producers as low as possible. Wholesale prices for coffee have fallen from $2.40 to just 50 cent per pound, the lowest for over 30 years.

This is having a detrimental effect on producer economies and is increasing the vicious cycle of poverty. Current terms of trade between developed and developing economies are unfair and are increasing the economic exploitation of developing countries.

GLOBAL ECONOMY AND TRADE
2008 QUESTION 13

*Examine the impact of global trading systems on **both** producer and consumer regions.* (80 marks)

GLOBALISATION/ TRADING PATTERNS

Globalisation and world trading patterns can be defined as the increasing interaction of economies and societies around the world, particularly through trade and financial flows and the transfer of culture and technology. Economic globalisation has been made possible by the establishment of multinational companies (MNCs, i.e. companies with production and marketing facilities in more than one country), increasing foreign investment and the expansion of international trade. MNCs allow the global movement of large amounts of capital in the form of foreign direct investment (FDI). The organisational structure of these companies has allowed a global system of production and marketing to develop. The global trading triad – the USA, Europe and Japan – is extending its influence over poorer regions of the world. Core global economies are becoming more interconnected as a result of trade, investment and improvements in transport and communication. The USA's influence extends into South America and South East Asia; the EU's influence, which is growing through enlargement, is significant in Russia, Africa and the Middle East (related to historical colonial links); and Japan's influence extends through South East Asia, Australia and New Zealand. In addition, China's economic influence is extending into Africa, Australia and the European Union. Over the coming years, China is likely to challenge the economic dominance of the USA, Europe and Japan.

In global free trade, the advantages reside with the developed world, which provides manufacturing output, while the developing world remains the main producer of primary products. Trade policies agreed between nations generally favour the developed world, and this economic situation is referred to as neo-colonialism.

IMPACT ON PRODUCER REGIONS

The development of manufacturing activities can have a positive impact on the economic and social composition of producer regions. Ireland was a late starter in terms of industrialisation; however, by the mid-1990s, the country had established a strong industrial base. Ireland's industrialisation was based to a large degree on its ability to attract MNCs, which resulted in the creation of manufacturing employment opportunities, the provision of industrial wages and an overall improvement in living standards. This has encouraged an increase in consumer demand in the domestic market. It was also anticipated that the MNCs would create a positive multiplier effect on the wider economy, based on the economic principle that growth brings growth and this trickles through the economy. It was also hoped that MNCs would create a seed bed of skilled workers, which would grow over time, and that the country would establish an international reputation for quality output based on the availability of a skilled and flexible workforce.

The growth of MNCs in Ireland did have significant positive impacts on the Irish economy and society. However, there have also been some negative impacts. During the period from the mid-1960s to the early 1990s, multinational investment was focused on establishing branch plants in Ireland. The MNCs were attracted by our low-wage economy, so wages in many MNCs during this period were low. Their plants were associated with limited job stability, and in the event of a global economic recession branch plants are the first to close. This resulted in rising unemployment during the economic recession of the mid-1980s. The increasing flexibility of industrial location in the global economy means that branch plants can easily relocate to cheaper labour markets. In many cases, links between MNCs and local economies were poor, and the positive multiplier effect was not as substantial as first anticipated. Many MNCs are often referred to as stand-alone capital intensive units with limited connectivity to local economies.

However, during the 1990s, Ireland adopted a new policy towards MNCs. The Industrial Development Authority (IDA) now began to look for investment in regional headquarters, which differ from branch plants in that they employ a more highly skilled workforce and put an emphasis on

- research and development (R&D)
- service development
- marketing and distributing goods to key regional markets, including the European Union.

From the early 1990s onwards, many such enterprises were attracted to Ireland. Examples include Boston Scientific in Galway and Cork, IBM in Dublin, Intel in Leixlip and Wyeth Healthcare, which has a number of different manufacturing and R&D operations throughout the country.

Regional headquarters are more rooted to their location (and, on the other hand, do not display the same flexibility in terms of location as branch plant systems do). Their high-end manufacturing and R&D have facilitated the development of a high value export economy, one which has continued to exhibit growth despite the current economic crisis. MNCs currently employ up to 150,000 people in Ireland and are critical to our economic recovery and employment creation potential.

Ireland's low 12.5 per cent rate of corporation profits tax has been a significant factor in drawing MNCs into the country. Following the EU and IMF (International Monetary Fund) plan to restore Ireland's near-bankrupt public finances in autumn 2010, there was much criticism of this low tax rate from some other EU countries, whose corporation tax rates are considerably higher. Maintaining – or changing – the 12.5 per cent rate will be a highly contentious issue in the future.

IMPACT ON CONSUMER REGIONS

The key consumer regions of the world are the developed economic core regions. In these areas, average incomes are high and disposable income has increased over time. The establishment of a global world trading system has allowed developed economies to source many products from the developing world. The price paid is controlled by the buyers, and many developed countries are now purchasing manufactured output from low-cost producers. Competition has also increased in the global market, resulting in lower prices for the average consumer. Global trading patterns have led to greater economic benefits for consumer than for producer regions.

Some goods are produced in developed economies and sold to the developing world. The consuming countries must ensure that the value of imports do not exceed exports: this would result in a trade deficit, which could have serious consequences. International research has highlighted the effect of importing processed food and food products on the production and consumption of indigenous foods. For example, in Ireland, Wyeth produces formula milk for newborn children and infants. The availability of baby formula food in developing countries means that fewer mothers breastfeed their infants, which can lead to poorer child nutrition. There are also problems associated with sanitation of feeding bottles and access to clean water for mixing formula. In addition, the ability of MNCs to produce and market commodities at low cost could be inhibiting the development of competing industries in consumer regions.

Global trading patterns have both positive and negative impacts on both producer and consumer regions. Consumer regions may benefit from greater availability of products and increased competition resulting in lower prices.

However, in some cases the availability of new products may be causing a societal change in consumption patterns and may have a negative impact on the production of local goods.

GLOBAL ECONOMY AND TRADE
2009 QUESTION 14

We live in an interdependent global economy. Actions or decisions taken in one area have an impact on other areas. Discuss. (80 marks)

GLOBALISATION

Globalisation is the increasing interaction of economies and societies around the world, particularly through trade and financial flows and the transfer of culture and technology. Over time, the world has become highly interconnected, and decisions and actions taken in one area have significant implications for other areas. This is sometimes referred to as the 'pebble, pool, ripple effect'. The development of a global system has been made possible by: improvements in transport (distance decay and time–space compression); developments in telecommunications (e.g. email, fax and mobile phones as well as TV and global satellites allowing for the efficient transfer of information and images); global banking and finance systems, international trade markets and stock exchanges (e.g. New York, Tokyo and London); free trade; the World Trade Organisation (WTO) and the opening up of new markets. Economic globalisation can clearly be seen in the interrelations which exist between major global trading partners. For example, the current economic recession experienced by the USA and the European Union is directly related to low levels of consumer demand within the two economies, and the global banking crisis.

Globalisation does not just impact on economic systems; it also has implications for the environment. Deforestation in the developing economies affects the global environment, and rising levels of air pollutants in mainland western Europe result in an increase of acid rain in Norway and Sweden. The significance of environmental globalisation can be seen in the efforts being made to establish a global response to the problem of climate change at a conference held in Mexico in December 2010.

MNCs

Multinational companies (MNCs) are companies that have production and services activities in more than one country. They are the main movers of global trade, production and employment creation, and they have a huge influence on the economic development of countries such as Ireland and India. Some of the large MNCs have greater capital resources than individual countries and have sales figures in excess of developing countries' GNPs. Important US MNCs include Walmart, General Motors, Ford Motors, Coca-Cola and Microsoft.

DELL   As the factors influencing industrial location have changed over time, MNCs have taken advantage of the flexibility of industrial location, and this can be clearly seen in an examination of Dell computers. Dell's headquarters is in Austin, Texas; the company has worldwide sales of approximately $35.5 billion and employs a global workforce of 39,000. The company has developed a global system of production and sales of computer systems. Dell Ireland, established in Limerick in 1991, expanded rapidly to create 3,300 jobs and was the production centre for Europe, the Middle East and Africa. It also opened a sales centre, call centre and central administration in Dublin that employed 1,200 people. However, in 2009, the company decided to relocate its manufacturing and production facilities from Limerick to Poland. This decision was taken at headquarters level in Austin, and despite significant representation from the Irish government and workers' unions, the company could not be persuaded to reverse its decision. The implications for the mid-west region have been, and will continue to be, significant. Dell employed a highly skilled workforce which enjoyed high wages and high standards of living. These people are now facing the prospect of unemployment as no replacement industry has been identified. The wider economy of the mid-west region will also be affected by a reduction in overall consumer spend and the closure of related industries, including transport companies and delivery services. Thus a decision taken in Austin, Texas, has had a significant impact on the economy of the mid-west region, while on the other hand the economy of Poland will reap significant economic and social benefits associated with the location there of a major manufacturing and production plant.

ACID RAIN   Fossil fuels release sulphur dioxide (SO_2) and nitrogen oxides (NO) during combustion. These are released into the atmosphere and react with water (H_2O) to create a weak acid. This falls to the earth as acid rain. Acid rain is airborne and thus does not respect national boundaries. The source of the pollution is not always the worst affected area, due to the influence of the prevailing winds. For example, Scandinavian countries are negatively affected by acid rain caused by the industrial economies of mainland western Europe.

Damage to forests occurs because the acid rain damages the ability of trees to photosynthesise. This results in stunted growth and makes forests more vulnerable to disease. It is estimated that 30–40 per cent of Sweden's forests and 25–50 per cent of Poland's are affected, and that one in four trees in western Europe suffer from the effects of acid rain. Acid rain also causes the chemical erosion of buildings, especially those built of limestone and sandstone. This process can be clearly seen in cities such as Athens and Dublin.

Rising levels of acidity in rivers, lakes and streams are also associated with an increase in the burning of fossil fuels and acid rain. This has resulted in the creation of up to 20,000 dead lakes in Sweden and Norway. These lakes have a pH level which cannot support living organisms. The application of lime reduces acidity but is an expensive solution. Acid rain can also result in the leaching of minerals from soils, thus having a negative effect on agricultural activity.

It is therefore clear that the consumption of fossil fuels, including coal, lignite, peat, oil and gas for domestic and industrial use, in one area can have negative implications for other areas. Acid rain is an airborne pollutant, and its origin and destination may not be the same. Thus it is a clear example of how actions taken in one part of the world can have implications for other regions.

MULTINATIONAL COMPANIES
2010 QUESTION 13

Discuss how the operations of multinational companies may contribute to the widening economic gap between developing and developed countries. (80 marks)

ECONOMIC POWER

A multinational company (MNC) is an enterprise that operates in more than one country. MNCs are the main drivers of global trade, production and employment, and they have a huge influence on the economic development of countries such as Ireland and India. Some large MNCs have more capital and higher sales figures than individual developing countries' GNP. The most important US MNCs are Walmart, General Motors, Ford Motors, Coca-Cola and Microsoft. MNCs have a three-tier organisational structure (global, regional and branch plant). The location of different tiers based on product cycle requirements allows them to take advantage of both core and peripheral regions. MNCs locate branch plant production line manufacturing activities in peripheral or developing economies because labour is cheaper, environmental standards are lower, and they may be offered financial incentives by destination governments. However, the economic power of MNCs means that the MNC rather than the destination economy reaps the benefits of expansion of the secondary sector. Destination economies may find that the key attraction for the MNCs is access to cheap labour and raw materials and that key economic decisions are taken by the MNCs rather than by national governments. The branch plants of MNCs are not tied to any particular location, and they can relocate when economic circumstances change. Many developing economies are over-dependent on MNCs, and this represents a significant economic and political risk.

UNFAIR TRADE PATTERNS

MNCs allow for the movement of large amounts of capital on a global scale in the form of foreign direct investment (FDI), and their organisational structure allows the development of a global system of production and marketing. Under global free trade, the advantages reside with the developed world, which provides manufactured output, while the developing world remains the main producer of primary products. Trade policies agreed between nations generally favour the developed world, and this economic situation is referred to as neo-colonialism. Many MNCs use the developing world as a source of cheap raw materials, energy and labour. The initial manufacture of products is undertaken in the developing world, and once this is successfully completed the goods are transported to core markets where final manufacturing and packaging is carried out. The goods are then sold on the global market. Manufactured goods are often sold back to the branch plant economy at a much higher cost than the cost of production. MNCs' use of labour and raw materials means that developing economies are unable to use them for their own benefit. Thus the power of MNCs to control manufacturing output in developing economies and to control global trade patterns may result in the continued underdevelopment of poorer economies. Unfair trading patterns ensure that economic power resides with the developed world; the developing economies' resources are used to the ultimate benefit of core economies. Unless a change occurs in trade policies, developing economies will remain locked in a vicious cycle of underdevelopment.

EXPLOITATION OF LABOUR

A key reason for the location of MNCs' activities in developing countries is access to a cheap and plentiful supply of labour. By using a branch plant system, MNCs can locate basic manufacturing tasks in areas where there is plenty of cheap labour. The global production of footwear and textiles is concentrated to a very large degree in peripheral developing economies, including India, Thailand and China. Branch plant production is based on the economic principle of mass production, which involves repetitive tasks requiring limited skills. Under these conditions, the only benefit to the host economy is the creation of employment opportunities, but in many cases the wages are very low and working conditions difficult. Some MNCs, including Apple and Nike, have been accused of exploiting labour in peripheral economies and of providing wages and working conditions that are well below acceptable standards. Gender exploitation of labour is also an issue in many developing economies, where women are entering the labour force in greater numbers. However, competition for jobs is high, and MNCs can exploit this situation by reducing wages. This exploitation of labour places workers in a vicious cycle of dependence on the MNCs and does nothing to encourage the economic potential of developing economies.

EXPLOITATION OF NATURAL RESOURCES

The natural resources of many developing countries are exploited by MNCs: examples include the hardwood timber resources of the tropical rainforests and the agricultural potential of huge tracts of newly cleared land. The deforestation of the tropical rainforests in the Amazon region has been driven by profit-hungry domestic and multinational companies keen to exploit the region's timber and mining resources. MNCs have been encouraged by successive Brazilian governments for the sake of short-term economic gain; but the long-term consequences are to exacerbate underdevelopment and to over-exploit natural resources. MNCs and national governments reap the profits, but local populations rarely benefit. MNCs are also involved in large-scale cattle ranching in newly cleared areas, and many of these ranches are run in an unsustainable manner, resulting in soil degradation and erosion, which in turn damages the country's economic potential. In many developing economies, large-scale production of cash crops such as rubber, sugar and coffee is controlled by MNCs, while domestic agricultural activities are confined to more unproductive crops. The global demand for cash crops encourages intensive large-scale agricultural activities which may result in the removal of local populations and the overuse of fragile soils, which may eventually lead to soil exhaustion and erosion.

L. WEDEKIND/IAEA

DEVELOPMENT AND UNDERDEVELOPMENT
2007 QUESTION 15

Examine the idea that attitudes towards development and underdevelopment are subject to change. (80 marks)

THE DETERMINIST VIEW

The deterministic approach to development was one of the first models that tried to explain why some regions experience high levels of development while others are underdeveloped. The model suggests that human development is determined by environmental factors, including climate, relief and soils; and that areas with poor environmental conditions will be unable to achieve high levels of economic development and will remain in a state of underdevelopment. In contrast, areas with suitable environmental conditions (i.e. mid-latitude locations) will be able to achieve high levels of development by using the competitive advantages of climate, relief and fertile soils.

CRITICISMS

This model was very popular during the nineteenth and early twentieth centuries. However, it has more recently been deemed to be too simplistic and

OPTION 2
GEOECOLOGY

OPTION 2: GEOECOLOGY

Questions 16, 17 and 18 in the options section cover Geoecology. The following instruction is given at the beginning of the section:
'It is better to discuss **three** or **four** aspects of the theme in some detail, rather than give a superficial treatment of a large number of points.'
Thus the following marking scheme is utilised throughout the Geoecology option:

MARKING SCHEME ✓

Number of aspects: **3 (27 + 27 + 26) (4 at 20 marks each)**
Identifying aspect: **4 marks**
Examination: **8 SRPs (6 x SRPs)**
Overall coherence: **7/6 marks graded (4 marks graded)**

Learning Outcomes

– *Explain, understand and evaluate the development of soils, dealing with both composition and characteristics.*
– *Explain, understand and evaluate the factors influencing the development of soils.*
– *Understand the effect of human activities on soils.*
– *Explain, understand and evaluate the principal characteristics of one biome students have studied.*
– *Understand the interrelation between the principal characteristics of a specific biome.*
– *Assess the impact of human activities on a specific biome.*

BIOMES: CHARACTERISTICS AND ADAPTATIONS **2006 QUESTION 17**

Examine the main characteristics of a biome that you have studied. (80 marks)

A biome is a large stable terrestrial ecosystem characterised by specific plant and animal communities. Each biome is usually named or classified by its dominant vegetation, as this is the single most identifiable feature and its presence is directly related to climatic conditions.

DESERT BIOME

The biome I have studied is the desert biome, with particular reference to the Thar Desert in India. The key characteristics of the Thar Desert biome include climate, soil structure and formation, vegetation and animals (flora and fauna), and human processes.

CLIMATE

The pattern of world climates has given rise to distinctive global ecosystems which are known as biomes. The climate of the Thar Desert is highly distinctive and is classified as a tropical desert climate. Two critical components of climate are temperature and rainfall. In the Thar Desert, the months of April, May and June are the hottest, and the average maximum and minimum temperatures during this period range from 41°C to 24°C. December, January and February are colder, with average maximum and minimum temperatures ranging from 28°C to 9°C. Temperatures in the Thar Desert are influenced by latitude, altitude and distance from the sea. The average rainfall of the region ranges from 100mm to 500mm; it is distributed very erratically, with the majority occurring between July and September. Winter rains are insignificant. The rains play a vital role in the life of all parts of the Thar Desert as the water deposits in the *tobas* (small ponds) are used for drinking, washing and other purposes. The *tobas* are the only source of surface water for animals and humans in the desert. Underground water is rarely found. Strong winds blow over large parts of the desert for four or five months, and dust storms are common during the summer.

SOIL STRUCTURE AND FORMATION

The development of soils in the Thar Desert is directly influenced by climate, parent material and living organisms. The soils of this arid zone are generally sandy to sandy loam in texture. The consistency and depth vary according to topographical features. About 10 per cent of the desert consists of shifting sand dunes; the remaining 90 per cent includes fixed dunes, inter-dunal areas, rock outcrops and salt pans. The low-lying loams are heavy and may have a hard pan of clay, calcium carbonate or gypsum. This is due to the process of calcification, which occurs as nutrients that were leached from the surface are drawn back up by capillary action: this allows for the creation of a hard pan which is nearly impermeable and will restrict the growth of plants with long root structures. Salination can also occur, and high levels of sodium lead to the creation of large salt pans. Some of these soils contain a high percentage of soluble salts in the lower horizons and can turn well-water poisonous. Their pH ranges from 7.0 to 9.5. The fertility of the soils improves from the west and north-west to the east and north-east, related to the changing topography of the region and its soil structure. The absence of organic matter is the result of low plant productivity, which thus restricts the soil structure due to the absence of critical micro-organisms that convert organic matter into humus. Due to a low organic content, these desert soils are a light grey colour. As there is limited vegetational cover, significant evaporation occurs, and this can result in a high level of dissolved minerals in the upper horizon, including calcite, sodium and gypsum; thus the soil is very alkaline in nature. The desert soils are regosols of wind-blown sand and sandy deposits derived from the disintegration of rock in adjacent areas and material blown in from the coastal zone and the Indus valley.

VEGETATION AND ANIMALS

The flora and fauna of the Thar Desert is directly related to climate conditions and soil composition and structure. Many areas in the desert are interspersed by hillocks and sandy and gravel plains. The natural vegetation of the desert is classified as northern desert thorn forest. The density, distribution and size of vegetation in the desert increases from west to east in response to an increase in rainfall levels. The natural vegetation of the desert is composed of trees and shrubs, many of which are stunted and thorny: these characteristics are adaptations to harsh climate conditions. The desert is also home to perennial herb species, which are drought resistant.

Due to its diversified habitat, the vegetation and animal life in this arid region is very rich. An estimated 700 different plant species are found, with 107 of these categorised as grass. These plants are deep-rooted and tenacious enough to withstand extended droughts and yet are efficient enough to rapidly gain biomass during a favourable season. About 23 species of lizard and 25 species of snake are found here. Some of the wildlife species which are declining rapidly in other parts of India are found in large numbers in the desert, and they include the great Indian bustard, the blackbuck, the Indian gazelle and the Indian wild ass. These animals have excellent survival strategies: they are usually smaller than other similar animals living in different conditions, and they are normally nocturnal. The Desert National Park in Jaisalmer, which covers over 3,162 square kilometres, is an excellent example of the ecosystem of the Thar Desert and its diverse fauna. This area is home to the great Indian bustard, blackbuck, desert fox, wolf and cat. Seashells and fossilised tree trunks in the park record the geological history of the desert. The area is also associated with many migratory and resident desert birds, including eagles, falcons and vultures.

HUMAN PROCESSES The Thar Desert is the most populated desert in the world, with a density of approximately 84 people per square kilometre. Population growth is also high: between 1901 and 1981 it stood at 249 per cent. (The corresponding figure for India as a whole was 187 per cent.) The population of the Thar Desert is dependent on agriculture and animal husbandry. In the last decades population numbers have increased, and this has resulted in increased agricultural activity in this fragile environment, leading to overgrazing and extensive cultivation, and vegetational resources have been negatively affected as a result. The increase in human and livestock populations in the desert has led to the deterioration of the ecosystem, resulting in the degradation of soil fertility. The living standards of the population are low, and many of the communities are nomadic, moving from one *tobas* to another. The density of livestock in the region has also increased, and the main types of livestock are sheep, goats, camels, cows and donkeys. Irrigation programmes have been developed in the desert, the most important being the Indira Gandhi Nahar Canal Project. However, despite these efforts, stress on the fragile desert environment is increasing due to expanding human and animal populations. It is estimated that the desert is extending at a rate of half a kilometre per year.

The Thar Desert is an example of a natural biome which is experiencing significant change and transformation due to human activity. Key activities that are resulting in increasing desertification include poor agricultural practices, increasing animal populations and variations in the arrival and intensity of rainfall, which is related to changing global climate conditions.

BIOMES: CHARACTERISTICS AND ADAPTATIONS 2008 QUESTION 18

*Describe and explain the main characteristics of **one** biome that you have studied.* (80 marks)

The biome I have studied is the boreal forest, also known as taiga. This biome is located in the higher northern latitudes, between the tundra and the temperate forests – approximately 52 to 66 degrees north of the equator.

CLIMATE The pattern of world climates has given rise to distinctive global ecosystems which are known as biomes. A biome can be defined as 'a large stable terrestrial ecosystem characterised by specific plant and animal communities'. Each biome is usually named or classified by its dominant vegetation, because this is the single most identifiable feature and its presence is directly related to climatic conditions.

The boreal forests are associated with sub-arctic and cold continental climates. They experience long, very cold winters, with mean temperatures below freezing for up to six months of the year. Temperatures range from –54°C to –1°C. Precipitation during the winter months falls as snow. Summers are short and temperatures vary significantly in relation to latitude and altitude: some areas will experience between 50 and 100 frost-free days during the summer. Temperatures during the summer can fall to –7°C with highs of 21°C. Summers are relatively warm and humid. Total precipitation during the year ranges from 30cm to 85cm. This precipitation falls as snow, rain and dew, with rain during the summer months. Spring and autumn periods do not exist in the boreal forests. Taiga is the world's largest land biome and accounts for 27 per cent of total world forest cover.

SOILS The soils in the boreal forests are influenced by climate, vegetation, parent material, topography and time. The soils are young and lacking in nutrients. The soil profile is limited and contrasts sharply with the rich organic soils of temperate deciduous forest regions. The thinness of the soil is directly related to cold temperatures, which hinder soil development and limit the range of vegetation. The humification of plant litter is a slow process, due to cold conditions, and this limits the development of the soils. Coniferous trees dominate the vegetation of the forest, and the tree litter from these is pine needles, which are very slow to decompose and are very acidic, which influences the pH content of boreal soil. These acidic soils encourage the growth of moss and lichens on the forest floor. During precipitation in the summer, leaching of nutrients from the top layer occurs, and this inhibits soil productivity. Podzolisation of soil also occurs in the boreal forests. The main soil type in the region is classified as podzol. Many areas of the forest floor experience permafrost conditions throughout the year.

VEGETATION AND ANIMALS The flora and fauna of the boreal forests are determined by climatic conditions. The dominant trees in the forests are needle-leaf coniferous trees, mainly evergreen spruce, fir, pine and some deciduous larch. The most common succession trees after felling are alder, birch and aspen, and over time these will be replaced by coniferous trees. The coniferous trees have adapted to the harsh cold and drought conditions in the winter and the very short summer growing season. Many of the trees are conical in shape, which enables them to shed snow, preventing the loss of branches that can occur from the weight of accumulated snow. Trees have also developed needle leaves, which have a narrow surface area that restricts transpiration of water, especially during the dry winter months. These needles also have a wax coating, which protects the stomata during the harshest weather. Coniferous trees do not shed leaves during the winter, and this allows the trees to photosynthesise quickly and efficiently during the short summer growing season. The dark colour of the leaves helps the trees to absorb maximum heat from the sun and to photosynthesise as soon as temperatures increase. The diversity of the forest is limited to coniferous trees and lichens and mosses on the forest floors.

Predatory animals dominate the fauna of the forests (for example bears, lynx, weasels, wolverines, bobcats and mink). These hunt on herbivores, including snow rabbits, red squirrels and voles. Some animals hibernate during the long cold winters. On the lower slopes where deciduous trees grow, red deer, elk and moose can be found. During the summer months, the forests support significant insect populations, and this encourages the migration of a large variety of birds which nest and breed in the forest. Resident birds of the forest include seed-eating finches and sparrows and omnivorous crows.

BIOMES: CHARACTERISTICS AND ADAPTATIONS **2007 QUESTION 18**

Describe how plant and animal life adapts to soil and climatic conditions in a biome which you have studied. (80 marks)

BIOMES: CHARACTERISTICS AND ADAPTATIONS **2010 QUESTION 16**

*Examine the influence of climate on the characteristics of **one** biome that you have studied.* (80 marks)

See answers to 2006 Question 17 (page 325) and 2008 Question 18 (page 327) and adapt these accordingly.

BIOMES: HUMAN INTERFERENCE
2006 QUESTION 18

Assess the impact of human activity on a biome that you have studied. (80 marks)

Tropical rainforest biomes have experienced significant change due to human activities, and impacts of both a local and global nature can easily be seen.

THE CARBON CYCLE

Deforestation increases the amount of carbon dioxide (CO_2) and other trace gases in the atmosphere. When a forest is cut and the outputs burned, to establish agricultural land or settlement areas, the carbon content of the trees is released (wood is composed of 50 per cent carbon). From 1859 to 1990, deforestation worldwide released 122 billion tonnes of carbon into the atmosphere. The release of CO_2 enhances the greenhouse effect, and this can lead to an increase in global temperatures, a fact related to global warming. The greenhouse effect results from the build-up of gases in the atmosphere. Many of these gases occur naturally, and their presence is essential to maintain temperatures on the earth's surface. Without these naturally occurring gases, average earth surface temperatures would be below −18°C. However, as a result of human activities, including deforestation, greenhouse gases have increased significantly, particularly since the 1950s. Solar heat is trapped within the earth's atmosphere, resulting in a rise in global temperature and causing climate change and, because the glaciers are melting, a rise in sea levels. Increasing levels of CO_2 and other greenhouse gases represent a critical problem for human and animal populations and for agricultural outputs.

THE LUNGS OF THE EARTH   Deforestation is thus having a negative impact on the carbon cycle. Forests provide one of the most important global sinks in terms of their ability to absorb CO_2. Trees clean the air by absorbing harmful air dust particles and gases, including sulphur dioxide, ozone and nitrogen. Due to the significant loss of tropical rainforests, overall global air quality standards may decrease; this will have major implications for human and animal populations. In addition, the accumulation of higher levels of CO_2 in the atmosphere will have very negative impacts on climatic conditions and on the glaciers in the polar and high latitude regions. Changing climatic conditions may result in more extreme weather patterns, which will have serious consequences for human settlement (as we have seen in recent flooding in Australia, mud slides in Brazil and droughts in the Sahel). Climate change will also impact on agricultural activities, especially in developing economies where food supplies and food security are serious issues of concern. Climate change will also have an effect on the biodiversity of both global and local fauna and flora, as species may not be able to adapt to rapid changes in their natural environment.

DEFORESTATION AND BIODIVERSITY   The tropical rainforests of the world contain over half the world's biodiversity in only 7 per cent of its total dry surface. Many rainforest plants and animals can only survive in these small areas because they require a very specific habitat. If this habitat is destroyed, these unique plants and animals may become extinct. Up to 137 species of plants and animals disappear worldwide each day as a result of deforestation. The loss of these species will have a huge impact on the planet. We are losing species that could be used in the prevention of cancers and as a cure for Aids. Many plant species from the tropical rainforests are used by the pharmaceutical industry: as many as one in four prescription drugs are derived at least partly from plant material. This loss of biodiversity, at a time when the value of biotic resources is becoming widely recognised, shows that current conservation strategies are inadequate. Natural ecosystems such as the tropical rainforests are a major source of new foods, new chemicals and new medicines, and are indicators of a healthy, functioning biosphere. However, due to poor management policies, we are facing a loss of genetic diversity which is unparalleled in human history.

NATIVE PEOPLE   The loss of tropical rainforests also results in the displacement of their indigenous people; for example, forcing the displacement of the native Indian population of the Amazon Basin into smaller and smaller areas is damaging their traditional culture and way of life. These populations have a unique knowledge of the plants and animals of the rainforests. Having sustainably used the forest resources for centuries, they could teach us a great deal about medicinal uses of the forests and sustainable management practices. The FAO estimates that 53,000 square miles of tropical forest was destroyed annually during the 1980s, and nearly 60 per cent of this destruction occurred in the Amazon Basin. However, the rate of deforestation varies from region to region. In 1970 only 1 per cent of the Brazilian Amazon Basin was deforested, but since then more than 15 per cent of the entire Amazon Basin has been cleared. The FAO estimates that, by continent, the loss of rainforests is over 50 per cent in Africa, 40 per cent in Asia and 40 per cent in Central and South America.

SOIL EROSION AND MINERAL LEACHING
When slash and burn techniques are used to clear tropical rainforests, nutrients are released into the soil. These nutrients increase the productivity of soils. However, during periods of heavy rainfall, they are washed away or leached by acidification, which reduces soil fertility. In as little as three years, the soil may lose all its inherent fertility and become nutrient deficient. Because the soil is now lacking in fertility, the cleared land is quickly exhausted by intensive agriculture, and fertility can only be maintained by using artificial fertilisers; however, this is rarely undertaken because of the high costs involved. These areas may then be abandoned as farmers move on to newly burned and cleared areas, but the replacement of vegetation is slow, and significant soil erosion may occur before natural vegetation is re-established. The regrowth of the natural forest takes time, and is gradually vegetated first by low bushes, vines and ferns.

BIOMES: HUMAN INTERFERENCE
2008 QUESTION 16

*Examine **two** ways in which human activities have altered the natural characteristics of a biome that you have studied.* (80 marks)

The natural characteristics of tropical rainforests have been altered by human activities, including: commercial logging; the conversion of forested lands for agriculture; fires; and the debt crisis.

COMMERCIAL LOGGING
Commercial logging is the major cause of primary rainforest destruction in South East Asia and Africa. Worldwide, it is responsible for the removal of five million hectares a year. Logging usually involves the transfer of control of the forests from local people, who have an interest in their long-term preservation, to commercial interests who utilise the timber resources for short-term profit.

Millions of hectares of primary rainforests are being destroyed in South East Asia as a result of commercial logging. This logging meets the increasing demand in developed economies for timber as a raw material for processing and for the paper and pulp industry. Furthermore, the creation of logging roads in tropical forests allows landless people access to newly cleared areas. In Africa, 75 per cent of land being cleared by peasant farmers is land that has been commercially logged previously. In Malaysia during the early 1990s, clear-cut logging practices were the main reason for forest loss as logging companies harvested huge tracts of primary forests. Today, commercial logging is still the most significant threat to forests in regions of Central Africa.

The removal of trees for commercial purposes is having a negative effect on natural vegetation, on soil composition and structure, and on the native biodiversity of these regions. Commercial interests, primarily from developed economies, are transforming the natural characteristics of tropical rainforests, and many of these changes are causing irreversible damage. Commercial logging is a clear example of the unsustainable management of an important natural resource in many developing economies.

LAND FOR AGRICULTURE Traditionally, indigenous people farmed the rainforests, felling trees to allow cultivation of crops and grazing space for animals, and moving on when the soil lost fertility. This practice is not a threat to forests, provided that it is undertaken in a sustainable manner, and that used areas are left to regenerate for long periods before repeating the process. However, difficulties arise when the land is not allowed adequate time to recover – intensive farming results in irreversible soil degradation.

Due to the needs of expanding populations, some sources identify shifting cultivation as the cause of 70 per cent of deforestation in Africa. Commercial ranching is another major cause of deforestation, particularly in Central and South America. In Central America, two-thirds of lowland tropical forests have been turned into pasture since 1950. Cattle ranching, in particular, is a key cause of deforestation in the Brazilian Amazon: government figures attributed 38 per cent of deforestation from 1966 to 1975 to large-scale cattle ranching. Ranching and the continuing consolidation of land ownership in fewer and fewer hands is forcing poorer populations into the rainforest in search of land. Furthermore, an increasing amount of deforestation is caused by the activities of subsistence farmers who are encouraged to settle on forest lands by government land redistribution policies. Between 1995 and 1998, land in the Amazon was granted by the Brazilian government to about 150,000 families. Cutting down the tropical rainforests for agricultural purposes in an unsustainable manner is causing irreversible damage to soil composition and structure and to native fauna and flora.

FIRES A significant amount of forest clearing by small farmers and plantation owners is carried out by burning. Though these fires are intended to burn only limited areas, they can spread from agricultural land and burn more of the forest. It is estimated that about 20 per cent of fires cause new deforestation. Using this 'slash and burn' technique, farmers remove ground shrubbery, the forest trees are cut, and the area is then set afire. The newly cleared area is planted with crops such as bananas, palms, maize or rice. After just two or three years, the productivity of the fragile soil declines and the farmers move and clear new forest areas for more short-term agricultural use.

The old, now infertile fields are used for small-scale cattle grazing or are left fallow. Meanwhile, the removal of the natural vegetation cover exposes the fragile soil to unsustainable rates of soil erosion, and as a result increases soil degradation in the tropical rainforests. The process is negatively affecting native fauna and flora as well as human populations.

Many of the fires are set during a three-month specified burning season and the smoke produced creates widespread problems, including disruption of air traffic and smoke pollution. The clearing of agricultural land and forested areas by burning produces carbon dioxide, carbon monoxide and nitrogen oxides. From July to October 1987, approximately 19,300 square miles of Brazilian Amazon forest was burned.

THE DEBT CRISIS The five countries with the largest rainforest areas are also among the world's most heavily indebted. They are under enormous pressure to cut and clear rainforests to finance debt repayments. Thus, the debt crisis has exacerbated environmental destruction in the Third World. Non-governmental organisations have highlighted the direct relationship between debt burdens and the unsustainable removal of tropical rainforest in many developing countries. However, despite the growing global awareness of this issue and worldwide appeals from nature conservation organisations and human rights groups for debt cancellation, creditor countries and institutions have failed to respond in a constructive manner.

The cash crop economy is an important part of Third World 'development', and the most productive land is used to produce output for the export market. Extensive areas of Brazil and Thailand now provide feed for Europe's cattle on land reclaimed from the rainforests. In Malaysia, over 3.5 million hectares of forest has been cleared for rubber and oil palm plantations. Worldwide, between 1.2 and 5.5 million hectares of forest is destroyed annually to grow tobacco. In the recent past the production of soybeans has become one of the most important contributors to deforestation in the Brazilian Amazon.

In the end, the income gained from this output may be used to service foreign debt rather than to aid the economic and social development of the countries involved. Meanwhile, due to land consolidation and changes in land ownership, many peasants are forced onto marginal lands, resulting in further deforestation, land degradation and poverty.

In conclusion, the natural characteristics of tropical rainforests, including soil, fauna/flora and human processes and activities, are being changed and destroyed at unsustainable rates – and much of the environmental degradation of these areas is irreversible. Human activities, especially those associated with large-scale commercial purposes, are transforming these natural environments, and the long-term impacts of these activities may result in deep-seated negative consequences, locally and globally.

BIOMES: HUMAN INTERFERENCE
2009 QUESTION 18

Assess how biomes have been altered by human activity. (80 marks)

The natural characteristics of desert biomes have been negatively affected by human activities, which have resulted in increased rates of desertification on a global scale. Desertification is a complex process. It involves multiple causes, including changing land use practices and increasing population pressure.

LAND USE PRACTICES

Droughts alone do not cause desertification. Droughts are common in arid and semi-arid lands, but well-managed lands can recover from drought when the rains return. However, continued land abuse during droughts increases land degradation.

The Sahel region is located south of the Sahara Desert. It has supported a human population for centuries, in particular nomadic herders who practised a form of agriculture that was in harmony with the natural environment. However, the agricultural economy of the region underwent a transformation as a result of colonialism, when the Sudan region turned to growing cash crops. Their production was based on a fixed agricultural system, utilising available water supplies and not using crop rotation.

During the same period, a new tribe (the Falani) entered the region. They were associated with animal production and less mobile herding. During the 1960s good outputs were achieved, and the number of animals in the region increased. This placed increasing pressure on available grazing land and resulted in greater movement of traditional nomadic herders. Furthermore, due to the greater human and animal populations in the area, there was more burning of vegetation cover and collecting of firewood. This resulted in the loss of vegetation cover, eventually leading to soil erosion and desertification. The over-exploitation of soil during the drought that began in 1968 and the land use practices in the region caused the death of more than 100,000 people and 12 million cattle by 1973.

By the 1980s the Sahel was overpopulated, and famine and early death were common. Many of the traditional populations are no longer able to attain the basic human requirements of food, water and shelter, and the region has experienced significant out-migration into surrounding areas. Climate modelling suggests that rainfall over the Sahel region may decline further as global warming continues. This, combined with increasing population and animal pressure and unsustainable soil management practices, may result in a significant increase in desertification in the area. At present, the annual rate of desertification in the Sahel is estimated at 5–9km per year.

POPULATION
PRESSURE

Increased pressure from humans and livestock on marginal lands has accelerated desertification. In some areas, nomads moving to less arid areas in search of grazing for their animals disrupt the local ecosystem and hasten the rate of soil erosion. The Thar Desert is the most populated desert in the world, with a density of approximately 84 people per square kilometre. Population growth is also high: between 1901 and 1981 it stood at 249 per cent. (The corresponding figure for India as a whole was 187 per cent.) The population of the Thar Desert is dependent on agriculture and animal husbandry. People's living standards are low. Many of the communities are nomadic, moving from one *tobas* (water pond) to another. Population numbers have grown in the last decades, and this has led to more agricultural activity – including extensive cultivation and animal grazing – in this fragile environment. The density of livestock, particularly sheep, goats, camels, cows and donkeys, has also increased. Vegetational resources have been negatively affected as a result. The increase in human and livestock populations in this desert has led to a deterioration in the ecosystem, resulting in the degradation of soil fertility.

Irrigation programmes have been developed, the most important being the Indira Gandhi Nahar Canal Project. However, despite these efforts, stress on the fragile desert environment is increasing due to expanding human and animal populations. It is estimated that the desert is extending at a rate of half a kilometre per year.

The Thar Desert is an example of a natural biome which is experiencing significant change and transformation due to human activity. Key activities that are causing greater desertification include poor agricultural practices, increasing animal populations, and variations in the arrival and intensity of rainfall, which is related to changing global climatic conditions.

Tropical rainforest biomes have also experienced significant change due to human activities, including commercial logging and the conversion of forested lands for agriculture.

COMMERCIAL LOGGING

Commercial logging is the major cause of primary rainforest destruction in South East Asia and Africa. Worldwide, it is responsible for the removal of five million hectares a year. Logging usually involves the transfer of control of the forests from local people, who have an interest in their long-term preservation, to commercial interests who utilise the timber resources for short-term profit.

Millions of hectares of primary rainforests are being destroyed in South East Asia as a result of commercial logging. This logging meets the increasing demand in developed economies for timber as a raw material for processing and for the paper and pulp industry. Furthermore, the creation of logging roads in tropical forests allows landless people access to newly cleared areas. In Africa, 75 per cent of land being cleared by peasant farmers is land that has been commercially logged previously. In Malaysia during the early 1990s, clear-cut logging practices were the main reason for forest loss as logging companies harvested huge tracts of primary forests. Today, commercial logging is still the most significant threat to forests in regions of Central Africa.

LAND FOR AGRICULTURE

In the past, indigenous people farmed the rainforests, felling trees to allow cultivation of crops and grazing space for animals, and moving on when the soil lost fertility. This is not a threat to the forests, provided that it is undertaken in a sustainable manner and that used areas are left to regenerate for long periods before repeating the process. However, problems arise when the land is not allowed sufficient time to recover – intensive farming results in irreversible soil degradation.

Due to the needs of growing populations, some sources identify shifting cultivation as the cause of 70 per cent of deforestation in Africa. Commercial ranching is another major cause of deforestation, particularly in Central and South America. In Central America, two-thirds of lowland tropical forests have been turned into pasture since 1950. Cattle ranching is the leading cause of deforestation in the Brazilian Amazon: government figures attributed 38 per cent of deforestation from 1966 to 1975 to large-scale cattle ranching. This industry in particular, and the continuing consolidation of land ownership, is forcing poorer people into the rainforest in search of land. Furthermore, a significant amount of deforestation is caused by the activities of subsistence farmers who are encouraged to settle on forest lands by Brazilian government land redistribution policies. Between 1995 and 1998, the government granted land in the Amazon to about 150,000 families.

SOILS: FORMATION **2008 QUESTION 17**

*Examine **two** of the natural processes which influence soil formation.* (80 marks)

CLIMATE AND PARENT MATERIAL

The formation and composition of soil is influenced by climate, parent material, living organisms, topography and time.

Climate is a major influence on the rate and type of soil formation, and the two critical components of climate are temperature and rainfall. Climatic conditions influence the rate and type of weathering (both chemical and physical) of parent material and also affect the type of local flora and fauna found in areas or regions. Ireland experiences a cool maritime oceanic climate, which has low to medium annual temperatures with high rainfall. This type of climate supports vegetational growth of deciduous woodlands, which encourages the formation of brown earth soils; these are inherently fertile and rich in organic matter. However, high levels of rainfall can cause the leaching of minerals from the upper horizon through the process of acidification, and this can reduce soil fertility. Acidic soil lacks calcium, magnesium and potassium, which negatively affects fertility.

The acidity of the soil may be increased by the leaching of bases, which can be counteracted by applying lime and fertilisers. In areas (e.g. the BMW region) which experience high levels of rainfall and have poor natural drainage, significant water logging can occur. This results in the formation of gley soils, which have low levels of inherent fertility and are not suitable for the intensive production of tillage or cereal crops.

PARENT MATERIAL   A soil's parent material is the underlying rock material from which soil is derived by physical and chemical weathering. Parent material can be classified as residual, i.e. underlying rock which has experienced weathering, disintegration and decomposition. Processes associated with the physical weathering of parent material include freeze-thaw action, which results in rock shattering and onion weathering or exfoliation. In Ireland's climate, freeze-thaw action is more common than exfoliation. Parent material can also be classified as transported weathered material, which has been transported and deposited by geomorphic agents, including rivers, glaciation and wind (e.g. the regosols of the Thar Desert in India). Many soils in Ireland are post-glacial in origin and thus are about 12,000 years old. These are considered to be young soils in terms of geological time. Chemical weathering of parent material is associated with the processes of hydrolysis, carbonation, hydration and oxidation. The type of parent material influences the texture and acidity of soils: for example, soils originating from granite are acidic (e.g. soils in Donegal and Wicklow), while soils originating from limestone can be alkaline or neutral (e.g. parts of the Central Plain), and soils from quartz and sandstone are sandy and free-draining (e.g. soils in the south-east of Ireland).

LIVING ORGANISMS   Living organisms range from micro-organisms to plants, animals and humans. In the upper horizons of soil, the presence of bacteria and fungi results in the decomposition of organic material such as tree litter and natural vegetation. High levels of these organisms occur in brown earth soils. The presence of earthworms, moles and rabbits in the upper horizons results in the mixing and aeration of soils, which has a positive influence on fertility and drainage. Plants have both a chemical and physical role in soil formation and texture. Root binding prevents soil erosion and can also increase the weathering of parent material as a process of biological weathering. Plants can encourage the breakdown of consolidated soils, allowing for increased aeration and improved drainage (e.g. brown earths and gleys). Over time, new organisms will colonise the area, eventually creating a rich organic layer on the surface. Humans have a very significant role to play in influencing soil formation processes, and activities such as ploughing, harrowing and using chemicals and fertilisers can significantly increase soil fertility and formation.

TOPOGRAPHY
AND TIME

The natural slope or relief of an area influences soil formation and structure and also affects the rate of drainage. Aspect will influence vegetational cover and growth. In general, upland areas with steep slopes are associated with shallow soils which experience significant leaching of minerals. These soils have poor levels of inherent fertility and may also experience significant erosion due to poor vegetational cover and surface water run-off. Areas in Ireland associated with these soils include the uplands of the west and south and the Dublin/Wicklow mountains.

In areas that have low-lying relief and undulating slopes, soils are generally deep and fertile with high levels of organic matter. However, drainage in these areas will be influenced by slope and soil composition, in particular texture. Deep fertile soils are found in the Golden Vale region in Ireland and in the south-east and parts of the Central Plain. Significant time is required for the accumulation of soil parent material and for the development of horizons in the soil profile. The maturity of a soil depends to a large extent on age: young soils show less horizon development than older ones. Soil formation is a slow process and can take thousands of years. Generally speaking, the greater the time frame involved in the formation of soil, the better the soil structure.

SOILS: FORMATION **2009 QUESTION 16**

*With reference to **one** soil type you have studied, examine how parent material, climate and organic matter influence the soil.* (80 marks)

See answer to 2008 Question 17 (page 338)

SOILS: COMPOSITION AND CHARACTERISTICS
2007 QUESTION 17

Examine the general composition and characteristics of any **one** *soil type that you have studied.* (80 marks)

2010 QUESTION 18

Describe and explain the characteristics of any **one** *soil type studied by you.* (80 marks)

2011 QUESTION 16

Soil characteristics are affected by their immediate environment and by a combination of processes operating in that environment.

Examine any **three** *soil processes that affect soil characteristics.* (80 marks)

THESE QUESTIONS ARE VERY SIMILAR AND ARE DEALT WITH HERE IN THE FOLLOWING ANSWER

The soil type I have studied is brown earth. Key characteristics of soil are texture, pH value, humus content, structure, moisture, air and colour. The key factors which influence these characteristics include parent material, climate, living organisms, topography and time and human activities.

SOIL TEXTURE   Texture is the most important characteristic of a soil. The texture of soil influences drainage, nutrient content and the degree to which plant roots can penetrate it. Many of a soil's physical, chemical and biological attributes are related to texture, and textural determination is one of the essential elements of soil analysis.

The texture of soil can be influenced by human activities, including ploughing, harrowing and the implementation of drainage programmes. Living organisms, especially burrowers, can also improve soil texture: moles, rabbits and earthworms can move and mix significant amounts of material over time. Parent material also has a significant role to play in influencing soil texture; for example, when sandstone disintegrates it creates sandy soils, as in the Munster valley region, while shales result in the formation of clay dominant soils.

Soil texture describes the size and distribution of individual soil particles, and the term usually refers to the amounts of sand, silt and clay in the soil. Soils are normally a mixture of these, and a soil can be classified (using a soil triangular graph, for example) as loamy, sandy or clay, according to the proportions of sand, silt and clay in it. Brown earths have a loamy texture. Loamy soil has a mixture of sand, clay and silt; it is well aerated (this increase soil productivity), has good drainage and retains minerals. Because of its fertility, farmers and gardeners prefer a loamy soil. In contrast, sandy soils contain more than 70 per cent sand; they are well drained but may lose nutrients (so they need extra fertiliser) and are vulnerable to drought. Clay soils are described as heavy, and because the clay particles prevent water percolation they can become waterlogged. They can be difficult to plough and are best suited to pastoral farming.

SOIL pH   The pH value of soil (its acidity or alkalinity) affects many aspects of crop production and soil chemistry, including the availability of nutrients and toxic substances, the types and activities of micro-organisms, the solubility of heavy metals, and the action of certain pesticides. Brown earths in Ireland are slightly acidic because of high rainfall and the leaching of minerals from the soil. The pH of a soil is determined by parent material, climate, native vegetation, cropping history, and fertilisers or liming practices. The addition of lime to soils reduces the pH level, thereby reducing acidity, while the addition of fertilisers can have varying effects on pH levels depending on the compounds used. CAN (Calcium, Ammonium, Nitrate) has an acidifying effect, but the calcium acts as a buffer. Cropping history can also influence the pH of soils; for example the use of monocultural activities can strip alkaline nutrients from the soil, leaving it acidic in nature.

The pH for most mineral soils ranges from 5.5 to 7.5, and the best pH value for agricultural soil is 6.5. A number of factors can cause soils to become acidic, including the leaching of basic ions (calcium, magnesium, potassium and sodium) by rainwater. In addition, carbon dioxide, which comes from decomposing organic matter and root respiration, dissolves to form a weak organic acid. Furthermore, strong organic and inorganic acids (e.g. nitric and sulphuric acid) can occur due to the decay of organic matter and oxidation of ammonium fertilisers. Acidic soils lack calcium, magnesium and potassium, and this reduces fertility. The type of parent material influences the texture and acidity of soils: for example, acid soils originate from granite (e.g. soils in Donegal and Wicklow), alkaline or neutral soils originate from limestone (e.g. the Central Plain).

HUMUS CONTENT

Humus refers to microscopic organic particles which are formed from decomposed organic matter. Soil organic material is made up of the decaying remains of plants and animals. While humus is a relatively small part of soil, it is very important in determining the soil's physical and chemical characteristics, including its fertility. Humus contributes to soil cation exchange capacity, water adsorption and soil structure stability. It also aids the formation of soil aggregates, which controls pore size distribution, and the flow of water and air into and out of the soil. Humus also helps protect soil from erosion. The accumulation of humus, which occurs in the O horizon, leads to the release of nutrients into the soil. The main factors that determine the levels of organic matter in a soil are moisture, oxygen supply, pH and temperature.

The humification rate varies according to climate: it is usually fast in hot, humid regions and slow in cool, temperate conditions. In Ireland, for example, humification can take up to ten years. The rich organic layer in the brown earth soils in Ireland is related to climatic conditions, which are favourable to the development of the natural deciduous forest biome. The addition of organic fertilisers (slurry and manure) and ploughing in of crop residues increases organic matter and humus over time. However, the use of chemical pesticides can reduce biological activity and in turn reduce the level of humus.

SOIL STRUCTURE AND RELATED ATTRIBUTES

Soil structure refers to the shape of the peds in soils: crumb, platy, block or prismatic. The structure of a soil determines its degree of drainage and aeration and affects its workability for agriculture. Brown earths have a crumb-like structure, which aids drainage, aeration, nutrient- and water-holding capacity. Moisture content is influenced by texture and structure. The amount of moisture in a soil is important because water carries dissolved minerals, encourages the growth of micro-organisms, helps the development of soil horizons and reduces soil erosion. The moisture content of brown earths is influenced by the time of year and the topography of areas. The optimum moisture content of soils is 25 per cent. Air content is also vital: oxygen is essential for seed germination, plant growth, respiration and the breakdown of organic matter. The air content of brown earths is influenced by climatic conditions (including rainfall and evaporation) and human activities (including ploughing, harrowing and crop type). Soil colour is important because it affects the soil's ability to absorb sun and heat. Dark brown soils, including brown earths, are warmer than other soils and have a high humus content, and these combined characteristics support germination and growth. The key geographic locations of brown earths in Ireland include the south, south-east and the midlands. Desert soils, on the other hand, are light in colour, reflecting limited organic material or humus (e.g. the Thar Desert in India).

SOIL: HUMAN INFLUENCES **2007 QUESTION 16**

Examine how overcropping/overgrazing and desertification can affect soils. (80 marks)

Soils are renewable natural resources, as long as they are used and managed in a sustainable manner. However, if good soil management practices are not followed, this vital renewable resource can experience significant degradation, resulting in irreversible damage and serious negative short-term and long-term consequences.

OVERGRAZING   Soil erosion can be caused by overcropping and overgrazing, which remove vital vegetation cover and expose the soil to agents of erosion and transportation. In particular, close-cropping animals such as sheep and goats can damage the root structure of vegetation, leading to reduced growth rates and eventual exposure of loose soil grains. It is believed that the limestone region of the Burren in Co. Clare once supported pastoral agriculture, but that overgrazing led to the removal of the vegetation cover, exposing the underlying soil to agents of erosion and transportation. The Burren is now a barren landscape with no soil cover, where vegetation is confined to sheltered grikes. In many upland areas in the BMW region, the overstocking of pastoral animals (sheep and goats in particular) resulted in the removal of vegetational cover and exposed soils to erosion by heavy rainfall. Similar problems associated with overgrazing by sheep and goats also occur in the upland regions of the south of Italy.

OVERCROPPING   Overcropping – the overcultivation of crops in particular areas – can result in the depletion of the soil's inherent fertility. Vegetation cover decreases, causing the soil to be exposed to climate conditions and agents of erosion and transportation. In a study on Niger, overcropping and monocultural activities were identified as causes of worsening soil erosion. During colonial times, peanuts were identified as a cash crop that could provide good economic returns. In the 1920s, local farmers and plantation owners were encouraged to establish large-scale peanut cultivation, production and marketing. Peanut exports from the Zinder region in Niger rose from 4,500 tonnes in 1928 to 78,900 tonnes in 1970, but then fell due to lower prices and diseased crops. As prices declined, farmers were encouraged to grow millet, and areas under cultivation rose from 72,000 hectares in 1970 to 162,000 hectares by 1980. This expansion of annual cropping resulted in a rapid decline of stable perennial vegetation, and soil erosion became common in many areas.

In the Thar Desert in India, the population is dependent on agriculture and animal husbandry. However, in the last decades, population numbers have grown, and this has resulted in increased agricultural activity in this fragile environment, which has in turn led to overgrazing and extensive cultivation, and vegetational resources have been negatively affected as a result. The growth in human and livestock population in the desert has led to a deterioration in the ecosystem, resulting in the degradation of soil fertility.

DESERTIFICATION   Desertification refers to the expansion of desert conditions due to the
AND SOILS   exposure and removal of layers of topsoil. In the 1930s, parts of the Great Plains

in the United States were turned into the 'Dust Bowl' by drought and poor farming practices. During this period, millions of people were forced to abandon their farms and livelihoods as vegetation was removed and the underlying soil was exposed to harsh climate conditions, resulting in dust storms and the removal of massive amounts of soil from the landscape. Better methods of agriculture and land and water management in the Great Plains have prevented that disaster from recurring, but desertification currently affects millions of people in almost every continent. Droughts are common in arid and semi-arid lands, though well-managed lands can recover from drought when the rains return. However, continued land abuse during droughts increases land degradation. By 1973, the drought that began in 1968 in the Sahel of west Africa and the land use practices there had caused the deaths of more than 100,000 people and 12 million cattle. The Sahel drought placed additional stress on its biological resources. Good resource management would have resulted in little, if any, permanent damage being caused by the drought. In contrast, poor resource management means that drought will accentuate the adverse impact of poor land management and accelerate land degradation and soil erosion. Key causes of desertification include climate change, population growth and poor land management practices, including overcropping and overgrazing.

SOIL: HUMAN INFLUENCES 2009 QUESTION 17

Discuss how human activities can accelerate soil erosion. (80 marks)

SOIL EROSION/
MINERAL LEACHING

When the tropical rainforests are cut down for agricultural land using the slash and burn technique, nutrients are released into the soil. These nutrients increase soil productivity. However, when the rains arrive these nutrients are washed away or leached through the process of acidification. This reduces soil fertility, and in as little as three years the soil may lose all its inherent fertility and become nutrient deficient. Due to poor soil fertility, the cleared land is quickly exhausted under intensive agriculture. Fertility can only be maintained by using artificial fertilisers, but this is rarely undertaken because fertilisers are expensive. Thus, these areas may be abandoned in favour of newly burned and cleared areas. However, the replacement of vegetation cover is a slow process, and significant soil erosion may occur before natural vegetation is re-established. Soil erosion occurs due to the exposure of loose soil grains to significant rainfall, which washes them away. Regrowth of the natural forest is slow, and the areas are gradually vegetated first by a mass of low bushes intertwined with vines and ferns.

It is a misconception that droughts alone cause desertification. Droughts are common in arid and semi-arid lands, and well-managed lands can recover from drought when the rains return. However, continued land abuse during droughts increases land degradation. By 1973, the drought that began in 1968 in the Sahel of west Africa and the land use practices there had caused the death of more than 100,000 people and 12 million cattle, and had resulted in the disruption of communities. In the 1930s, parts of the Great Plains in the United States were turned into the 'Dust Bowl' as a result of drought and poor farming practices, and millions of people were forced to abandon their farms and livelihoods. Huge improvements in agricultural methods and land and water management in the Great Plains have prevented that disaster from recurring, but desertification currently affects millions of people in almost every continent. Droughts, however, are not the cause of desertification: humans are. The Sahel drought from 1968 onwards served only to place additional stress on the biological resources of the Sahel. If resource management had been good, little, if any, permanent damage would have been caused by the drought. But unwise resource management allows droughts to accentuate the adverse impact of bad management and accelerates land degradation. This is what has happened in the Sahel and elsewhere.

Soils are renewable natural resources when they are used and managed sustainably. If soil management is poor, however, soil can suffer significant degradation, resulting in irreversible damage and serious negative short-term and long-term consequences. Soil erosion can result from overcropping and overgrazing. These processes remove vital vegetation cover and expose the soil to agents of erosion and transportation. Overgrazing occurs when too many animals, particularly close-cropping animals such as sheep and goats, are allowed to remove vegetational cover: the root structure of vegetation is damaged, resulting in reduced growth rates and eventual exposure of loose soil grains. Researchers believe that the limestone region of the Burren, Co. Clare, once supported pastoral agricultural activity but that overgrazing led to the removal of the vegetation cover, exposing the underlying soil to agents of erosion and transportation. Today the Burren is a barren landscape with no soil cover, and vegetation is confined to sheltered grikes.

Overcropping – the overcultivation of crops in particular areas – can result in the depletion of the soil's inherent fertility; as this occurs, vegetation cover decreases, exposing the soil to climatic conditions and agents of erosion and transportation. In a study of increasing rates of soil erosion in Niger, overcropping and monocultural activities have been identified as a critical cause. In the Thar Desert in India, the population is dependent on agriculture and animal husbandry. However, in recent decades, population numbers have increased and this has resulted in increased agricultural activity in this fragile environment. Overgrazing and extensive cultivation have damaged vegetation resources. The increase in human and livestock population in the desert has led to the deterioration of the ecosystem, resulting in the degradation of soil fertility.

SOIL: HUMAN INFLUENCES **2010 QUESTION 17**

*Examine **two** ways in which human activities have impacted on soils.*
(80 marks)

Human activities can have significant implications for soil structure and composition, and these implications can be both positive and negative. First I will deal with the positive impact of human activity on soils.

FERTILISATION   All soils have an inherent soil fertility, which refers to the natural presence of elements essential for plant growth. Soil is composed of both organic and inorganic matter and is an important natural renewable resource because it has significant implications for vegetation cover and food production. Humans can enhance soil fertility, thus maximising plant growth, by adding both organic and inorganic elements. Inorganic elements, such as nitrogen, phosphorus and potassium, can be applied by spreading fertilisers, while organic material, including slurry and manure, also adds to these important trace elements. The development of adequate nutrient management plans can enhance soil productivity without causing negative environmental effects to surface or groundwater supplies.

Enhanced soil fertility leads to better agricultural output, which benefits both the producer and consumer. Developing economies, which are experiencing increasing population growth, need to improve their agricultural output, and this can be achieved by proper soil management that increases inherent soil fertility. This has been successfully undertaken in India as part of the Green Revolution.

SOIL MANAGEMENT   Farmers can also improve soil structure and composition by employing soil management techniques that increase productivity in a sustainable manner. Soils consist of four main components: mineral matter (45 per cent), organic matter (5 per cent), air (25 per cent, variable) and water (25 per cent, variable).

Activities that can strengthen soil structure and composition include ploughing, which improves drainage and soil aeration and mixes organic humus material. Arterial drainage schemes and deep ploughing can improve drainage and help remove surface water, which can cause gleisation and podzolisation. Applying lime to soil can also reduce its pH level and thus improve productivity. Crop rotation conserves soil structure, maintains pH levels, improves soil fertility and prevents the build-up of pests, weeds and diseases associated with particular crops. Other techniques include harrowing, rolling and ploughing. Under the Rural Environment Protection Scheme (REPS), farmers are encouraged to use organic sources of fertilisers, to use clover to fix nitrogen, and to utilise mixed grazing by cattle and sheep, which increases pasture productivity and protects soil structure and fertility.

SOIL EROSION

However, human interference with soils can also result in negative consequences, the most detrimental being soil erosion. For example, ploughing on slopes that were formerly under grass can result in the destabilisation of soil structure and possible erosion by water due to surface run-off or mass movement.

In tropical rainforest areas, the problem of soil erosion and the leaching of minerals is a major issue. When slash and burn is used to cut down the rainforests for agricultural land, nutrients are released into the soil; but when the rains come these nutrients are washed away or leached through acidification into the lower horizons. This reduces soil fertility, and in as little as three years the soil can lose all its inherent fertility and become nutrient deficient. Because the soil is lacking in fertility, the cleared land is quickly exhausted by intensive agriculture. Fertility can only be returned to the soil by applying artificial fertilisers, but this is rarely undertaken. The area is then abandoned in favour of newly burned and cleared areas, but the replacement of vegetation is a slow process, and significant soil erosion may occur before natural vegetation is re-established. Regrowth of the natural forest is slow, and the areas are gradually vegetated by a mass of low bushes intertwined with vines and ferns.

OVERUSE OF FERTILISERS AND HEAVY MACHINERY

In recent decades, intensive agriculture has become associated with using more mechanisation and applying fertilisers to increase productivity. Both of these can have adverse impacts on soil structure and composition. The use of large agricultural machinery increases soil compaction and damages soil structure, resulting in poor drainage and surface waterlogging. If this happens over a long period of time, gleisation can result.

Organic and inorganic fertilisers are increasingly used in batch application, i.e. once-off application, which is economically efficient. However, soils and vegetation only absorb fertilisers in small amounts, so over-application can result in leaching and the subsequent deposition of additional nutrients in rivers, lakes and streams, thus causing eutrophication. The growing reliance of intensive agriculture on artificial fertilisers is also leading to the depletion of inherent organic material.